The Making of the 20th Century

This series of specially comm~
tion on significant and o~
themes of world history in th~
provides sufficient narrative a
comer to the subject while o~
study, detailed source-referen
together with interpretation and
of recent scholarship.

    ~,
~the light

    In the choice of subjects there is a balance between breadth in some spheres and detail in others, between the essentially political and matters economic or social. The series cannot be a comprehensive account of everything that has happened in the twentieth century, but it provides a guide to recent research and explains something of the times of extraordinary change and complexity in which we live. It is directed in the main to students of contemporary history and international relations, but includes titles which are of direct relevance to courses in economics, sociology, politics and geography.

The Making of the 20th Century

Series Editor: GEOFFREY WARNER

David Armstrong, Lorna Lloyd and John Redmond, *From Versailles to Maastricht: International Organisation in the Twentieth Century*
S. R. Ashton, *In Search of Détente: The Politics of East–West Relations since 1945*
V. R. Bergham, *Germany and the Approach of War in 1914*, second edition
Raymond F. Betts, *France and Decolonisation, 1900–1960*
John Darwin, *Britain and Decolonisation: The Retreat from Empire in the Post-War World*
John F. V. Keige, *France and the Origins of the First World War*
Dominic Lieven, *Russia and the Origins of the First World War*
Sally Marks, *The Illusion of Peace: International Relations in Europe, 1918–1945*
Philip Morgan, *Italian Fascism, 1919–1945*
R. A. C. Parker, *Chamberlain and Appeasement: British Policy and the Coming of the Second World War*
Anita J. Prażmowska, *Eastern Europe and the Origins of the Second World War*
G. Roberts, *The Soviet Union and the Origins of the Second World War*
Alan Sharp, *The Versailles Settlement: Peacemaking in Paris, 1919*
Zara Steiner, *Britain and the Origins of the First World War*
Samuel R. Williamson, *Austria-Hungary and the Origins of the First World War*
R. Young, *France and the Origins of the Second World War*

Eastern Europe and the Origins of the Second World War

Anita J. Prażmowska

First published 2000 by
MACMILLAN PRESS LTD
Houndmills, Basingstoke, Hampshire RG21 6XS
and London
Companies and representatives
throughout the world

ISBN 0–333–73729–6 hardcover
ISBN 0–333–73730–X paperback

A catalogue record for this book is available
from the British Library.

This book is printed on paper suitable for recycling and
made from fully managed and sustained forest sources.

10   9   8   7   6   5   4   3   2   1
09 08 07 06 05 04 03 02 01 00

Typeset in Great Britain by
Aarontype Limited, Easton, Bristol

Printed in China

 Published in the United States of America by
ST. MARTIN'S PRESS, INC.,
Scholarly and Reference Division
175 Fifth Avenue, New York, N.Y. 10010

ISBN 0–312–23352-3 (cloth)
ISBN 0–312–23353-1 (paper)

To Miriam and Janek

To Marieke

for an excellent

PhD.

Anita J. Praxinska

24.09.00

Contents

List of Maps

Preface and Acknowledgements

Men make their own history, but they do not make it just as
they please; they do not make it under circumstances chosen
by themselves, but under circumstances directly encountered,
given and transmitted from the past.

(Karl Marx, 'The Eighteenth Brumaire of Louis Bonaparte',
in Karl Marx and Frederick Engels, *Selected Works*, Lawrence &
Wishart, London, 1970, p. 96)

The burden of history weighs heavily upon Eastern Europe. This
simple fact is easily overlooked in West European countries which
have experienced fewer territorial and political changes during
the twentieth century. This in turn has affected Western European
understanding and at times even its willingness to understand the
fate of that part of Europe. The natural inclination is to consider
the fate of the smaller and politically weaker East European states
during the inter-war period, and especially in the run-up to the
Second World War, as no more than an outcome of Big Power rivalries. The aim of this book is to suggest that this was not the case.
In each of the many small and large crises which affected the
region, the states of Eastern Europe were active, though not
always willing, participants. This was a region riven with rivalries,
unforgiving of slights and unyielding in its peoples' desire for independence. These attitudes played a role in the events preceding
the outbreak of the war. It cannot be denied that the Eastern European governments of the inter-war period became victims of
much bigger international crises, in most cases beyond their control. As individual countries became objects of German aggression, their neighbours became willing participants in the process
of dismembering those countries. The Second World War merely
added to that burden of history.

The idea for this book was conceived when *History Today* com-
missioned an article on Eastern Europe during the inter-war
period. This appeared in the October 1990 edition (Volume 40),

ix

and it is reproduced here, with kind permission of the *History Today* editors, as the Introduction. I am grateful to past students whose credulity in the face of the apparent passivity of the Eastern Europeans led me to conclude that this book is long overdue.

ANITA J. PRAŻMOWSKA

Acknowledgements

The author and publishers wish to thank the following for permission to use copyright material: C. Hurst & Co. for the map of the Baltic States from Georg von Rauch; *The Baltic States: The Years of Independence, Estonia, Latvia, Lithuania, 1917–1940*, 1974; Cambridge University Press for the map of the Balkan States after the First World War from Barbara Jelevich, *History of the Balkans in the Twentieth Century*, vol. 2, 1965; Macmillan Press for the map of the reconstructed Poland from Latawski, *The Reconstruction of Poland, 1914–1973*, 1992, for the map of the administrative boundaries of the Kingdom of Yugoslavia, 1929–41, from F. Singleton, *Twentieth-Century Yugoslavia*, 1976, and for the map of Czechoslovakia after Munich in 1938 from Norman Stone and Eduard Strouhal (eds), *Czechoslovakia: Crossroads and Crises, 1918–88*, 1989. Every effort has been made to trace all the copyright-holders, but if any have been inadvertently overlooked the publishers will be pleased to make the necessary arrangement at the first opportunity.

Introduction

'The Versailles powers created the new states of Eastern Europe' is a comment that just slips off the tongues of most experienced historians. The phrase is incorrect, but nevertheless it is a widely acceptable generalisation that does not challenge the prejudices of our audiences. It is easy to imagine the great statesmen at Versailles pondering, deciding, and adjudicating, in between taking puffs at their cigars or tapping out their pipes. A caricature perhaps, but one that is almost a cliché.

The real problem is that while it is difficult to overlook the influence, direct and indirect, of the Big Powers on the affairs of the small states, the precise degree of that influence is not always easy to discern. Once we come to deal with the causes of the Second World War the European Big Powers seem to come into their own. We study, teach and therefore view the problem almost exclusively from the perspective of the European balance of power, the contest between Germany, Italy, France and Great Britain, and occasionally the Soviet Union. The small states figure as objects of policy, victims and at times a nuisance necessitating action by one of the Big Powers.

The case of Danzig and German aggression against Poland is a very good example of this approach. A. J. P. Taylor's revisionist work on the origins of the war has unfortunately also defined the Danzig problem as a mistake made by the British in their dealings with Germany. Had the British government not guaranteed Poland, he argues, the Poles would not have been so obdurate in their dealings with Germany, over Danzig and their common border. The quarrelsome Poles would not have been able to precipitate the war in this way. This view conveniently overlooks the question of whether the British guarantee was indeed seen by the Poles as a commitment to the defence of their security and whether it did therefore cause them to make their foreign policy more disagreeable (in the presumed belief that the British would protect them). Only the study of Polish foreign policy shows conclusively that this was in fact not the case.

1

The study of history from the perspective of the Big Powers obscures the question of the extent to which the small states of Eastern and South Eastern Europe decided their own fate and responses to difficulties. Looking only at Big Power relations, we fail to appreciate the extent to which those smaller states did not look to the Big Powers, either for assistance or advice on matters relating to their security. The small states might rarely have had the means of implementing their policies, and frequently their internal and foreign policies might have been imprudent and deplorable in their consequences. Nevertheless a lack of statesmanship is not exclusively found in small, impoverished and backward states.

In Eastern Europe the decision to create new states and to define their boundaries was determined by the force of national aspirations in given people, by the degree of their organisation and by their military presence at the time of the collapse of the German–Austrian effort. Although the Central Powers were in a better position to influence directly and exploit the strength of national self-determination than were the Allied Powers, they only acted in so far as it suited them. At times a number of provisional authorities emerged, vying for the support of the Big Powers. On other occasions self-appointed committees which emerged within the region came into conflict with those which were formed outside. In the case of Yugoslavia the Serb government in exile, supported by Tsarist Russia, confined itself to trying to obtain the incorporation of Bosnia-Hercegovina and securing access to the Adriatic. Simultaneously, in Italy a committee was formed with the aim of uniting all the South Slavs, that is the Serbs, Croats and Slovenes. This proclaimed itself the Yugoslav Committee. These two managed to arrive at some understanding and in December 1918 they committed themselves jointly to the creation of a South Slav Kingdom. Similar movements had in the meantime emerged in Zagreb and Montenegro campaigning for the creation of a united Yugoslavia.

The Polish case presents an equally interesting variety of committees and organisations reflecting both political differences and international orientation. In Paris a National Committee emerged with the explicit aim of obtaining the Allied states' support for the creation of an independent Polish state. Meanwhile the German occupation authorities in Warsaw sought to harness

Polish nationalist sentiments by similar promises. As the German armies withdrew from Warsaw Józef Piłsudski emerged as both a politician and national hero of sufficient standing to head a provisional administration. In the meantime in Lublin a socialist 'People's Government of the Polish Republic' emerged, while in what previously had been Prussian Poland another Polish governing body appeared. It was some time before agreement was reached between these assorted aspirants to the status of a provisional government.

There were losers in the battle for national self-determination. The Ukrainians, who throughout the war campaigned for independence and whose case had been supported at one and the same time by the German authorities and by the American State Department, were from the outset aware that the creation of an independent Polish state would spell the end of their hopes.

Territorial claims and readjustments were made in an equally haphazard manner. The collapse of the European Empires, which had hitherto governed that part of Europe, created a vacuum. None of the Eastern European states exercised circumspection in claims to territorial readjustments. As the boundaries of the pre-war order were irrevocably destroyed, the victorious Big Powers were neither willing nor able to affect the course of change. The result was that borders established by 1920 were invariably unfair to inhabitants of a disputed region or neighbouring states. Causes for tension, disunity and instability in Eastern Europe were legion.

The signal features of Eastern European politics during the whole of the inter-war period were dictatorship and political disunity. The strength of nationalism and a determination to justify territorial acquisitions prevented the states of that region from combining together against any common foe (even if such could be defined), while their national minorities were antagonised and shamefully mistreated.

With hindsight one feels that surely Germany was the most likely aggressor towards Eastern European states. That was in fact never the case and it did not appear so at the time. Yugoslavia was hostile to Italy, with whom there had been a conflict over the Istrian peninsula and political interference in Dalmatia and Albania. With Austria there was a conflict over the Klagenfurt region and with Hungary over Baranja, Bácska and Bánát. Additionally

Yugoslavia had bad relations with Romania over the Bánát region and with Bulgaria over the Dragoman Pass.

Romania, which had nearly doubled her territories, created for herself innumerable sources of conflict: with the Soviet Union over the region of Bessarabia, with Hungary over Transylvania, occupied by the Romanian troops in a war of intervention against the Red regime of Béla Kun. The two million Hungarians thus included in Romania were far from grateful.

Further north, Poland occupied the town of Vilnius and its surroundings in a rather spurious coup by General Lucjan Żeligowski in 1920 which created a source of friction between the Poles and the Lithuanian government. This was not rectified by the somewhat crude expedient of issuing an ultimatum to the Lithuanians during the Anschluss, demanding that diplomatic relations be restored if hostilities were to be avoided. They were restored but, not surprisingly, neither the old territorial claims, nor the boorish manner of resolving the diplomatic impasse, created the preconditions for good relations. The Poles had obtained the Poznań region and the Corridor, a strip of land dividing German-held Western Prussia from Eastern Prussia. This gave them direct access to the sea, but the area was inhabited by a sizeable German minority. Their claims to the town of Danzig were thwarted by the Versailles Powers, who instead created there a Free City protected by the League of Nations. These and several inconclusive plebiscites, followed by uprisings by local Poles in the Silesian region, all meant that Polish–German relations were characterised by deep distrust and anxiety. Polish–Czechoslovak relations were strained throughout the inter-war period over the region of Teschen, which the Czechs had occupied during the Soviet–Polish conflict in 1920.

But the Eastern European states were at least united in seeing the Soviet Union as the common enemy during the inter-war period, either because of genuine territorial differences, as in the case of Poland and Romania, or because of anxieties about the nature of the Communist regime. States which had brutal internally repressive regimes used anti-communism as part of their propaganda. Hungary after 1919, and Poland after the Piłsudski *coup d'état* in 1926, were outstanding examples.

Internal security and external dangers were inextricably linked in the eyes of the Eastern European regimes. Persecution of national minorities, religious dissidents, and even those who did not fit into any of these categories, was rife. Discrimination against Jews, and on occasion their active persecution, was symptomatic of more general developments in this period.

For both economic and political reasons the states of Eastern Europe looked to the big and wealthy states of Western Europe for aid and assistance. They all subscribed to the ideas of the League of Nations, either in the hope that their grievances would be supported, or because they sought to obtain guarantees of the status quo which had been favourable to them.

Of the Western European powers Britain was most heavily involved economically in Eastern Europe. But this was rarely, if ever, translated into political dependence and economic contacts tended to be unsupported by the British government. In any case, with the exception of Greece, Eastern Europe lay outside the British zone of political influence and therefore only attracted attention in an impending crisis or a conflict in which France might be involved.

French involvement in the political, territorial and economic developments of Eastern Europe was always more apparent and more weighty. Anxiety about the loss of the Russian partner and unease about the absence of British involvement in European politics meant that French politicians took a direct interest in that region. They wanted Eastern European unity, preferably of an anti-German character. French banks and industrialists sought to replace investment opportunities lost in Russia, and trading partners scattered with the break-up of the Austro–Hungarian Empire. French support for the Czechs during the Polish–Czechoslovak crisis over Teschen in 1920 is explained by their desire to obtain good coking coal from Czechoslovakia. But French political involvement in Eastern Europe was neither single-minded nor consistent and fluctuated depending on a variety of factors, including the changing fortunes of relations between France and Britain, Germany and the Soviet Union. Business investment, in particular that supported by the government, varied depending on the state of the French economy. The import of cheap agricultural foodstuffs from Eastern Europe became a bone of contention at a time when French farming was in recession.

The result was that while the Eastern European states looked to France for political and economic assistance, that country could not exercise consistent, effective and exclusive political patronage over them. For this reason, and because of their own inconstancy, the Eastern European governments were permanently on the look-out for other opportunities. At times of close co-operation between France and states east of Germany, excessive familiarity merely led to deep distrust rather than allaying it.

Poland was a very good example of this type of perverse relationship. Politically Poland appeared to be closely bound to the French camp. The political agreement signed in 1921 was subsequently augmented by a military convention. French military contacts with Poland were extensive. The Polish military academy had been established by the French, and French military teaching and ideas were the ones to which the Polish military leaders (who ruled the country from 1926) subscribed. After the death of Piłsudski in 1935, military men were placed in senior banking and civil service posts, as well as in the government. These men were French speaking and frequently trained in France.

The result of this French influence was the opposite of what might have been expected. In 1932 the new Minister for Foreign Affairs, Colonel Josef Beck, was virulently anti-French. Financial and political contacts were maintained and extended, but these were always characterised by distrust and suspicion. Petty jealousies and intrigues permeated Polish–French relations even at times of crisis. The French Ambassador to Warsaw during the crucial period prior to the outbreak of the war, Leon Noël, on the whole advised his government to resist the temptation to strengthen military and political commitments and subsequently blamed the September defeat on the Poles exclusively. His reports and memoirs are characterised by half truths and recriminations against the Poles in which historical veracity was only respected if it placed the French in a good light.

In spite of these differences, the Eastern European states did try to establish some regional pacts. The Little Entente and Josef Beck's 'Third Europe' were the two best known. The first consisted of a series of bilateral treaties initiated by Romania in the years 1920–1 and included Czechoslovakia, Yugoslavia and Romania. Though France was credited with being the architect of the agreements it was the Romanian Foreign Minister's brain child. France clearly took an interest in the Little Entente which complemented her own policy in the region. The maintenance of the status quo was its main object, but anxiety about Hungarian revanchism was the only foreign policy issue uniting the signatories. In reality it was aimed against any attempt by Hungary to regain the territories in Slovakia, Transylvania and Yugoslavia, which had been removed from Hungarian control at the end of the First World War.

From the outset it was hoped that Poland, Bulgaria and Austria would join it, but Poland refused to join, even though Polish–Romanian relations were good. Anti-Hungarian feelings were not shared by the Poles. Rather, fear of the Soviet Union and the determination to limit Soviet influence and territorial readjustments were the common foreign-policy objectives shared by Poland and Romania. During the crisis years of 1938 and 1939 the Little Entente was of no significance either to its members or the French.

Beck's subsequent 'Third Europe' initiative took a similar form. He conceived the idea of a middle-European bloc, opposed on the one hand to Germany and on the other to the Soviet Union. At its most ambitious it was to span the Scandinavian states, the Baltic States, the states of Eastern Europe and the Balkans. A less ambitious version of the 'Third Europe' was to be confined to Poland, Hungary, Romania and Yugoslavia.

Beck's problem was that the Scandinavian states, though interested in some sort of Baltic pact, looked no further than that. But relations between Hungary and Romania were the most obvious obstacle. Whereas the Hungarian government was not prepared to abandon Transylvania, the government in Romania was not likely to return it to Hungary. Mediation and conciliation between the two states could only be partially successful and only if some prize could be offered to Hungary. Interestingly the Soviet and Romanian governments had been able to reach a limited accommodation over Bessarabia in the mid-1930s and therefore neither anti-Soviet nor anti-German policies appealed to the Romanian government. The French came to view Beck's policy as an attempt to oppose the spread of French influence in Eastern Europe and clearly they had good reason to be distrustful of any initiative from Josef Beck. Close Franco–Czechoslovak economic ties and the excellent political relations that were associated with them were sources of particular irritation to the Poles.

The emergence of a Nazi government in Germany in 1933 had little immediate impact on Eastern Europe. Only the Polish and Czechoslovak governments had reasons for concern. In any case the Polish government appeared to have been uniquely successful in removing all obstacles to the negotiation of all grievances with her western neighbour when, in January 1934, a Pact of Non-Aggression was signed with Germany.

The Nazi war of nerves against Czechoslovakia in no way suggested that the Eastern European states needed to close ranks. In fact the governments of Poland and Hungary watched the developments with the aim of exploiting Czechoslovakia's weaknesses rather than resisting Germany. Both states informed the government in Berlin that they would not view the break-up of Czechoslovakia as undesirable. The Poles resentfully castigated Czechoslovakia for being France's stooge in Eastern Europe and looked forward to resuming control of the Teschen district. The anti-Polish activities of Ukrainian nationalists, which had been encouraged and financed by the Czechs, provided additional justification.

The Poles envisaged the break-up of Czechoslovakia into the Czech, Slovak and Ruthenian areas, of which Ruthenia would be incorporated into Hungary, and a puppet regime under Polish control would be established in Slovakia. They looked forward to being able to offer the Hungarians the prize of Ruthenia, to enable them to re-establish good relations with Romania without loss of face. Bringing Hungary into the 'Third Europe' in this way, together with territorial adjustments in Poland's favour, was to enable Poland to emerge as the controlling power in Eastern Europe.

During the Czechoslovak crisis of 1938, and in particular during its final stages in September and October, the Poles and the Hungarians joined Germany in bullying Czechoslovakia into submission. For Poland the prize was snatched from their hands when French and British co-operation enabled Hitler to destroy the Czech state. The political vacuum thus created was filled by German power. Hungarian territorial readjustments were completed by a series of Vienna Agreements in the autumn of 1938. Although Poland's demand for the return of Teschen was satisfied, her failures were more significant.

By 1938 a process which had been taking place since 1936 had yielded fruit. Gradual but nevertheless aggressive economic penetration of the Eastern European states by Germany had resulted in both economic dependence and a pro-German orientation of the ruling elites and therefore also of their foreign policy. By the autumn of 1938 Hungary and Romania looked to Germany for economic assistance and political cues. Poland was not merely isolated; she now became the object of German aggression. The return of Danzig to the Reich, and an extra-territorial link across the Corridor, were connected with propaganda claims that the German minority in the Corridor and the Poznań region was being mistreated. Polish attempts now to capitalise on good relations with the Italian dictatorship and the Yugoslav government elicited positive statements, but in reality neither was prepared to jeopardise their relations with Germany to support Poland. Nor was it possible for the Poles to obtain any further mileage from their anti-Soviet policy. To the Romanians good relations with Germany appeared to be a more tangible guarantee of security.

In March 1939 Britain made an unusual break with her traditional policy of dissociation from Eastern European affairs. Acting on a tip-off that Germany was planning to establish total control over the Romanian economy, including its strategic oil production, Britain took the initiative in attempting to act as doyen of an Eastern European collective security system. Resolutely determined to pledge nothing of her own economic and military potential, the British government nevertheless hoped that the vision of Eastern European unity would in some way cause Hitler to hesitate before his next aggressive step.

After some hesitation the Polish Foreign Minister, Beck, extracted from the initial British proposal (which was for a set of interlocking agreements between Britain and a number of Eastern European states, most notably Poland and Romania) a bilateral Polish–British agreement. Still confident that he could handle Hitler, he declined to work for the extension of that agreement to other states. In any case the only tangible goal which the Polish and Romanian Ministers for Foreign Affairs shared was a desire to see the removal of the Jewish communities from their respective states. The economic penetration of Romania by Germany was not something to which Gafencu, the Romanian Foreign Minister, was opposed in principle. While both were opposed to the Soviet Union, Beck was unwilling to entertain any agreements – even in the face of a direct German threat. Gafencu, on the other hand, believed that the inevitable economic dependence on Germany could be offset by improving relations with the Soviet Union.

The signing of the Ribbentrop–Molotov Pact of Non-Aggression confounded everyone in the European capitals. It was that, rather than either the actions of the Western democracies or the unconvincing attempts of the small Eastern European states to defend the status quo, which set the pace for the revision of the borders of the region. The union of the two powers which had a direct interest in the balance of power in that region, and which dominated it militarily, was decisive. The reasons for their unlikely unity of purpose are not important here. What is important is that they were able to effect territorial adjustments in their own favour, most notably when they occupied Poland, and when, in 1940, the Soviet Union reclaimed Bessarabia and Bukovina from Romania.

The wisdom of standing together might have, in retrospect, been obvious. But to the Eastern European states during the inter-war period the question was not whether to stand resolute but against whom to stand resolute.

1 Friends? France and Britain

France

Of all the major European powers, France retained the most consistent interest in developments taking place in Eastern Europe and the Balkans. The need for security against Germany explains France's involvement in that region. But, as the newly emerged Successor States and Yugoslavia were to find out, this did not mean that France would always support them. Lack of consistency between the theory of France's eastern alliances and the reality was due to the fact that, within French military thinking, the doctrine of an Eastern Front was never accepted as the only means of guaranteeing French security. While accepting in principle the idea that a pro-French orientation in Eastern Europe should be cultivated, the French government never fully worked out just how this was to be done. Throughout the inter-war period other methods of strengthening French security continued to be debated with the same vigour as was that of the Eastern Front. French thinking on the subject of the Balkan and Eastern European states tended to vary over time, depending on a number of factors. The British and United States' willingness, or the lack of it, to uphold the Versailles Treaty decisions was one example of an issue which decisively affected all internal French debates on the subject of the Eastern Front. Of consequence was the fact that Britain, the US and Italy at various times, in varying degrees, showed a reluctance to make commitments to guarantee French security against Germany. This in turn made the French more willing to clutch at straws in Eastern Europe.

Other factors and considerations further distracted French politicians and military thinkers alike from concentrating exclusively on Eastern European states. During the course of the late 1920s discussions on the Soviet Union came to dominate all debates on Eastern Europe. In the mid-1920s the German government's willingness to cease publicly attacking the Versailles decisions and to accept the principle of reparations strengthened arguments put forward by those who felt that Eastern Europe was a drain on France's military and economic resources. In the mid-1930s Italy became the main focal point of French diplomatic endeavours to decrease threats to France's metropolitan and imperial interests. This fact contributed further to the acceptance by French military leaders of the need to reduce involvement in Poland, Czechoslovakia and Yugoslavia.

If at times it seemed as if France lacked commitment to her eastern allies, this was not because at any one time during the inter-war period the doctrine of an Eastern Front was rejected outright. As East European statesmen noted, the growth of British interest in France's security was invariably accompanied by a decrease of French interests in the build-up of the East European alliances. Similarly, the economic crisis of the middle 1930s, which led to the peasant voters putting pressure on the French government to limit imports of cheap foodstuffs from Eastern Europe, had implications for foreign policy. The decrease of funds for trade and investment in that region undermined pro-French sentiments within the ruling elites of those countries and raised doubts about France's commitments. This impression was difficult to counteract in the years before the war. Notwithstanding anxiety about the loss of influence in Eastern Europe, French policy makers always concentrated on the security of French territories and that of her colonies as an absolute priority. The fate of the eastern allies was inevitably subordinate to that consideration. This obvious fact was not one which Eastern European politicians liked to hear repeated too often, preferring instead to operate on the assumption that their and France's security considerations overlapped. This attitude, maintained by both sides, led to numerous misunderstandings and frequently stood in the way of a realistic appraisal of the ways in which France and her eastern allies co-operated.

An analysis of French foreign policy towards Eastern European states cannot be adequately conducted without taking into account France's own security considerations. Internal priorities and economic restrictions all played a vital part in defining the attitudes of successive French governments towards the eastern allies. French politicians and military leaders were never entirely convinced of the relevance of the eastern alliances to French security, nor were they free to plan for an Eastern Front. Therefore in order to understand French motives one has to dwell on factors which directly contributed to, and ultimately inhibited, political and military discussions in Paris.

French post-war policies towards Eastern Europe are frequently analysed as if they had started with the Versailles Conference decisions. This is not correct, as France had always taken an interest in the fate of nations east of Germany. Not surprisingly during the 1914–18 war, the implications of the collapse of the Austro–Hungarian Empire upon France's post-war European position were considered at the highest level. The obvious conclusion was that were the Eastern European nations to assert their claim to sovereignty, France would work towards securing good relations with them. As a result of these debates the French were sympathetic towards the various Eastern European exile authorities which established themselves in Paris during the First World War. At the same time a governmental committee was established with the express purpose of studying possible post-war settlements. The Comité d'Etudes, which started its deliberations in February 1917, discussed papers written by eminent scholars relating to a number of topics of which Eastern Europe was one.[1] During meetings and lectures over which the Comité presided, ideas were aired, though none led to concrete proposals. Although throughout the First World War the French assumed that the fate of Eastern European nations would be of direct interest to them, the end of military activities found them in a weak position to influence the course of events. In the first place the outbreak of the February Revolution in Russia in 1917, followed by the anti-war Bolsheviks assuming power in October, clearly damaged the Allied war effort. The Brest–Litovsk Peace Treaty ending war between Russia and the German Empire, signed on 3 March 1918, came at a militarily very difficult time for the French. When their fortunes were reversed and the Central Powers collapsed, France still trailed behind developments east of Germany. The French High Command had little influence over events unfolding in the region. The definition of new frontiers and the establishment of civilian authorities in areas previously under German, Austrian and Russian administration proceeded with the French having no say in the matter. The outbreak of the Revolution in Russia and the civil war which followed suggested to French politicians that, when the time came to consider future allies, Russia would have to be discounted at least until some political stability was re-established. Thus the idea of strengthening Poland and Czechoslovakia as a counterbalance to Germany and a substitute for Russia, took root in 1918. In the course of the war France had already committed herself to the creation of an independent Poland and Czechoslovakia. Therefore the extension of the discussion to include both countries in the scope of military debates concerning the Eastern Front was inevitable.

From the outset the French found the East Europeans unmanageable and unpredictable. In the case of Czechoslovakia this was not as serious a problem as it was in Poland. In June 1918 the French government recognised the Czechoslovak National Council as the official representative of that country. This was made easy by the fact that the Czechs had succeeded in establishing their own administration in Czech and Slovak territories of the Austro–Hungarian Empire. It was generally appreciated that they were able to do so without acrimonious and public conflicts taking place between various *émigré* and home-based groups. This bode well for the future. In October a first provisional government was formed. Tomáš Masaryk became President and Edvard Beneš was appointed to head the Foreign Ministry. Both were known and respected in France. France was eager to recognise the new state as an allied nation. At this stage in the war French friendliness towards Czechoslovakia was motivated, at least in part, by the desire to see the militarily valuable Czech Legion, which had been formed in Russia, evacuated to the West. In 1918 this Legion had found itself trapped in the midst of the revolutionary upheavals which affected all Russian territories.[2]

Czechoslovakia did not figure as an issue which divided the decision-makers at the debating tables of the Versailles Conference. The new state's territory and its future role in Central Europe had been settled as a result of direct negotiations between the new government and Hungary, possibly its main rival in the region. Thus from the outset Czechoslovakia benefited, in particular when compared with Poland, from the general impression that it was a state which did not create difficulties and whose objectives were likely to coincide with French foreign policy objectives. Neither Britain nor the United States raised objections to stated Czechoslovak territorial aims, nor did they feel that French influence was excessive.

In contrast, the newly emerged Polish state appeared to elude French tutelage, while gaining powerful enemies. In France, doubts concerning the wisdom of supporting the Polish cause were widespread. Both during the war and after the Revolution in Russia questions were asked about Poland's usefulness to France. A strong Russia would have been a preferred choice. But as long as first the Revolution, then the civil war, and finally the imponderable course of Soviet policies, limited all discussions concerning that country, Poland was considered to be an important, though never tractable, substitute. Unfortunately problems associated with Poland tended to multiply. As the war ended the French initially backed Roman Dmowski's Polish National Committee, which had established itself in Paris, against the Piłsudski-led Government which emerged in Warsaw in November 1918. This turned out to have been a miscalculation, as Piłsudski was better placed to bring together various provisional and regional organisations which had mushroomed in Poland during the course of the war. French blundering was further highlighted by attempts to get the Poles to support the Russian White General Denikin. The Whites were opposed to the creation of an independent Poland. As a result Piłsudski, in common with other prominent Polish military leaders, came to view the French with deep suspicion.

At the Versailles Conference, the Polish issue became central to the debate on the German question. During the course of discussions the French faced British opposition to the strengthening of French influence in Europe, in particular in Central and Eastern Europe. Their task was not helped by the Polish delegation, which because of the arrogance of its members and total preoccupation with the Polish case, to the exclusion of other larger questions, generally made a bad impression on the French and on other delegations. The Poles had been determined to put their case independently of the French and because of that only succeeded in confusing matters further. The French delegation nevertheless fought hard to increase Polish territories in the West at Germany's expense. Lloyd George, taking the view that France had obtained security on the Rhine, used all his wiles to oppose it. As a result of conflicts between the key decision-makers territorial readjustments frequently reflected compromises rather than clearly thought-out territorial aims. The ancient Baltic port of

Danzig provides a good example of such bungling. It was denied the Poles, who claimed that they needed a port and it lay at the mouth of the main river that ran through Polish territories. The majority population was German but the town was not allowed to be part of the German state. Instead it became a Free City, the status of which was protected by the League of Nations. It quickly emerged that no one was satisfied by this solution. Although Poland obtained the Poznań region and access to the Baltic Coast, plebiscites determined the fate of Allenstein and Mairnwerden in Eastern Prussia and Upper Silesia. At this early stage France recognised that although her security would depend on the continuing French influence east of Germany, it was equally important to retain US and British goodwill. Thus France's policies towards Poland would henceforth be determined by her success, or the lack of it, in drawing the two world powers into upholding the post-Versailles order.[3]

During the ensuing years France vacillated between the desire to strengthen and build up her eastern alliances and the realistic acceptance that only British support would guarantee full security against Germany. In the early 1920s French diplomatic initiatives went in the direction of consolidating relations with Eastern European partners. Since Poland and Czechoslovakia could not be induced to co-operate, an attempt was made to form a Danubian Union based on Hungary and including Romania and Yugoslavia. When that failed due to Czechoslovak opposition, the French settled for a patchwork of agreements. Following the still-born Danubian Union, the French gave their support to a regional initiative which came to be known as the Little Entente. This was a loose system of agreements between Czechoslovakia, Romania and Yugoslavia, countries which had little in common other than the strong desire to forestall the resurgence of a strong Hungary, from whose dismemberment they had recently benefited.[4] The Poles too were responsive to French approaches. Motivated by a shared anxiety about German revanchism and deeply hostile to the Soviet Union, they needed French aid. In February 1921 the Polish–French Alliance was signed. Unlike the Little Entente it provided for joint co-operation against German aggression.[5]

It is too easy to overstate the importance of these agreements to French security. The reality was that even the alliance with Poland, which was the treaty most clearly documented and obvious in its anti-German aim, was opposed by a number of prominent French military leaders. Although a military convention accompanied the agreement, it could not be said that all ambiguities had been removed. The key questions of just exactly what each side was supposed to do when faced with German aggression against its own territory or that of its ally were never clarified. Only in 1939, on the eve of the outbreak of the war, did Anglo–French staff talks, aimed at coordinating military responses, take place. Even then General Maurice Gamelin, Army Chief of Staff, refused to admit openly what had become an axiom in military planning of the time, namely that France, when faced with German actions eastward, would take no other than limited action against the common enemy.[6]

Of less military importance, but equally contradictory, was the Franco–Czechoslovak Treaty of January 1924. This provided for mutual consultations in the event of aggression. In May 1935 the signing of the Franco–Soviet Treaty obliged the Soviet Union to give Czechoslovakia assistance in the event of German aggression. The illusion that this was a comprehensive East European security arrangement was compounded by the signing of a Czechoslovak–Soviet Treaty, also in May 1935, which provided for the latter aiding Czechoslovakia in the event of France first taking action to protect Czechoslovakia against German action.[7] In June 1926 France had agreed an accord with Romania promising consultations in the event of aggression. In 1927 a similar commitment was made to Yugoslavia.

No one, least of all French military and political leaders, deluded themselves about the East European alliances. The complex network of arrangements, in all cases lacking clear definition of what military support would be given in all circumstances, failed to convince anyone that France could depend for her security on an Eastern Front. Each treaty could, at best, be an element in a broader scheme, but since that very basic pre-requisite needed to galvanise France's allies together, namely a common enemy, was missing, so France's eastern alliances were no more than a loose collection of diplomatic gestures. Countries east of Germany had little in common. That much was obvious. Nevertheless the situation was made worse by the fact that each of France's allies was more committed to regional squabbles and territorial disputes than to the vague concept of a French anti-German bloc. Most

obviously France had failed to reconcile Poland and Czechoslovakia, which were divided not only by regional rivalries
but also by a dispute over the rich coal-mining region of
Teschen, which Czechoslovakia had snatched from Poland in
1921. But while Poland remained anxious about Germany and
hostile to the Soviet Union, Czechoslovakia had no anxiety
about the latter. Polish–Hungarian friendship further precluded
Polish–Czechoslovak co-operation, in spite of the shared anxiety
about Germany. Hungary was Czechoslovakia's biggest rival
throughout the inter-war period. In the longterm Poland preferred to strengthen ties with the perceived historic ally, Hungary,
while Czechoslovakia remained committed to the Little Entente.
Clearly Polish and Czechoslovak regional aims would have been
difficult to resolve. Unfortunately all French plans for an Eastern Front were based on the need for Czechoslovak and Polish
co-operation.

France faced the most complex dilemma in relation to the
Soviet Union. It was generally accepted that, notwithstanding
the havoc and instability caused by the Revolution and the civil
war, the country still possessed the economic and possibly even
military potential to become once more France's ally against Germany. Difficulties in evaluating the consequences of changes
which were taking place in the Soviet Union throughout the
inter-war period accounted for France's unwillingness to enter
into binding agreements. It was known that, until the Second
Five Year Plan, the Soviet Union did not have the industrial
potential to re-arm the Red Army. Prejudice, nevertheless, continued to play a part in the apparent timorousness of successive
governments to commit France to developing military collaboration with the Communist state. Post-war economic problems explain why politicians preferred to avoid the issue of
the Soviet Union. The French *rentier* class had been heavily hit
by the nationalisation policies of the Bolsheviks, which made
Russian bonds held in France worthless. In addition internal politics, with conflicts between the left and right and a general tendency to overestimate the strength of the French Communist
Party, increased hostility to any form of collaboration with a state
governed by a hostile ideology. These ideas and prejudices were not
just common to the wider public, but were also shared by military
men, who visibly dithered between, on the one hand, supporting

the generally unsatisfactory patchwork of eastern alliances, while on the other wishing to bring the Soviet Union into closer colla-boration with France. Even those wary of closer ties with the Soviet Union accepted that it would have been a good idea to deny Germany access to Soviet resources.[8] The decisive push to respond to Maxim Litvinov, the astute Soviet Minister for Foreign Affairs, who badgered the French for closer collaboration throughout the 1930s, came in 1935. The suggestion is that anxi-ety about the growth of German military power, combined with an uneasy suspicion that Britain was seeking closer collaboration with the new Nazi regime, pushed Pierre Laval, the Minister for Foreign Affairs, to initiate talks with the Soviet Union in earnest.[9]

Had France proceeded to develop military and economic ties with the Soviet Union after 1935, this process would have eroded most of her agreements with the Eastern European states. Poland and Romania in particular were bitterly opposed to the Soviet Union and refused to consider any agreements which would have drawn it into regional security arrangements. As it turned out, having initiated talks with the Soviet Union, Laval then post-poned the ratification of the concluded agreement until February 1936. The diplomatic implications were serious, for the gesture signalled neglect. This impression was confirmed by the failure to initiate military talks and lack of any further developments in Franco–Soviet relations. Since Franco–Soviet talks were closely monitored in European capitals, the failure to conclude them was widely interpreted as a snub to the Russians. Germany and Britain assumed that France was still hoping to resume direct talks with Berlin and London. The Poles concluded that, notwithstand-ing the establishment of contacts between France and Russia, the former still wished to maintain existing agreements with the small East European allies.[10]

In France the general wisdom of retaining all options open for the Eastern Front was confirmed when in March 1936 Germany re-militarized the Rhineland. This led Paris to review once more its commitment to the eastern allies. Poland benefited directly by the receipt of 8000 million francs from what became known as the Rambouillet loan for the purchase of French industrial goods and armaments. Unfortunately French industry proved incapable of supplying the required goods, thus making political nonsense of the gesture.[11] This apparent inability to decide whether the eastern allies were in the long term vital or merely necessary to French security continued to characterise debates which took place on the highest level. Even in 1936 the paralysis, which was the inevitable consequence of so many contradictory considerations, affected all debates concerning Eastern Europe and with it the Eastern Front. Internal political instability stood in the way of a consensus emerging and successive governments found that support for Eastern Europe was an issue more likely to cause dissent than unity. They thus generally shied away from new initiatives, preferring to concentrate on trying to defuse the causes of conflict between France and Germany, and after 1936 increasingly with Italy.

East European leaders tended to be critical of France's preoccupation with Britain and the United States. What they refused to accept was that to France this was a necessary precaution, not merely to guarantee French security but also as a means of upholding post-war peace. That does not mean they doubted France's determination to uphold the Versailles Treaty. They generally realised that some revision of the more restrictive clauses was necessary, but they feared that this would be at the expense of their security and France's commitment to Eastern Europe. The Eastern European states knew that the Western European Powers were willing, in their discussions with Germany, to consider the revision of their borders with Germany.

During the inter-war period France gave proof of its continual willingness to discuss issues with the German state. Thus in the mid-1920s, inspired by the hope of economic recovery, Aristide Briand, the Foreign Minister of the Centre-Left Government, led the way in negotiating directly with Germany.[12] He found his counterpart in the person of the German Minister for Foreign Affairs, Gustav Stresemann. The Weimar Republic's willingness to enter into talks for the restructuring of reparations payments and the acceptance of the loss of the provinces of Alsace and Lorraine, which had been returned to France after the First World War, inspired hopes that stability would prevail and that the League of Nations would replace war as a means of resolving international conflicts. The upshot of the Franco–German rapprochement were the Locarno Treaties signed in October 1925. As a result of these Germany's frontiers with Belgium and France were recognised by all sides and their security guaranteed. Since the main territorial grievances related to Germany's eastern border it was always difficult to square the Locarno Treaties with France's East European agreements.

Locarno was meant to be the beginning of a major process of re-integrating Germany into European politics.[13] This hope was not realised, as Stresemann refused to extend talks to include Germany's eastern frontier and as a result France failed in her half-hearted attempts to match the Locarno guarantees with an Eastern Locarno. Negotiations between France and her East European allies had been conducted throughout 1925, in fact simultaneously with talks with Germany. While the Poles were very keen to sign an anti-German regional pact, Beneš was not inclined to have his hands tied. He believed that Czechoslovakia's international standing was such as to allow for hope that the country could resolve its outstanding problems with Germany by direct talks rather than have its negotiating position limited by joint representations with Poland and France. The ambivalence, which had prevailed up till then and which would continue to bedevil French assessments of the usefulness of her eastern allies, manifested itself fully. Briand publicly refused to accept that the Locarno Treaties would at one single stroke render all the eastern alliances invalid. It has been suggested that what he had really wanted was to destroy German co-operation with Moscow. At the risk of appearing to neglect France's eastern allies, Briand fought a diplomatic battle to unzip Berlin from its Rapallo Treaty agreements which had been signed with the Soviet Union in April 1922. This agreement had raised the spectre of Germany using Russian economic and manpower resources to rebuild her dominant position in Europe.[14]

France's reasons for seeking to draw Germany back into European politics were complex. A genuine desire to scale down international tension, the prospect of breaking the impasse concerning reparations, the desire to limit German co-operation with the Soviet Union and finally the need for unity with Britain, which could only take place on the background of a decreased likelihood of conflict in Europe, all played a part in French considerations. In the search for security, which Locarno seemed to have briefly offered, France was prepared to run the risk of offending her Eastern European allies. In 1925 France finally obtained German co-operation on a number of outstanding issues, most notably the repayment of reparations. Without that she would have faced the financially draining task of imposing upon an unwilling Germany demands for reparations and of policing the state for signs of breach of military restrictions. However unsatisfactory, the Locarno Treaties represented an improvement on the militarily dubious and fragmentary Eastern Front doctrine which the French had succeeded in putting into operation up to that date.

Britain, a signatory to the Treaty of Mutual Guarantee, the central plank of the Locarno Treaties, approved of the Franco–German rapprochement. In January 1923, infuriated by German unwillingness to make reparations payments, the French government had authorised the occupation of the Ruhr region. Britain disapproved of this action. In the long term, the exploitation of the occupied region proved to be financially disastrous. The result was that France was keen to mend fences with Britain. British support for Briand's initiatives raised hopes that Britain would once more assume a direct interest in European security. In due course it became apparent that British support for France was qualified and was certainly not intended to be a blank cheque. It in particular did not extend to France's eastern alliances. The unresolved issue of Germany's eastern frontiers remained a source of anxiety.

In France's relations with countries of that region, the Locarno Treaties would henceforth act as a warning light signalling that France would, if the circumstances were right, dissociate herself from the states of Eastern Europe. In many ways Locarno increased those states' lack of commitment to France, if only because it encouraged them to investigate possible means of guaranteeing their own security by opening direct contacts with Germany. Psychologically a barrier had been crossed and, even though France was not ready to divest herself of her eastern alliances, the East European states were henceforth less inclined to take their cue from Paris.

1936 was the beginning of the final chapter in France's search for the means of guaranteeing her security and the deliberations on the role which the East European states would play in any war against Germany. The debates of that year set the pace and direction of discussions which would alter little until the outbreak of the war in September 1939. In 1935 the Ethiopian crisis focused attention on Italy. The view advocated by the General Staff was that it was important to placate Mussolini in order to gain Italy's assistance in the maintenance of peace in Central Europe.[15]

The German remilitarization of the Rhineland on 7 March 1936 led to an assessment of Germany's future objectives. In January 1935 Maurice Gamelin had been appointed Commander in Chief Designate. His attitude was that henceforth Hitler would concentrate on an offensive in the east. This conclusion still left unanswered the question of what France was to do in face of the German violation of the Versailles Treaty decisions concerning Eastern Europe. Ultimately both politicians and military leaders decided to do nothing.[16] The recognition of a major strategic dilemma seemed to paralyse decision-making. The impetus to make a move against Germany was ultimately sublimated into the opening of tripartite talks with Belgium and Great Britain. The securing of a British commitment to French security replaced anxiety about the need to formulate a response to Germany.

French paralysis in the face of the obvious growth of German belligerence was compounded in May 1936 by the election of a Popular Front government headed by the Socialist Léon Blum. In the first months of its tenure the new government tried to address problems already identified but left unresolved by the previous administration. The task was to reassure the Eastern European allies, primarily Poland and Czechoslovakia, and to secure the support of the Little Entente governments. Reasserting and strengthening ties with the Soviet Union became a personal quest of Pierre Cot, the Aviation Minister.[17]

But within weeks of coming to power the Popular Front's efforts lost their momentum. Internal conflicts played a key role in this process. The election of a government committed to major social reforms exacerbated internal tensions. Waves of strikes, the mobilisation of the extreme right wing, conflicts between the government and major banks and between the government and the military leadership, created a sense of tension which ultimately paralysed the government. The outbreak of the Spanish Civil War, which taxed the loyalties of Blum who would have wanted to support Cot in aiding the Republican side, only made matters worse. These were not circumstances conducive to the continuation of further military talks with the Soviet Union, already portrayed by the right-wing press as the instigator of strikes in France and the evil force behind the civil war in Spain. The Poles and the Czechs continued to be as difficult as they had previously been about co-operation in the face of possible German aggression.

The need to secure Polish support for Czechoslovakia became a priority. Polish actions in signing a Non-Aggression Treaty with Germany in 1934 confronted the French with a spectre of Poland moving into the German camp and co-operating in the revision of the Eastern European balance of power. The unthinkable scenario was that of Poland co-operating with Germany in military action against the Soviet Union. Personality clashes account for some of the difficulties experienced by the French. In France it was believed that the Polish Minister for Foreign Affairs, Josef Beck, was virulently anti-French, a view encouraged by the French Ambassador to Warsaw, Leon Noël. None-too-subtle efforts were made to build up in Poland a pro-French group headed by the Chief of Staff, General Rydz-Śmigły. These crude attempts to interfere in the internal working of the military coterie which dominated Polish political life after 1935 had the disastrous consequence of only further alienating the Poles from the French. Problems between the Poles and the French went deeper. In spite of extensive political and military talks which had been conducted in 1936 and on the eve of the war in 1939, no precise obligations were made by the French to the Poles, while Staff Talks yielded only oblique, loosely worded commitments to fighting in the event of Poland being the object of German aggression.[18] In 1937 Gamelin already accepted that France would not pursue offensive action against Germany in the event of an attack east. Despite this, in the autumn of 1938 French leaders were bitterly disappointed that the Poles had joined Germany in intimidating Czechoslovakia. The fact that Poland had benefited territorially from the break-up of Czechoslovakia in 1938 increased the public perception of an unreliable and treacherous Polish ally.

The final opportunity for the French to try and influence the Poles to fall in with French policies in Eastern Europe, whatever they were, came in the spring and summer of 1939. At that time the Poles and the French had resumed military talks, in the course of which Gamelin appears to have promised that direct military action could be taken against Germany. By a crude ruse of linking the outcome of the military talks to the conclusion of the political talks which had been taking place at the same time, Gamelin avoided the responsibility for the final outcome of this brief reconciliation. Since the political agreements were not ratified, commitments undertaken during the military talks were not

binding on France.[19] In the course of the Franco–British Staff talks
which started in February 1939 and continued intermittently
throughout the year, inconsistent attention was paid to the question of how to induce the Poles to accept co-operation with the
Soviet Union. The French High Command was unclear on
whether the Soviet Union had anything to offer and conducted
talks with the Soviet side in bad faith. Military talks with the
Soviet Union collapsed, then commenced and collapsed again on
24 August 1939. Marshal Klimenti Voroshilov, Soviet Defence
Commissar, forthrightly questioned the French and British delegations on the issue of the Polish response to a German attack.
Both delegations had to admit that they had not secured Polish
permission for the passage of the Red Army across Polish territory,
even though they had come to Moscow to ask the Soviet Union to
attack Germany in the event of the latter taking action against
Poland.[20] The Soviet side withdrew from talks with the British
and French when the Polish predicament remained unresolved.
All sides knew that the Soviet Union demanded a more serious
undertaking to prepare for war than either France or Britain was
prepared to make at that stage. France and Britain were nevertheless pained to hear that the Soviet Union and Nazi Germany were
able to find common ground and sign the Ribbentrop–Molotov
Pact of Non-Aggression on 23 August 1939, just a few days after
the collapse of their own talks with Voroshilov.

The continuing dilemma of the role of the Soviet Union time
and time again highlighted French ambiguities and shortcomings
in its foreign and military policy towards that part of Europe. For
if Poland had been elevated to the role of the linchpin of France's
policy towards Eastern and Central Europe, the position of
Czechoslovakia in the overall scheme was most obviously left
unresolved. After the German remilitarization of the Rhine in
March 1936, it was assumed generally in France that Germany
would next concentrate her attention on Czechoslovakia. Events
unfolded differently and on 12 March 1938 Hitler's troops occupied Austria. France had no commitment to defend Austrian independence. In any case French military leaders had come to terms
with that possibility, which had been anticipated by their intelli-
gence service since 1936.[21]

Since France did not propose to take offensive action against
Germany the security of Czechoslovakia could not be assured

unless one of France's other allies was willing to co-operate. In effect this meant that either the Soviet Union, bound by the Czechoslovak–Soviet Treaty of Mutual Assistance signed in 1935, would defend Czechoslovakia, or that Poland would have to be induced to do so. During the crucial period 1935–7 Poland was accorded disproportionate attention and talks with the Soviet Union were played down. The suggestion is that the military leaders, hostile to co-operation with the Soviet Union, concentrated on massaging the uncooperative Poles into the un-likely role of the defenders of Czechoslovakia in order to avoid having to face the distasteful need to enter into discussions with the Soviet Union. Since the Poles refused to enter into any commitments with Czechoslovakia, the latter were left exposed and undefended.[22]

But the growth of German belligerence towards Czechoslovakia faced French politicians and military leaders with a considerably more complex dilemma. The French were in a quandary as to whether the events unfolding east of Germany were of sufficient gravity to cause them to assume military action. Underlying all considerations relating to Czechoslovakia was the assumption that Germany's military strength was greater than France's. The army advised the politicians not to risk war in circumstances where they believed France would not be prepared to face Ger-many for another two years. At the same time the Minister for For-eign Affairs, Georges Bonnet, did all he could to avoid France's commitment to Czechoslovakia. He therefore welcomed Cham-berlain's solution of a negotiated settlement as a means of defusing a situation into which he did not want France drawn.[23]

The question of Czechoslovakia hinged in equal measure on the anticipated responses of the Soviet Union, of Poland and of the other states of the Little Entente, Romania and Yugoslavia. And even in the latter case, French foreign policy was blighted by a self-imposed paralysis. The focal point in the case of all debates con-cerning the Little Entente was Italy, and the conviction which prevailed was that it could still be induced not to associate directly with Germany. French military thinking on the subject of Eastern Europe was, after 1936, determined by a preoccupation with Italy and the Mediterranean. The consequence of the outbreak of the Spanish Civil War was a realisation that French Mediterranean and imperial interests were severely threatened by the growth of

Italian influence in the region. This preoccupation with Italy
meant that the German threat was increasingly seen as secondary
to the more likely possibility of an Italian attack on French interests. French diplomacy concentrated on trying to defuse the
potential threat posed by Italy to French interests in North and
East Africa, to Corsica and to the mainland.[24] As a result France,
the state which had encouraged and facilitated the build-up of a
regional understanding, found itself in the second half of the
1930s unable to make use of it. The importance of Italy in France's
Mediterranean policy was such as to inhibit the High Command
from recommending action which might be disapproved of by
Italy. Thus any attempts by the government to strengthen ties
with Yugoslavia or Romania were discouraged. In effect this also
meant that Soviet attempts to reach an accommodation with
France, in the course of which the Romanian–Soviet territorial
issues could have been a factor, were also avoided.[25]

The defensive nature of French military planning after 1936
relegated all debates concerning Eastern Europe to the question
of what these states would do in the event of a German attack on
France. Plans for French initiatives, should there be a German
attack against Poland or Czechoslovakia, were never worked out.
The logical consequence of such an approach to the narrowing
down of the French security debate was that at the beginning of
1938, when Gamelin examined France's military situation, he
concluded that while both Germany and Italy were likely to pose
a threat to France's interests, of the two Italy was in a position to
inflict greater damage. This would form the basic framework for a
discussion of France's political and military options during the
forthcoming Czechoslovak and Polish crises. Gamelin judged
that France's security forces were in the first place committed to
the defence of metropolitan France and her imperial interests.
The second priority was to be prepared to take action against
Italy across the Alps and in North and East Africa. Assistance to
the East European allies, when under attack from Germany, was
the third priority of the French security forces.[26] Once military
priorities were confirmed they acted as a guiding principle during
Staff talks with the British and the Poles. During these talks the
French never wavered from their determination not to take
the offensive unless French interests in the Mediterranean and
North Africa were directly threatened.

By the time of the German attack on Poland, twenty years of French deliberations on the subject of an Eastern Front had yielded few tangible results. The dilemmas posed by the Eastern Front concept never were resolved. Moreover, as a result of General Gamelin's influence on military thinking, military doctrine on the defence of France had been narrowed down to the singular solution of defending and conserving French resources in anticipation of a German attack.

On 3 September, following the German attack on Poland, France declared war on the aggressor. In spite of the military convention which accompanied the alliance with Poland and contrary to expectations generated by the recent Polish–Staff talks, France had no legal obligation to defend Poland.[27] The decision to go to war with Germany was made reluctantly and not in order to defend or even relieve Poland. It was done because of the fear that Hitler's aggression would result in Germany capturing economic resources. The assumption continued to be that the war was going to be long and economically exhausting: a country's ability to sustain a long campaign would be of decisive importance. In August 1939, French politicians and military leaders made the decision not to defend Poland or even to punish Germany, but to put a halt to Germany establishing control over the economic resources of Eastern Europe.[28] The result was that even though France declared war on Germany, her main, if not only, preoccupation was not with the plight of her ally, but with her own military situation. All calls for military action against Germany were mitigated by cautionary warnings that not only would this interfere with France's preparations for war, but would also provoke Germany at a time when France still needed time to complete her war-plans.[29]

Plans for the destruction of the Romanian oil field were briefly discussed. All proved unworkable. French prestige, as did Britain's, fell as the neutral countries of the Balkans took note of those countries' impotence in the face of German aggression. At the end of 1939 the Balkans still attracted some attention when the Salonica Front was discussed. As the subject was tentatively touched upon, the will to invest in the proposal evaporated. On 19 December in the course of the fourth meeting of the Supreme War Council the British delegation was informed by Daladier that France was not able to provide a force for the Balkan Front. Since British plans for Salonica and Constantinople were developed on the assumption that France would provide the infantry, preparations for the Balkan Front went no further. The pace and direction of the war was dictated by Germany, France was reduced to the role of a hapless observer of developments in Eastern Europe. On 10 May 1940 Germany attacked France by moving through Holland and Belgium. On 22 June the Government of Marshal Philippe Pétain signed an armistice with Germany.

Great Britain

Unlike France, Britain had traditionally not sought direct involvement in Eastern Europe. In the long term neither France, Germany, nor even Russia posed a threat to the security of the British Isles or to their vital economic interests. The result was that during the inter-war period any concern about the balance of power in Eastern Europe tended to be short-term and usually caused by some crisis. The same attitude characterised Britain's attitude towards Europe as a whole. Stability on the European continent was clearly seen as a desirable precondition for the maintenance of British security and economic wellbeing. Nevertheless Britain did not wish to commit herself to any one European state in advance of any conflict. During the inter-war period the prevailing view was that Britain's economic prosperity depended on economic links with her Empire. During the Depression of the 1930s Britain sought to increase and strengthen trade with her overseas possessions and the Dominions. The First World War had taught all European states that they would only win the next war if they had the capacity to sustain an economically draining long offensive. Thus the need to maintain Britain's links with the Empire was seen as a priority in any future war. Upon the military services fell the burden of defending the British Isles, the Imperial possessions, and the communication routes to those distant territories. Not surprisingly any involvement in the affairs of the European continent was carefully evaluated from the perspective of those priorities.

While geographically Britain is undeniably part of the continent of Europe, politically and even strategically Europe was on the periphery of British considerations during the whole of the inter-war period. In 1938 the government, led by Neville Chamberlain, lost sight of the distinction between, on the one hand, upholding a stable balance of power in Europe and, on the other, assuming an active role in maintaining it. In 1938 none of the politicians involved in the talks initiated with Germany on the subject of the Czechoslovak crisis fully understood the implications of that decision. None had intended to pitch Britain into the turbulence of European affairs. As it turned out, once the decision to mediate between Czechoslovakia and Germany had been taken, the next inevitable step was to assume responsibility for decisions made and for their implementation. In September 1938 the British government broke with past British policy and unwittingly involved Britain directly in the maintenance of the European peace. In the process, Chamberlain also deviated from previous policies of not making commitments to countries east of Germany.

Both Britain's earlier limited interest in the fate of Eastern Europe and her late conversion to becoming the champion of small states are worthy of comment. Within English-language writing the historian A. J. P. Taylor was the first forcefully to criticise Britain for her ineptitude in her handling of Germany during the inter-war period. His book *The Origins of the Second World War* raised the uncomfortable issue of whether Britain's policy of appeasement did not lead Nazi Germany to presume that the revision of the frontiers, in particular those in Eastern Europe, would be tolerated. The resulting study of appeasement has led countless secondary school pupils and undergraduates to ponder the question of Britain's responsibility for failing to support France, for allowing Germany to presume that aggression would be tolerated, and for the collapse of British prestige and standing in the world. No less than British responsibility for the outbreak of the Second World War has become the main objective of studies of appeasement. When put in this way it becomes difficult to defend the argument that Britain's preoccupation with the Empire, her trading routes and her own security was based on a sound assessment of choices facing the British Empire at the time. Those determined to see the study of appeasement as an opportunity to judge Britain interpret the turning of a blind eye to the true nature of Germany's policies towards Eastern Europe, not as an oversight, but as evidence of a conspiracy or at least of complicity. Notwithstanding the tragic implications of the Second World War upon Britain and Europe, that view cannot be sustained, in particular if Britain's strategic and economic policies are studied in the context of the time, rather than with hindsight. Circumstances at that time determined Britain's policies towards Germany, and in turn dictated the degree of commitment which could be made to helping any victim of German aggression. Our understanding of these broad factors is essential to the full analysis of Britain's role in the outbreak of the Second World War.

During the First World War British politicians and their advisors, in common with their counterparts in Europe, took into account the possibility that the Austro–Hungarian, Russian and Ottoman Empires would collapse after the war. The vulnerability of these big empires to internal pressures was well known. National leaders from the Balkans, Poland and Czechoslovakia had sought British commitments to their causes. British lack of enthusiasm for the small nation states was based on a pragmatic realisation that however unstable, the three European empires were preferable to a patchwork of quarrelsome, aggressive and unstable new states. In any case, the need to leave the doors open for Austria to abandon Germany dictated caution in making declarations of support to the Eastern European and Balkan national groups. Hence there was a marked reluctance to make any commitments to the break-up of the Austro–Hungarian Empire.

Two developments alerted British political leaders to the fact that this attitude might not be in the long term advisable. In 1916 Germany initiated negotiations first with Polish and Lithuanian, and then with Belorussian and Ukrainian national leaders in territories occupied by the German Army. The German High Command sought to secure their support for the German war effort.[30] Germany's promises to recognise the rights of these national groups to independence was seen by Britain and France as creating a dangerous precedent. In February 1917 revolution broke out in Russia. The disintegration of the central authorities in Petrograd was followed by the establishment of regional administrations. The British Foreign Office was only too well aware that its own interest could be threatened if outlying regions of the Russian Empire, notably the regions of the Black Sea and the Caucasus came to be dominated by a power hostile to British interests. While little sympathy was expressed for the political aspirations of the people of the ex-Russian Empire, German support for

Ukrainian, Belorussian and sundry Cossack groups during the Revolution and the civil war in Russia confirmed the need to keep an eye on developments in areas adjoining British spheres of influence. Nevertheless as the war in Western Europe drew to a close Britain had no plans to use her troops for action in other parts of the world. Inconsistent and half-hearted support for the White Generals during the civil war yielded few tangible results. Similar action in the Caucasus region, motivated by anxiety about threats to British spheres of influence in the Middle East, only served to confirm that unless Britain was in the long term prepared to commit troops and equipment to these areas, any victories and agreements with local national leaders were likely to be ephemeral. By 1920 the desire to end involvement in peripheral theatres was overwhelming. Instead there was felt a need to concentrate on economic relations with the Empire territories, which were to form the basis of Britain's post-war economic recovery.

Policy toward Poland and Czechoslovakia was likewise affected by larger considerations. While the newly emerging authorities in Poland came to view Britain as hostile to their interest, reality was more complex. In effect, in her desire to see a balanced post-war redistribution of territories, Britain was apprehensive of French support for the nation states east of Germany. This accounts for the opposition of the British delegation at the Versailles Conference to the incorporation of the city of Danzig into Poland and British support for German claims to Upper Silesia. The need for stability in Europe pushed successive British governments towards supporting initiatives either confirming the peaceful status quo, or allowing for the major European Powers to agree jointly on a peaceful process of territorial revision. This accounts for British condemnation of the Franco–Belgian occupation of the Ruhr in January 1923 and the contrasting British support for the Locarno Treaties which drew Germany into the concert of Europe. French efforts to follow up the Locarno guarantees of West European frontiers with similar security treaties for Germany's Eastern borders met with British disapproval and were finally dropped. British politicians were only too well aware that Germany did not consider her borders with the Successor States as final. If Britain desired to bring Germany back into the concert of Europe, the contentious issue of Germany's relations with her eastern neighbours had to be avoided. In the 1930s Britain supported Italian

efforts for a Four Power Pact which would have united Britain,
France, Germany and Italy in their commitment to the peaceful
revision of territories.

It is not surprising that the states of Eastern Europe interpreted
British policies as being opposed to their interests. British preoccupation with imperial and domestic economic problems was seen
as a sign of hostility. Beyond the eastern borders of Germany support for a European balance of power and a search for Big Power
consensus amounted to policies favourable to Germany. Some
believed that Britain was encouraging Germany to seek spheres
of influence in Eastern Europe. In any case nothing short of direct
military commitments, backed by extensive economic involvement, would have convinced the insecure and divided states of
Eastern Europe that Britain was not hostile to their interests.

From 1919 the biggest single factor constraining Britain's military commitments was finance. Basing itself on the assumption
that Britain and the Empire were unlikely to be at war with any
country during the following ten years, the Treasury cut the military budget to one fifth of its war-time level.[31] As a result of what
came to be known as the Ten-Year Rule, the services were starved
of resources even though anxiety about Germany continued to be
a permanent feature of all future discussion on the subject of continental security. At the same time difficult relations with France,
and a general prejudice against the French, bedevilled attempts to
plan for a European role in any future war. But the political and
military leaders were unable to escape the conclusion that French
and Belgian security was, and would continue to be in the foreseeable future, of direct concern to Britain.[32] In 1932 the Ten-Year
Rule was set aside and the Treasury authorised increased expenditure on defence. At the time the growth of Japanese belligerence
ensured that all discussions of defence and strategy concentrated
on issues relating to the Empire. To the airforce was assigned the
role of defending the British Isles, to the navy the protection of the
seas, while the infantry units designated for action in Europe had
their budget cut. Funds to maintain the British Army's continental
role were further cut in 1935. Neville Chamberlain, the new Chancellor of the Exchequer, was hostile to plans for Britain's involvement in Europe, seeing it as a waste of scarce resources. In 1937
Chamberlain decided that the Field Force destined for continental
action should have its rearmament budget cut further.[33]Even

though this coincided with the German programme of rearmament, the service departments were unsuccessful in bids for further funds. The Treasury was able to overrule all opposition to its policies because the government had decided its main priority was the achievement of balanced budgets. This was seen as the only way of securing economic stability. In any case military planning was based on the principle that Britain would not be waging any offensive war and therefore only needed a defence capability.[34]

Appeasement, in effect an effort to define the limits of Britain's military and political influence in accordance with her economic capabilities, resulted in Britain confining her involvement in areas vital to Britain's economic wellbeing and stability. Eastern Europe and the Balkans did not have a place in those considerations, though developments which might affect the security of Britain's communication routes through the Mediterranean, or the fate of her investments, did occasionally merit attention. This accounts for British concern about Italian conflicts with Yugoslavia and the extension of German economic influence into Eastern and South Eastern Europe.

In March 1936 Germany reoccupied the demilitarised zone of the Rhineland. Neither the political nor the military leaders in London could think of a reason for Britain to take any action which would signal condemnation of the German move.[35] But anxiety about Germany's long-term aims in Eastern Europe was expressed at the time of the Austrian crisis in February and March of 1938. Nevertheless at the time the Chamberlain Cabinet still believed that Britain should not take action to either dissuade or threaten Germany. The Austrian crisis at least initiated a debate on the implications of Germany's revisionist policies upon Europe. British politicians were forced to consider the likelihood of a threat to European peace flaring up as a result of a territorial conflict east of Germany. This possibility clearly defined the limits of any action which could be considered in the event of this happening. Britain would have found it difficult to send troops to that part of Europe. Furthermore she had no major economic and strategic interests to defend there.[36] When Nazi propaganda succeeded in focusing European attention on the crisis which developed between the Czechoslovak government and its Sudeten German minority in 1938, British politicians had by then at least prepared themselves to consider the issue in advance of events actually taking place. But the situation was made more worrying by the fact that Czechoslovakia had a security treaty with France and France had in turn obtained Soviet commitment to aid Czechoslovakia. The latter was made conditional on France taking action to defend Czechoslovakia in the event of a German attack. As the British politicians and strategists saw it at the beginning of 1938, German aggression against Czechoslovakia was likely, at least in theory, to cause Eastern European countries to invoke the French obligations to the defence of their security. British politicians were thus moved by an anxiety about the possibility of such an escalation of events, rather than by a wish to defend the integrity of the Czechoslovak state. This brought them into direct contact with Eastern Europe in a way in which, until 1938, they had believed unnecessary.

The British government had thus transformed the Czechoslovak crisis into a European issue. Acting in defence of European peace, it took the matter out of the Czechoslovak government's hands. Spurred on by an anxiety that the French government might, by aiding the Czechs, irresponsibly plunge Europe into a war, Chamberlain and his government assumed the role of mediators, initially between the Czech government and the leadership of the Sudeten minority and then between the Nazis and the Czechoslovak government.[37] The initiative ended in the convening of the Munich Conference in September 1938 and the signing of the Four Power agreement which sought to resolve the German–Czechoslovak conflict. As a result of the agreement Germany, France, Britain and Italy undertook to guarantee the security of the Czechoslovak state, once territorial claims made by Germany, Poland and Hungary had been dealt with. Thus in a manner which had been neither planned nor thought out, Britain committed herself to becoming a guarantor of the integrity of an Eastern European state; furthermore it was one with which Britain had few traditional links and in the fate of which Britain had no interest, beyond not wishing it to provoke Germany into aggression.

The Munich Conference turned out to be a short-term solution to a much bigger and imponderable problem of understanding Germany's long-term aims. Few politicians were able to understand the dynamic of the Nazi state and to separate propaganda statements from defined objectives. Whereas in the autumn of

1938 the British initiative had indeed defused the tense situation, in the early spring of 1939 Chamberlain was to accept that it had not dampened Germany's appetite. On 15 March 1939 Nazi troops occupied the Czechoslovak capital and the Bohemian and Moravian districts.[38] This coup worried the British government because it not only signalled Hitler's lack of respect for agreements made at Munich but also suggested that Germany might be preparing for a full-scale war. Having assumed the responsibility for arbitrating in the Czechoslovak crisis, the Chamberlain Government found itself drawn further into the affairs of Eastern Europe. News of German attempts to subjugate economically the oil-rich state of Romania was followed by rumours of German claims on the Free City of Danzig. The latter threatened to pitch the German state into a direct conflict with the apparently unpredictable Poles. Having once broken with her traditional approach to the Eastern European affairs, the British government thus moved from merely trying to defuse a crisis to building an anti-German alliance. From March 1939, however ill-prepared Britain was to assume this burden, she had no alternative but to consolidate opposition to aggression. Neither by September 1939, when the war broke out, nor by May 1940, when the British Expeditionary Force went into action against German troops invading France, had Britain succeeded in building up a system of collective security. Most decisions to prepare for war were made too late and with little consistent planning. Britain's irresoluteness in the face of Germany's initial aggression can be explained largely by the fact that it was directed towards areas where British political influence had traditionally been minimal. Geography as much as economic and military priorities stood in the way of comprehensive planning for war against Germany in the east.

In Britain's policy of appeasement, economic and political motives have to be viewed as interrelated. Thus any attempt to understand Britain's response to the growth of German belligerence and initial lack of interest in Eastern Europe must be seen against the background of domestic and economic constraints.[39] These did affect Britain's ability to prepare for any future war. Britain tried to avoid being drawn into security arrangements requiring investment in rearmament programmes which would in turn upset the delicate balance of the domestic economy.

During the 1920s Britain did invest in Eastern Europe, most notably in the three Baltic States. Most of the loans were private ones and the government did not attempt to link these to political co-operation. In terms of volume British finance played an important role but this did not give rise to pro-British policies on the part of the recipient states.[40] In the early 1930s concentration on domestic and imperial priorities reduced Britain's economic involvement in the Baltic and Danubian States, areas where trade with Britain had exceeded that with Germany.[41] During the mid-1930s the British Foreign Office noted the growth of German trade with the Danubian states, but also with Poland, Czechoslovakia and the Baltic States. They were unsure of its implications for British economic and political interests but were definitely worried by its rapidity. German preference for making payments by means of blocked accounts meant trade with Germany led to economic and in due course also to political dependence. There was anxiety within the Foreign Office that Germany's aggressive methods would reduce British trade with those regions.

In 1936 a Foreign Office enquiry addressed this trend.[42] The question was whether Eastern and South Eastern Europe were becoming an exclusively German sphere of influence and whether this was desirable from the point of view of British interests. The discussion which ensued, though confined to the Foreign Office, was a wide-ranging debate on German long-term political and economic objectives and of the desirability or otherwise of Britain opposing this process. The Foreign Office Heads of Departments were in a quandary. On the one hand they recognised that it would be generally undesirable for Germany to establish monopoly control over any part of Europe. Britain subscribed to the principle of free trade and even though British economic links with those areas were limited, it was generally not a good idea for Germany to exclude other states from this traditionally volatile area. On the other hand, as even Chamberlain recognised, economic expansion eastward would give German industry an outlet denied them in Western Europe and this was likely to lead to the scaling down of international tensions. The Foreign Office continued to debate this issue inconclusively. By the end of 1937 the state of affairs was tacitly accepted, partly because the Treasury had let it be known that it would oppose the extension of legislation to permit government loans for political reasons to the areas under discussion.

The most obvious obstacle to the expansion of British trade with South Eastern Europe was economic. The countries in that region were primarily agricultural states with little industry. What they had to offer for sale was not appropriate for British markets. Balkan tobacco was not popular in Britain, where Virginia tobacco was preferred. Goose eggs, down and fat were more appropriate to the French market. Bacon available in quantities was unlikely to sell well as leaner cuts were preferred in Britain. Though ostensibly Eastern European and Balkan governments were very keen to expand trade with countries other then Germany, they refused to settle old debts. Any attempts to grant loans to Hungary and Romania in order to stimulate trade were opposed by the Treasury because the governments of both countries refused to discuss pre-war financial obligations.[43]

After the 1938 Munich Conference the question of German economic and thus also political expansion eastwards acquired a new urgency. And still inconsistency prevailed. Governmental agencies pursued policies which they believed to be in line with Britain's foreign policy objectives and with her long-term economic capabilities. Each of these had its own interpretation of Britain's priorities. The Board of Trade, the Treasury and individual ambassadors sometimes duplicated and at times contradicted each other. Neville Chamberlain's preference for personal emissaries undermined the authority of the Foreign Office. British ambassadors were not sure whether they were to attempt to persuade governments to which they were accredited to look to Britain for loans and financial assistance for their rearmament programmes, or to discourage enquiries on the grounds that the scaling-down of international tensions and negotiations continued to be the most important objective in Britain's policy towards Eastern Europe.

After March 1939 British diplomatic staff in Romania and Warsaw believed that a pro-British orientation should be cultivated within the ruling circles. Howard Kennard, British Ambassador in Warsaw, encouraged the Poles to send a financial delegation to London. Reginald Hoare, British Minister in Bucharest, warned that Britain's prestige would suffer unless she was seen to be helping Romania to prepare for war. In London decisions concerning spending, including aid for allied states, was still controlled by the Treasury. Expenditure which was likely to

affect Britain's ability to fight a war was vetoed.[44] The Board of
Trade on the other hand pushed for continuing trade with
Germany.[45] It was inevitable that where new diplomatic initiatives were at variance with actual financial commitments, as was
the case with Poland and Romania, Britain's prestige suffered.
On the eve of the war Poland was offered what the Poles saw as a
paltry sum of £8 million, and that only in the form of credit guarantees. They had asked for a minimum of £24 million for the purpose of armament purchases. In the case of Romania, Britain's
economic and political policies were even more bewildering.
In late March 1939, at the time when attempts were being made
to draw Romania away from Germany, the Export Credits
Guarantee Department of the Board of Trade withdrew authorisation for credits on grounds that it had become a risky venture.
Economic talks which followed resulted in an offer of £5 million
of credit guarantees. Their use was constrained by such complex
conditions that it was impossible to utilise them for immediate
arms purchases.[46]

Britain's economic policy was only one part of a larger picture.
The need to secure economic stability in Britain, to conserve British resources and to try to defuse the Europe crisis were all of equal
importance. Political appeasement was thus, even in 1939, mirrored by efforts to deal with the world's economic crisis and
to build preconditions for economic stability. Political efforts to
warn Germany against resorting to aggression led to Britain
making a commitment to defend Polish security on 31 March.
This was followed by similar commitments to Romania and
Greece on 13 April. At the same time unofficial attempts continued to reach a general economic settlement with Germany.
Between November 1937 and September 1939 the Chamberlain
Government made five major approaches to Germany with the
aim of negotiating an economic détente.[47] These initiatives took
precedent over agreements with Eastern European states, for
with them were associated hopes for a permanent solution to economic crises which could arise between industrialised states. They
were unsuccessful because Nazi Germany did not respond.

Questions relating to Britain's military capability to defend her
interests by means of defensive or offensive strategies were always
dominated by financial considerations. In that context the Empire
increasingly became a drain on British resources while imposing

constraints on plans for involvement in Europe. At the end of the First World War the British government extended its control over larger parts of the world than before the war. What followed was increased commitment to the defence of the Empire. Furthermore the governments of the Dominions, which had provided troops and finance for the British war effort, henceforth demanded to have a voice in military decision-making. Australia, New Zealand, Canada and South Africa imposed a wider perspective into discussions dealing with the security of the British Empire and the safety of routes to outlying areas. At the end of the First World War the importance of the European continent once more diminished. Commitments to the upholding of the post-Versailles order were subordinated to the needs of the Empire.[48]

While British politicians prided themselves on the fact that international standing bestowed upon Britain the responsibility to act as arbiter in European conflicts, European states expected more from Britain. It has been noted that British involvement in attempting to defuse the Czechoslovak crisis in 1938 gave rise to conflicting interpretations of British objectives. While diplomatically Britain was taking the lead and actively seeking to reduce the likelihood of war breaking out, her lack of military commitment to France tended to remind European states forcefully that Britain viewed continental security as an issue apart from that of the security of the British Isles.[49]

In February 1939 growing German belligerence caused the Cabinet finally to increase Britain's commitment to fighting on the continent. Conscription was introduced, though its scope was so limited that it had only a minimal impact on preparations for war. The Territorial Army was doubled and financial commitments were made to the rearming of the Field Force. Decisions to increase British commitment to fighting Germany were motivated by a desire to be seen responding to what was a crisis situation.[50] In September 1939 four divisions of the Field Force sailed for France badly equipped, in obsolete vehicles and, as was apparent to all onlookers, badly trained.[51]

On 8 February 1939 the Cabinet accepted the need to open Staff talks with the French. These started on 29 March and periodic meetings continued until the fall of France. At first precise military talks evolved around the pre-agreed theme of 'The Military Implications of the Anglo–French Guarantee to Poland and

Romania'.[52] During the course of discussions the British Chiefs of Staff maintained that neither Poland nor Romania was in a position to mount a successful counter-offensive against Germany. It was tacitly accepted that whether they held out for some time or were rapidly defeated would make no difference to British strategic plans for the defeat of Germany.[53] Britain did not plan to assist Poland and no attacks on Germany were envisaged. French plans, naturally, were more precise in addressing what in essence was an old dilemma of France's concept of an Eastern Front. Unlike their British counterparts, the French military leaders did see that some benefit could be derived from Polish resistance to Germany. Poland was credited with an inspirational ability to galvanise Romania and the other Balkan states to resist Germany. The sting nevertheless came in the closing sentence of the French report, in which it was admitted that Polish resistance would only be of use if it brought about the creation of 'a long, solid and durable front'.[54] The last statement would henceforth act as an exclusion clause, explaining why it was not worth taking the initiative against Germany in the west, and justifying a failure to grant Poland aid and ammunition in her preparations for war against Germany. British military planners saw in the phrase merely a confirmation that France would do nothing until British commitments were increased. Plans for the Eastern, and also the Western, Fronts proceeded inconclusively, with the latter ultimately becoming more precise. Nevertheless even these were confined to taking defensive action.

In the months preceding the outbreak of the war in September 1939 the Poles demanded the opening of Staff talks with the British, initiated financial talks and finally sent to Britain a military mission with the aim of purchasing vital equipment. The British response to all this was to refuse to be drawn into arrangements which would reduce Britain's war capacity and which would distract from the long-term objective of preparing for the impending war. In British military planning the concept of an Eastern Front never developed beyond the vaguest notions of a diplomatic initiative.

Clearly in 1939 an air of unreality hung over all the military measures which the government was introducing rapidly and without due consideration for other long-term priorities. The new-found determination to persuade Germany that Britain would come to the assistance of victims of aggression was rarely if ever underpinned by careful planning of resources and capabilities. Poland and Romania had willingly accepted British guarantees. They nevertheless were not willing to allow Britain to control their foreign policies. Instead they had hoped to strengthen their hand in dealings with Germany. Neither country wished to be associated with any military arrangements that would include the Soviet Union. Both put forward a number of explanations for refusing to see the British guarantee extended to include the Soviet Union. The Poles believed that they would not need Soviet assistance. Beck had persuaded himself that in the event of a war with Germany Polish bravery and determination would tip the military balance in Poland's favour. In addition there was a realistic suspicion that once the Red Army entered Polish territories it would not willingly depart. Chamberlain was indifferent to the first argument while being wholly in sympathy with the second. Romania too feared the Soviet Union. King Carol had come to view the Soviet threat as more serious than the German one. The Soviet Union let it be known that it wished to reopen talks on the subject of the contested regions of Bessarabia and Bukovina. Thus Britain, Poland and Romania all agreed that plans to resist German aggression did not require the co-operation of the Soviet Union. During the tense last two weeks of March, at the time when the proposal for a concerted response to German aggression was first mooted, the Cabinet sought the military leaders' advice. The Chiefs of Staff did not express strong feelings on the subject of the Soviet Union. They estimated that Romania would not be able to resist a German attack. Poland was credited with the ability to fight for only a limited period. Neither France nor Britain proposed to attack Germany in the west and finally neither was willing to station troops and prepare ammunition dumps in Eastern Europe prior to the outbreak of the war. Throughout the months preceding the outbreak of the war, and as Britain continued military contacts with the Poles and conducted Staff talks with the French, the British concept of an Eastern Front became hazier.[55]

At the beginning of April British statesmen hoped that without actually entering into any agreements with the country, they could secure Soviet support for their proposals to oppose Germany. On 18 April the Soviet Ambassador put to the Foreign Office a proposal which, as was to become apparent in the coming months, was the only basis on which the Soviet Union was prepared to conduct talks with the British and French. What the Russians wanted was a pact of mutual assistance. The Baltic States, Poland and the Balkan countries were to be included in the scope of the agreement. Chamberlain was uncomfortable at the eager determination of the Soviet Union to treat seriously his earlier, loose proposals for Eastern European countries to form a bloc opposed to German aggression. France's willingness to go along with the Soviet proposal only increased his concern.[56] Unprepared to go beyond the granting of guarantees to Poland and Romania, with no clear idea of how they were to operate in the actual event of a German attack, the British government found itself drawn into negotiating a treaty with the Soviet Union, the successful conclusion of which it had tried to avoid, and the very implications of which it found embarrassing. Buffeted by demands from within his own party and vocal calls from the Opposition, Chamberlain agreed on 24 May to the opening of formal talks with the Soviet Union. The Chiefs of Staff had in the meantime realised that Britain's commitments to Poland and Romania placed Britain in a difficult situation. They knew that the British government had no way of honouring them. Furthermore they came to the realisation that only a war on two fronts could offer the hope of defeating Germany. They had come round to the view that Soviet assistance was vital to Britain's plans for opposing Germany. Unfortunately for them, Chamberlain had set his mind against any alliance with the Soviet Union.[57]

What followed was to be predicted. Initially the British hoped that the talks could be kept at a low key and conducted through the ambassadors. At the beginning of June approval was given to the sending of a British negotiator to Moscow. William Strang, Assistant Under Secretary in the Foreign Office, was an able negotiator. He nevertheless was not a person of sufficient standing to persuade the Soviet leaders that Britain attached any importance to the talks. By the 19 July it became clear that the Soviet Union would accept nothing short of a full tripartite pact. While grimly indicating that it might accept the inevitable, the Foreign Office conceded that military talks should be initiated as a means of keeping the Soviets at bay, while at the same time hoping to obtain additional information about the Soviet military situation.[58] When the Franco–British military delegation arrived in Russia, the instructions held by them, which excluded authorisation to sign agreements, as well as finally an open admission that neither Britain nor France would do anything in the event of a German attack on Poland, revealed to the Soviet military leaders more than was actually conveyed in words. On 24 August, while the French and British military missions were still in Moscow, news was released that Germany and the Soviet Union had signed a Pact of Non-Aggression.[59] What British politicians had refused to accept, namely that all calculations concerning Eastern Europe inevitably had to take into account the role which the Soviet Union was bound to play, Nazi Germany had fully assimilated. The text of the Secret Protocol to the German–Soviet agreement was not known to the British politicians. Nevertheless it was not difficult to guess the basis of co-operation between the two states. Few doubted that the fate of Poland and Romania was sealed. British and French plans for an Eastern Front, vague and unclear as they had been, evaporated into thin air.

News of the German attack on Poland reached the British government early on 1 September. Between then and 11 p.m. on 2 September the British Cabinet dithered, hoping Germany would either withdraw from Poland or perhaps would even agree to the convening of a conference. When it became clear that neither was likely to happen Nevile Henderson in Berlin was instructed to deliver an ultimatum. This expired at 11 a.m. and Britain, together with France, found herself at war with Germany. Since the Agreement of Mutual Assistance signed by Britain and Poland on 25 August 1939 did not provide for military action, none was taken to aid Poland.[60] When Soviet troops entered Polish territory on 17 September, all Polish attempts to interpret the agreement as covering the case of attack from the east were rejected.

The declaration of war on Germany was not a commitment to either defend or even liberate Poland in its pre-war borders. It signalled only a decision to oppose Germany. For the time being action against the enemy was confined to attempts to bully the Romanians into assisting the Poles and not allowing Germany access to oil resources. In both, the British government was unsuccessful. The Polish government and High Command crossed to Romania only to be interned for the duration of the war. British attempts to purchase Romanian oil pre-emptively foundered on the Romanian unwillingness to enter into agreements with

British representatives. Britain's failure in relation to Romania marked a more fundamental loss of authority. British inactivity signalled to the Balkan states weakness. By the end of November 1939 Romania increasingly looked to Germany. The Foreign Office briefly deluded itself that Bulgaria, because of her willingness not to attack Romania, was following British requests to maintain unity in the region. This proved an illusion and at the beginning of 1940 loss of British influence in the region was fully recognised. The fact that Britain was not willing to declare war on the Soviet Union further decreased British influence in the region. The Balkan states stood to gain or lose too much, depending on Germany's long-term plans for the Soviet Union. By the end of 1939 British plans for the Western Front took precedence over discussions of Eastern Europe and the Balkans.[61]

2 The Soviet Union: The Ideological Enemy?

The revolutionary origins of the Soviet Union pose specific problems in our understanding of its short- and long-term foreign policy objectives during the inter-war period. In 1917 the Bolsheviks saw themselves as the vanguard of the world revolution. They furthermore believed that they did not represent the interests of any single national group but of all 'oppressed and exploited masses'. Subsequently Soviet security considerations appeared to be very similar to those of the Tsarist regime. Thus, in addition to securing its Asian interests, it sought to maintain a foothold in the Black Sea. Bessarabia continued to be a bone of contention between Romania and the new Russian regime. On the Baltic coast defence of Petrograd (renamed Leningrad) and the naval base at Kronstadt required negotiations with the Finns and newly established Baltic States. The fear that a weak Poland could be used by hostile powers intent on attacking Russia was paralleled by a desire to keep Poland weak lest it seek to settle old grievances with Russia, most obviously in the Ukraine.

In early March 1918 the revolutionary regime decided that it did need to have a diplomatic service and a well-functioning Ministry for Foreign Affairs. The failure of the European working class to stage further revolutions, on which the Bolsheviks had counted, and the onset of the civil war, changed the previous diplomatic disinterest. It became very important to maintain relations with the outside world, if only for the purpose of dividing enemies and attracting potential allies.[1] Though revolutionary in its origins, the Soviet government had to think of security as a priority and that consideration determined its foreign policy.

In view of the apparent overlap between the foreign policy objectives of the Soviet Union and those of Tsarist Russia, the inevitable question which has to be considered, in particular in relation to its Eastern European neighbours, is whether Soviet leaders did abandon revolutionary principles. Did the Communists become merely a ruling party which continued mouthing revolutionary statements, whereas in reality it had long abandoned them in favour of a much simpler defence of Russian territories? To contemporary observers this continues to be a dilemma. The fact that Soviet foreign policy of the period is characterised by statements suggesting a continuing commitment to revolutionary objectives and enigmatic initiatives lends credence to the suggestion that the real aim of the Soviet regime was revolutionary. If analysis is confined to the treaty signed with Germany, the Brest-Litovsk Agreement of March 1918, when the Allies still faced the full force of the German attack on the West, the Rapallo Agreement in 1922, and the Ribbentrop-Molotov Agreement in 1939, one could only too easily come to the conclusion that the main, if not the only, foreign policy objective of the Soviet leadership was to assist Germany and to destroy the post-Versailles European order and ultimately, by collaborating with the aggressive aim of the Nazi regime, to establish a Soviet sphere of control over Eastern Europe, the Baltic States and the Balkans.

This approach could only be sustained if one successfully overlooked the internal motives for foreign policy decisions. Indeed it would be possible to find in all the initiatives made by the Soviet Union during the inter-war period evidence that the sole aim of the Soviet regime was the fomenting of instability in the world. Once Soviet foreign policy is discussed in the context of international objectives, against the background of economic and political constraints, including the evolutionary nature of the regime, then a more complex picture emerges. This is not to suggest that the revolutionary nature of the Soviet regime should be overlooked. On the contrary, since all members of the policy-making bodies had played key roles either in the Revolution of 1917 or the civil war which followed, and most likely in both, it would be impossible to maintain that Communist ideology did not motivate the decisions made by these men. The fact that the Soviet Union embarked on the process of developing a diplomatic service, the purpose of which was to nurture relations with the capitalist countries whose hostility to the Soviet Union was presumed to be constant, does not conclusively prove that the ultimate objective of a world revolution had been abandoned. The defence of the revolution could not be guaranteed without dividing enemies. Lenin was willing to accept that a coexistence of the mutually hostile socialist and capitalist systems was possible in certain circumstances. In 1918 there was no inherent contradiction between the postponed revolutions in Europe and the need to deal with European governments whose hostile actions could be delayed or deflected.[2]

During the Stalinist period and in particular during the great upheavals of the first two Five Year Plans which laid down the basis of Soviet industrial progress and when collectivisation was implemented, the theory of peaceful coexistence was further extended to cover economic issues. The Soviet Union needed time to consolidate its economic achievements, its rearmament programmes and its borders in the east. Each of these major objectives individually and collectively provided an absolute rationale for maintaining working relations with the capitalist states. The revolutionary objectives and the institutions whose function it was to liaise with other Communist Parties received less attention and became subordinate to the first priority. They nevertheless were never abandoned.[3] Far from shackling the Soviet leadership to an increasingly unworkable programme, the ideological commitment to the continuation of the revolution beyond Russian boundaries gave them the freedom to pursue it as and when it was possible. Thus collaboration with the enemy and economic and military alliances with capitalist states were a valid means of defending the Russian Revolution while offering time for the revolutionaries to consolidate their resources against internal enemies.

The Decree on Peace was the first foreign policy initiative made by the Second All-Russian Congress of Soviets after October 1917. Far from being a reflection of wild idealism, it encapsulated the Bolsheviks' revolutionary, but nevertheless reasonable, conviction that peace was desired by all workers, peasants and soldiers, irrespective of nationality. At the same time, and from the Soviet point of view, it was startlingly realistic in postulating that only the abandonment of annexationist aims could form the basis of fair settlements which would guarantee stability in postwar Europe.[4]

The revolutionary leadership did not consider relations with other states as an issue separate from the question of internal stability. In fact, Lenin and his collaborators saw the fate of the revolution which had taken place in Russia as inextricably linked to the fate of the capitalist world in Europe. Since 1905 Lenin had believed that a revolution could break out in Russia, a state with limited industry and only a small working class. He assumed that the revolution in Russia would be the beginning of the world-wide revolution. The survival of the Russian Revolution was totally dependent on the spread of the upheavals to the industrial countries of Western Europe. The capitalist systems endured and the Russian revolutionaries were faced with the need to fight both internal and external enemies without any assistance. In March 1918 the mutiny of the Czech Legion against Bolshevik authority marked the beginning of the civil war. Disparate groups temporarily found unity in their opposition to the Bolsheviks. By summer foreign intervention added difficulties to the already dramatic situation. During the next three years the Bolsheviks mounted military campaigns against the White opposition, nationalist groups and foreign intervention. Lack of unity between these forces, and the indecisiveness of the governments which had initially intervened in Russia, constantly drew the Bolsheviks' attention to the need for diplomacy as a means of dividing the enemies.

During these years of civil war and foreign intervention the Russian leadership had to make often painful decisions to limit assistance to Soviets and revolutionary administrations which had emerged in outlying regions and to concentrate all resources on the defence of regions which they had some hope of holding. Thus, in the fight against the White opposition and foreign intervention, diplomacy was deployed to divide those European states which were not entirely committed to intervention in Russia from those which had a clearer motive for supporting the Whites. One such example was in April 1919 when France was willing to negotiate with the Bolsheviks who were moving into Bessarabia, the Ukraine and the Crimea region. Britain continued to support the increasingly unpopular anti-Bolshevik groups. By obtaining the agreement of the French commanders to avoid direct conflict with the Bolsheviks the latter were able to reduce the effectiveness of the British initiatives.[5]

From the outset Lenin identified Germany as Russia's main enemy. Only Germany had the capacity to destroy the Russian Revolution militarily. Thus the negotiation of a treaty with the German High Command was the first major test of the Bolshevik's ability to deploy diplomacy as a means of reducing the military threat. The drawn-out Brest-Litovsk negotiations were conducted at the end of 1917 and the beginning of 1918, when Germany was still hopeful of a final military victory in the west and the east. The Soviet delegation was forced to accept the loss of the Baltic region and Ukraine. Notwithstanding the humiliating nature of these conditions, the wisdom of establishing relations with the capitalist state, for the purpose of dividing the enemy bloc, was established.[6]

In the summer of 1919 the Bolsheviks took the initiative in negotiating with the Baltic States. Britain had hoped the Baltic people would co-operate with the White forces in defeating the Red Army. As it turned out the White leader, General Yudenich, and a number of assorted adventurers were more of a liability to the anti-Bolshevik cause. The Whites' unwillingness to concede the Baltic people's right to independence created an insurmountable obstacle to any co-operation. The Bolsheviks seized the initiative and expressed willingness to recognise the independence of the Baltic States. While ostensibly a political issue, in reality this was a military decision caused by fear of losing Petrograd. Negotiations between Estonia and the Bolsheviks dragged on, but by October fear of Finnish intervention in the Baltic added an impetus to negotiations with the Baltic States.[7] In February 1920 the Soviet Union and Estonia signed the Treaty of Peace at Dorpat. Latvia soon followed Estonia.

To revolutionaries, and the Soviets which had been created in the outlying regions of the Tsarist empire, it spelled the end of any hopes of unconditional support for their own revolutionary aspirations. As early as 1919 the Bolshevik leadership was making difficult compromises to concentrate all military resources on areas which they could defend. While support for revolutions continued to be the objective of Russian Communists, during the formative period of the civil war they displayed pragmatism which contradicts any suggestion of blinkered dogmatism. It has been suggested that the Bolsheviks had been successful in the pursuit of their objectives during the civil war precisely because, unlike their opponents and the foreign powers which intervened in Russia, they were able to define their priorities. Economic criteria were placed at the top of the list of priorities. Resources needed for a military victory were located in the areas defined by the line Petrograd–Moscow–Baku. They embraced the grain-producing regions of the Ukraine and Western Siberia and the oil producing regions of the Caucasus. During negotiations other disputed territories were sacrificed in order to concentrate on those which were absolute priorities.[8] When revolutions broke out in other European states, notably in Finland and Hungary, Soviet military and diplomatic support was limited because the Russian regime was not able to assist them. The process of assessing what could be lost and what territories needed to be defended defined the limits of support which would be given for purely ideological causes. The result was that Hungarian and Finnish Communists who had sought to establish revolutionary regimes in their countries received fraternal support, but notably little military assistance. The Russian revolutionaries had learned not to squander their resources on peripheral revolutions.

Historians differ in their assessment of the precise moment when Russian revolutionaries abandoned their commitment to an early world revolution and instead concentrated on fostering internal stability.[9] Most agree that the war with Poland in 1920 defined the limits of realistic Soviet aspirations in Eastern Europe. That the two were bound to face a confrontation was obvious. The defeat of Germany and the earlier collapse of the Tsarist Empire created a political vacuum in Eastern Europe. The emergence of an independent Polish state at the time when Bolshevik power was still weak whetted Polish aspirations. Polish territorial ambitions extended to Lithuania and the Ukraine. The Allied Powers, in particular France, wanted Poland to co-operate with the White generals. This was impossible because the Whites refused to recognise the emergence of an independent Poland. The Polish leadership was therefore content to see the Whites and the Bolsheviks fight it out as long as neither appeared to be winning. In autumn 1919 Jósef Piłsudski, the Polish Head of State, was unwilling to attack the Red Army which at the time was engaged in fighting the White General Denikin in the Ukraine. By April 1920 he felt that the time was right for a contest over the control of the Ukraine.[10] Polish failure to secure a swift victory created a host of dilemmas, which were not only military in nature. By July the Red Army reversed the Polish offensive and pushed towards Warsaw. Britain and France tried to halt their progress by opening negotiations with the Soviet Union with a view to agreeing armistice terms acceptable to the Poles. This was the point at which the Soviet leadership reversed its previously cautious policy towards the Polish question. In Moscow the matter was discussed during the Second Congress of the Comintern. Buoyed by the false hope which the military victory had stimulated, the Soviet leadership and the leadership of the Comintern spoke of a Polish fraternal revolution assisting the Red Army.[11] When defeat came it was both a military and a political one. The Polish counter-offensive pushed the Red Army back. By September both sides were willing to negotiate. The Red Army had failed to make progress in Poland, but by the same token, the Poles had realised that they could not enter deep into Soviet territory without first securing communication routes. On 12 October an armistice was signed. Poland gained Belorussian territories in excess of the Curzon Line, earlier proposed by the British.

The Polish debacle had taught the Soviet leadership not to move into territories where there was no prior sympathy for either the Russians or for the revolutionary ideals associated with the Soviet Union. The Red Army had been able to gain a foothold where there had existed some indigenous revolutionary movement. This had not been the case in Poland. The Polish campaign had been a military one and to confuse it with political objectives had been a dangerous departure from already-accepted principles of dividing enemies by means of negotiations.[12] The Soviet leadership fully assimilated the lessons of this campaign.

At the beginning of March 1919 representatives of Communist Parties and socialist movements from 19 countries met in Moscow for the founding Congress of the Third International which was subsequently to be known as the Comintern. Laying claim to being the natural heir to the defunct Second International, this revolutionary organisation was to bear the hallmark of its origins. It has been stated that

> What had taken place in Moscow in March 1919 was not in fact the fusion of a number of national communist parties of approximately equal strength into an international organisation, but the harnessing of a number of weak, in some cases embryonic and still unformed, groups to an organisation whose main support and motive force was necessarily and inevitably the power of the Soviet state. It was Soviet power which created Comintern and gave it its influence and prestige; in return, it was natural to expect that international communist

propaganda and action should help to defend that power at a moment when it was threatened by all the reactionary forces of the capitalist world.[13]

After the civil war the Comintern failed to assert itself and remained subordinate to Soviet foreign policy. From the outset the Comintern did not enjoy organisational independence. The Soviet Union provided finance for Communist Parties in other countries. During the years 1920–2 the Bolshevik organisational model and the example of the Russian Revolution was accepted by other Communist Parties.[14] The Comintern had the powers to investigate any member party with a view to purging its ranks. During the following years the Comintern came to mirror all the ambiguities which characterised internal ideological conflicts in the Soviet Union.[15]

Whereas in the first months after the October Revolution the Ministry for Foreign Affairs was seen as a minor bureau subordinate to the larger objectives of the world revolution, by the early 1920s the roles had been reversed. Georgy Chicherin, People's Commissar for Foreign Affairs from 1918, constantly laboured under the suspicion that his initiatives and pronouncements were not as authoritative as those made by leaders of various Communist movements.[16] As has been pointed out, 'The two objectives, world revolution and normal and friendly relations between Russia and the capitalist countries were . . . incompatible. One of them would have to be sacrificed or, at any rate, subordinated to the other.'[17] During the civil war and the war with Poland a hard lesson had been learned, that long-term diplomatic aims and the building of bridges between the Soviet Union and Western Europe had been damaged by European suspicions about the role of the Comintern.

On 21 January 1924 Lenin died. The battle for the leadership of the Communist Party affected all aspects of Soviet life. After 1924 Stalin further reduced the Comintern's influence and independence. This he did by placing his men in key positions and by purging 'Trotskyites' and 'Rightists' from various Communist Parties. When the conflict between Stalin with Bukharin in one corner and Zinoviev, Kamenev and Trotsky in the other reached its peak in 1926–7 the Comintern was no more than a battleground. In December 1928 Stalin, after expelling his opponents from the party, initiated a policy of 'Socialism in One Country'. Developing the Soviet Union became an article of absolute faith. The Comintern's policies followed this diktat. Communist parties were obliged to embark on a policy of confrontation with other socialist parties, now viewed as the main enemy. The mock ideological battles conducted by the Communist Parties under the Comintern's instigation were of little direct relevance to the Soviet Union. A suggestion has been made that Stalin attached scant importance to their actions.[18] What concerned him more was that the Comintern should not pose a challenge to his authority.

Hitler's assumption of power in Germany and in particular the refusal to continue the collaboration initiated with the Rapallo Treaty in 1922 had a sobering effect on the Soviet leadership. The Comintern was given a new role. In 1934 it was instructed to set aside previous instructions, which had prevented any contacts with socialist parties and trade unions, and to embark on a policy on collaboration and mobilisation of the working class in the fight against fascism and nazism. The Comintern's role, arguably the clearest and most constructive which it performed during the inter-war period, came about at a time when the organisation had no independence and was a compliant tool of Soviet foreign policy.

In 1920 the Soviet desire to establish diplomatic relations with European states was the outcome of the realisation that the Soviet regime would survive. In January 1920 the Allied Supreme Council lifted the blockade of Russia. Individual states therefore felt free to enter into direct negotiations with Soviet representatives. Nevertheless the biggest break came with the signing of the Rapallo Treaty. In 1919–20 the only power which had been capable of defeating Russia was Germany. Had the Allied Powers so wished, they could have allowed Germany to take action against the newly established revolutionary government in Russia. Fortunately for Lenin, the war-time allies were unclear about their long-term objectives in relation to the still rapidly evolving situation in Russia, while at the same time they were hesitant to see Germany establish herself in the political vacuum which emerged in Central Europe. The Bolshevik leadership had been fully alert to this possibility, hence Lenin's determination to counter the German threat at all costs. After the signing of the Brest-Litovsk Treaty Germany had shown her willingness and ability to interfere in peripheral areas where Soviet-style governments had sprung up. Thus in the spring of 1918 German troops had been active against leftist insurrections in the Ukraine, Crimea and Finland. At the time, by means of astute negotiations in the course of which the Soviet leadership held out the promise of economic co-operation, mutually destructive military conflicts were averted.[19] Nevertheless Germany remained central to all future considerations. Peace and co-operation with Germany was thus not merely a guarantee that the West European powers would not be able to gang up against the Soviet Union, but would also neutralise German aspirations.

The Soviet realisation that Germany was a vital factor in its plans concerning the Baltic region and Eastern Europe had its counterpart in Germany where, within military circles, strong views were expressed in favour of cultivating the Soviet Union as a counterbalance to the hostile Franco–British bloc.[20] Military contacts between the two had taken place even before the conclusion of the RapalloTreaty on 16 April 1922. West European governments had failed to agree on what advantages could be derived from negotiating with the Soviet government and by this indecisiveness had unwittingly offered German and Soviet diplomats an opportunity to discuss new openings. The result was an agreement whereby both sides repudiated all claims to each other's territories and to reparations payments. Both sides undertook to establish full diplomatic relations. For the Soviet Union the agreement led to fruitful military contacts and trade. The diplomatic advantages far outweighed those gained on the military and economic fronts. Most important for the Soviet Union was the fact that the treaty bound Germany to co-operation with the Soviet Union on all possible levels. Until Hitler's decision to renounce the treaty, the Rapallo Treaty was the linchpin of Soviet security in Europe.

Nazi electoral successes in 1930 had disturbed the Soviet leadership sufficiently to cause it to renew attempts to build an alternative security system in case anti-Soviet groups gained the upper hand in Germany. First the French government and then the Polish government, also disturbed by Nazi victories in Germany, sought contacts with the Soviet Union. The government in Warsaw let it be known that it would not renew an anti-Soviet agreement it had with Romania.[21] At this stage little came of these tentative manoeuvres. The decisive push towards a new foreign policy came with the Manchurian Crisis in 1931 and the growth of Japanese belligerence. Preparations for war with Japan placed an unbearable burden on the Soviet economy and war industry. Economic and strategic considerations focused Soviet attention on the need to decrease the possibility of a simultaneous war with Japan and a European Power. In 1932 suspicions were raised about the possibility of France co-operating with Japan. At the same time Poland, whose relations with Japan seemed to be unusually cordial, was suspected of trying to rally the Baltic States and Romania for a joint war against the Soviet Union. None of these speculations were entirely correct. Nevertheless they gave a strong impetus for negotiations with all countries in Europe.[22] Between January and July 1932, driven by very real anxiety, the Soviet Union concluded non-aggression pacts with Finland, Latvia, Estonia and, finally, with Poland.

On 12 December 1933 the Soviet Politburo authorised a major change in foreign policy. Henceforth collective security became the main policy pursued both by the Commissariat for Foreign Affairs and the Comintern. This reassessment of priorities, in common with all previous initiatives, was characterised by consistent pragmatism. The Communist dictators had no fraternal feelings for the German Nazis, they did not share their radical aims, and neither approved nor disapproved of their anti-democratic methods. Even after the previous policy of 'Socialism in One Country' was replaced with the new collective security idea, Stalin and his recently appointed Commissar for Foreign Affairs, Maxim Litvinov, continued to seek means of dividing the West from Germany.[23] What happened in late 1933 was an admission that the previous belief, that Soviet security could be based on separating Germany from the West, had under-estimated the aggressiveness of the German Nazis. Collective security was aimed at preventing Germany and the Western Powers from co-operating. The Soviet Union would henceforth concentrate on securing the assistance of the West European Powers against Nazi Germany.

In May 1935 the Franco–Soviet Pact of Mutual Assistance was signed. Negotiations between the two nevertheless revealed the near impossibility of drawing the Balkan, Baltic and Eastern European countries together into any form of regional agreement. Furthermore, their respective attitudes towards the Soviet Union and France, not to mention the degree to which each felt threatened by Germany, clearly contradicted the very principle of collective security. In the course of negotiations France's initial determination to proceed with the negotiations cooled. Britain's disapproval of the likelihood of France's increased involvement in the east hung ominously over the course of negotiations. The Franco–Soviet agreement became a devalued currency soon after its signature. Rumours of Italy reintroducing the idea of the Pact of Four, aimed at consolidating co-operation between Italy, Germany, France and Britain, and excluding the small states and the Soviet Union from negotiations of contested issues, dampened hopes that the signing of the joint agreement had marked a watershed. Maxim Litvinov continued to search for a new role for the Soviet Union in Europe, although he was left in no doubt about the enormity of the task. The Soviet Union's entry into the League of Nations in 1934, at a time when the international organisation had so little authority, was of scant significance to the Soviet Union's search for security. But it did facilitate Litvinov's contacts with other European statesmen. The period 1934–9 was a time of hope and of bitter disappointments for the Soviet Union. By the time Czechoslovak–German relations reached crisis point in 1938, collective security, a concept which was meant to draw the Western states into underwriting Soviet security by making it synonymous with the ideas of European security, had yielded very modest results.

Poland was the first state to secure what appeared to be an exceptionally advantageous agreement with Nazi Germany. The signing of the German–Polish Pact of Non-Aggression in January 1934 removed from the list of immediate anxieties the most likely sources of tension in Central Europe. In October 1933 Germany had left the League of Nations. The Poles flirted briefly with the idea of a non-aggression agreement with the Soviet Union. When they finally opted for a treaty with Germany, the Soviet leadership realised that the Poles had used the Soviet proposal as a ploy in their negotiations with the Germans. The fact that the Poles had refused to guarantee the security of the Baltic States, a direct route to the heartland of Soviet territory, indicated that Polish–German plans against the Soviet Union were being considered, if not in detail, then at least as a distant possibility. The German threat to the Soviet Union increased because it was felt that the Poles would either co-operate or at least connive with Germany.[24]

The Czechoslovak–Soviet Pact, which was signed on 16 May 1935 following the signing of the Franco–Soviet Pact, was a crumb of the larger Eastern Locarno concept which had been bandied around East European capitals since 1925. According to the Soviet agreement with France, the latter was committed to assisting the Soviet Union in the event of German attack. The relevance of the undertaking was diminished by a clause which stated that the League of Nations' recognition that unprovoked aggression had indeed taken place was necessary before France was obliged to take military action. In the event of a German attack against Czechoslovakia the Soviet Union was only required to take action if and when France had first taken action in defence of the eastern ally. Complex and qualified, both pacts reflected the Soviet inability to commit the Western democracies to action against Germany. Not surprisingly therefore the result was to increase Soviet insecurity. Those in the Soviet political and military leadership who advocated retention of open channels with Germany had no difficulty in putting forward their arguments. In April 1935 the Soviet Union and Germany had concluded a credit agreement for Reichsmarks 200 million.[25] In relations between the two states economic factors played as important a role as did alliances and guns. The Soviet Union's bitter disappointment with France's inconsequential response to its initiatives repeatedly reinforced the desire to bind Germany by economic means to peaceful relations with the Soviet Union.

In relation to Poland Soviet policy had failed, whereas Soviet–Czechoslovak relations had resulted in a dubious victory. In contrast, Soviet–Romanian relations appeared to have been a victory of *realpolitik* over national chauvinism. During the 1920s and early 1930s the two countries appeared to have been divided by the conflict over Bessarabia. The Soviet Union was Romania's main security concern. Shared hostility towards the powerful eastern neighbour brought the Poles and Romanians together and led them to sign an alliance in 1921. In the early 1930s the Romanians felt betrayed by the Poles, who had signed a Pact of Non-Aggression with the Soviet Union on 25 July 1932. The Poles had wanted the Romanians to conclude a similar agreement with the Soviet Union, but the Bessarabian issue stood in the way of any accommodation. The consequence of this Polish miscalculation of their influence over Romania was Bucharest's determination to assert its independence. Thus in 1934 Nicolae Titulescu, the Romanian Minister for Foreign Affairs, urged on by the French, decided to open direct talks with the Soviet Union with the aim of resolving the Bessarabian problem. In return for relinquishing claims to the contested region, the Soviet Union hoped to obtain permission for its troops to cross Romania's territory. The possible conundrum of just how the Red Army was to assist France or even Czechoslovakia, with which no frontier was shared, had not been resolved during the Franco–Czechoslovak talks. Romania was one possible route, since the Poles had absolutely refused to discuss granting the Red Army the right to cross its territory. During the years 1934–6 Romanian–Soviet relations were characterised by optimism. But this was short-lived. Polish intrigues and the Romanian King's weakness led to the fall of Titulescu in August 1936 and with this to the reversal of friendly policies towards the Soviet Union.[26] The Soviet response to the breakdown of relations between the two states was to reaffirm their claim to Bessarabia.[27]

The Seventh Congress of the Comintern which met in the summer of 1935 signalled a reversal of hitherto-consistent opposition to rearmament programmes, co-operation with socialist parties and trade unions. In its place the Congress advocated a policy of support for anti-Fascist forces in Europe. This change had been approved from above and was in line with the foreign policy approved earlier by the Soviet Politburo. Nevertheless the role of the individual Communist Parties cannot be dismissed. For them the Comintern's official sanction of policies which they had wanted to pursue since Hitler came to power in 1933 became a source of strength. Events in Austria and France had mobilised the radical Left. Italian and Hungarian exiles, and socialists from Poland and Romania, had been torn apart by factional conflicts when trying to define their response to the growth of authoritarianism in Europe. The Comintern's approval for a new line of action cut through these and imposed a policy which met with full approval from the rank and file of European Communist Parties.[28] Co-operation with anti-Fascist forces did not mean the abandonment of the commitment to the ultimate establishment of socialism, nor was it a transitory stage. It was a necessary expedient, a tactical manoeuvre necessitated by the fact that Fascist and Nazi regimes were recognised as more dangerous enemies than 'bourgeois' democracies.[29]

At the very top the new strategy had not been fully thought out. The Comintern's new policy was superimposed on previous internal conflicts and only vaguely coordinated with the Soviet foreign policy initiatives. Thus while the European Communist Parties on the whole enthusiastically responded to the new line, which freed them from an increasingly unpopular passivity in the face of the growth of Fascism, they were left without clear guidelines on issues relating to rearmament programmes and strikes.

In the Spanish Civil War the Soviet Union supported the Republicans. Nevertheless other considerations came into play. The emergence of another totalitarian regime in Europe would have weakened France. The reverse side of the coin was the possibility that republican victory would challenge Soviet domination of the radical Left. Republicans in Spain received the support of Anarcho-Syndicalist and Anarchist groups, ideological enemies of the Communist movement. In addition, a Republican victory was likely to fan the anxieties of the middle-class-dominated regimes of Europe and of the US, thus making its more difficult for the Soviet Union to pursue its foreign policy objectives.[30] The Soviet Union therefore gave support to the Republican side but at the same time the Spanish Communist Party was instructed not to push for radical economic and social reforms. As it turned out that proved insufficient to allay the suspicions of the Western democracies. In August 1936, in order to retain the goodwill of the democracies, the Soviet Union made an announcement that it was discontinuing supplies to Spain and accepted the policy of non-intervention.[31] In reality Moscow increased supplies to the Republicans. At the same time Soviet military advisers arrived in Madrid to guide the government in military and associated political matters. The Republican side's main internal weakness was its disunity. The advisers advocated total consolidation of socialist–communist forces and the disarming and subjugation of the syndicalist and anarchist militias.

The rambling course of Soviet policy in relation to Spain was shaken by the consolidation of the Rome–Berlin Axis in October 1936 and the emergence of a German–Japanese understanding which in November took the form of the Anti-Communist Pact. These were ominous developments.[32] By the end of 1937 Litvinov was under attack though no alternative to collective security was put forward. Stalin's internal struggle against any form of opposition spilled over to the army and the Ministry for Foreign Affairs. Henceforth Litvinov, on the defensive because of the failure of collective security, was under increased pressure to come up with results. In 1936 Andrey Zhdanov, who replaced Sergei Kirov, the assassinated Leningrad Party Secretary, was appointed to head the Supreme Soviet's Commission for Foreign Affairs. This dangerous duplication of Litvinov's functions was followed by Zhdanov's direct attacks on the Commissar and on his foreign policy. At the end of 1938 criticism came from Viacheslav Molotov, who was to replace Litvinov in April 1939. This was far more dangerous in its implications.

On 12 June 1937 Deputy Commissar of Defence Marshal Mikhail Tukhachevsky was executed. Only a month earlier he had been arrested on suspicion that he had been plotting with foreign powers to overthrow the Soviet state. The wide-ranging purge which had touched all civilian institutions in the Soviet Union now gripped the army. That an organisation so closely associated with great victories in the civil war, and showcase of Soviet achievement, should be purged, was not surprising. The highest ranks of the Communist Party had already been decimated. What is more surprising is the fact that this should have taken place at a time of danger and an increased feeling of encirclement by Germany and Japan. With hindsight it would seem to be a blow aimed against the very organisation which should have been strengthened in preparation for the inevitable attack. Historians are divided as to the reasons for the purge being instigated at the high point of international tension. If one is to discount the idea that Stalin was an irrational dictator and instead look for a reasoned explanation, the internal dynamic of a state under siege might be considered. One suggestion is that the well-organised and united officer corps of the army group did make preparations to stage a coup to topple Stalin.[33] This assumption is qualified by a suggestion that

Stalin must, therefore, have had weighty reasons for deciding that the Red Army's best brains and leading personalities were expendable. In liquidating the most independent section of the high command, Stalin rid himself of the last potential source of a leadership which could rival his own, having sent or being in the process of sending his political opponents to the wall. The action was not so much to prevent a conspiracy but to block an eventuality.[34]

We can only speculate that the possibility of army opposition to Stalin's internal and foreign policy was, in the circumstances, sufficiently critical to justify its destruction in spite of the military consequences. The purges rolled on until the end of 1938, in the process decimating the High Command more than the lower echelons of the army. It was inevitable that Soviet war preparedness was severely affected and that in turn had implications for Soviet foreign policy.

In European capitals the Anschluss rather than the remilitarisation of the Rhineland gave rise to the first serious debates of Germany's aims. In Moscow the response was muted. It has been suggested that the trial of a number of prominent Communist leaders, notably of Bukharin, overshadowed all other issues. Nevertheless the Austrian crisis in the long term merely added to the ongoing debate on the desirability of continuing the policy of collective security. British and French inactivity in the face of so blatant a breach of the Versailles Treaty clauses ordaining the separation of Germany and Austria confirmed Russian suspicions that both powers were tacitly willing to tolerate the Nazis.[35] On 11 March 1938 the Polish government took advantage of the fact that international attention was focused on Austria and issued an ultimatum to Lithuania. The demand was for the restoration of diplomatic relations between the two states, broken off after the Polish occupation of Vilnius in 1919. This incident galvanised the Soviet Ministry for Foreign Affairs to think of ways of warning the Poles that they should not consider the Baltic as their sphere of influence. But a diplomatic warning to the Poles carried the threat of accelerating Warsaw's slide into the German camp. The Soviet leadership had been anxious about Poland's co-operation with Germany ever since the signing of the Polish–German Pact in 1934. The result of deliberations was that the Lithuanians were advised by Moscow to accept the Polish demand for the resumption of diplomatic relations. At the same time the Poles were warned not to interfere in Lithuania's internal affairs. The spectre of Polish–German co-operation nevertheless became more real. The suspicion that Poland was acting on Germany's behest was further confirmed by Poland's part in the dismemberment of Czechoslovakia during 1938.[36]

The Soviet Union watched closely the way in which the Western Powers handled the issue of German demands on Czechoslovakia. Germany's bullying of the Czechs, French unwillingness robustly to defend her Eastern ally, Britain's disingenuous mediation which led to the Munich Conference, from which the Czechs and the Soviet Union were excluded, were actions which individually and jointly spelled the failure of Soviet efforts for a system of collective security against German aggression. The Soviet Union realised that it had failed to break out of its isolation. The Anschluss and increased Polish–German cooperation brought the German threat closer to the Soviet Union.

At the same time none of the East European states, whose growing dependence on Germany increased the Soviet Union's military vulnerability, were willing to accept Soviet assistance. In the course of the 1938 crisis, Czechoslovakia had asked the Soviet Union about its likely response to German pressure. Moscow's response, though guarded, suggested that the Czechs should in the first place make the decision to defend their territory. Nevertheless it soon became clear that the Soviet attitude towards German pressure on Czechoslovakia was of scant concern to the Czechs themselves. Czechoslovak policy was almost entirely dependent on French willingness to honour her undertaking. As it turned out neither France nor Britain considered it wise to confront Germany over Czechoslovakia. The road to mediation taken by the British Prime Minister, when he suggested that the Czechoslovak government request British help, excluded the Soviet Union from the picture.[37] Neither Poland nor Romania was willing to discuss the possibility of the passage of Soviet troops through their territory. Any action taken by the Red Army would be interpreted as aggression.

The Munich Conference completed the picture. The Soviet Union was not invited to attend and the Czechs had first bowed to British pressure to request mediation, and then had accepted its results. The sense of betrayal and bewilderment in the Soviet Union was acute. During the months following the Munich Conference attempts were being made to understand Western European motives for what was seen as a lack of foresight in their dealings with Germany. Inevitably the Munich crisis weakened

Litvinov's position and strengthened groups which were hostile to accommodation with any of the European capitalist powers. A factor moderating the urge towards strict isolationism was the realisation that the Soviet Union was militarily in no condition to fight Nazi Germany on its own. The suspicion that the Western Powers would welcome a conflict between the two was an added argument against a hasty break with Britain and France.

The period of bewilderment and of internal struggle for control over foreign policy was dramatically cut short by two events. On 10 March 1939 in a speech to the 18th Party Congress Stalin made a rare public statement on foreign policy matters. To those whose ears were finely tuned to the nuance of Stalin's interventions, it signalled a dramatic reversal of policies pursued hitherto. Unfortunately few West European statesmen cared what Soviet leaders thought and thus missed Stalin's suggestion that negotiations with all countries on a business-like basis were necessary. Berlin however picked up the message. On 3 May came the announcement that Maxim Litvinov had resigned and had been replaced by Vyacheslav Molotov. The removal from the political scene of this well-known Soviet statesman whose name was inextricably linked to collective security was not analysed seriously. Only with hindsight was it realised that the replacement of the Jewish architect of collective security opened new possibilities, which could not have been convincingly pursued unless a change of personnel had taken place.

During the remaining months of peace the Soviet Union considered two options. On the one hand Franco–British willingness to negotiate a general agreement offered an opportunity of salvaging some crumb of the defunct collective security concept. On the other, more decisive than hitherto, responses from Germany gave rise to the hope that German aggression could be forestalled or perhaps delayed by means of direct negotiations. The Soviet leadership was prepared to consider both options, the question was which one was most advantageous.

Franco–British responses to the Soviet Union and the course of negotiations for a Three Power agreement conducted during the period May to August left Molotov in absolutely no doubt that neither European Power was serious in its commitment to co-operate with the Soviet Union. On 8 May the British Foreign Office implied to Moscow that it hoped that the Soviet Union would make a commitment to the defence of East European states against German aggression. No suggestion was made that Britain and France should assist the Soviet Union.[38] On 2 June the Soviet Union made it clear that it expected Latvia, Estonia Finland, Romania, Poland and Turkey to be jointly guaranteed. A willingness was expressed to consider guaranteeing states vital to British and French security, namely the Netherlands, Switzerland, Luxemburg and Belgium. This was of no avail.

The stark truth was that Britain and France had no concept of how the Eastern Front was to work.[39] Britain's sensitivity to the wishes of the Baltic States and their apparent respect for Romanian and Polish objections appeared to be surprising to the Soviet leaders. Romania and Poland had recently been granted virtually unconditional British guarantees of security, and still were not expected to make any concessions to Britain's broader plans for fighting Germany. Both states had emphatically restated their opposition to Soviet entry on to their territories. The defence of the Baltic States, so important to Soviet security, was not an issue which the British had wanted to discuss. British politicians had little sympathy for the concept of 'indirect aggression', which they saw as no more than a Soviet attempt to legitimise its interference in the internal affairs of sovereign states. The matter remained unresolved, but to the Soviet leaders this attitude symbolised British and French lack of serious commitment to opposing Germany. Political talks between British and Soviet representatives made little headway and on 5 August military talks were opened as a means of breaking the *impasse*. In order to force the British and French military delegates to make viable proposals, Marshal Voroshilov, head of the Soviet negotiating team, demanded to know what would be the basis on which Soviet troops would be allowed to enter Polish or Romanian territory in order to engage German troops in battle. Since neither the shockingly low-ranking British nor the French military delegations had been prepared to discuss this basic problem, the military talks were terminated. It could be claimed that Colonel Beck's unwillingness to give the matter any serious consideration was the reason for the collapse of the talks. Tentative enquiries with the Poles only elicited a confirmation that the entry of the Red Army onto Polish territory would be treated as aggression. But the responsibility for the breakdown of the talks cannot be moved on to the shoulders of a minor player. The lamentable truth was that neither France nor Britain wanted an alliance with the Soviet Union. The Soviet leaders were left in little doubt about this.[40]

On 23 August Ribbentrop arrived in Moscow to sign a non-aggression pact. The timing of the German offer was opportune. Earlier Molotov had harboured the suspicion that negotiations initiated by Germany were merely aimed at forestalling a Soviet–French–British alliance. Since May credit and trade talks had acted as a basis for testing each other's intentions. The Soviet Union made it clear that it wanted to improve trade with Germany, but before economic agreements could be completed, political relations between the two had to improve.[41] By mid-August the Russians had no doubt that the Western democracies had nothing to offer. In the circumstances the German wish to discuss all contentious issues was not an opportunity which the Russians could have rejected.

Negotiations conduced by Ribbentrop in Moscow were brisk and to the point. Stalin knew that the German Army was poised to attack Poland. What mattered was that in response to a Soviet commitment not to interfere in the forthcoming German–Polish war, Germany was willing to make a commitment not to proceed beyond an agreed line. The Soviet strategic situation, which would be dramatically altered by a German entry into Poland, was to be safeguarded by a joint commitment to spheres of influence. As a result of the Non-Aggression Pact signed by the two, the Soviet Union and Germany undertook not to assist any country which might attack either of the signatories. In accordance with the Secret Protocol, Nazi Germany declared that it had no interest in Bessarabia, thus freeing the Soviet Union to pursue its own grievances. In relation to Poland, the demarcation line was fixed along the line of the three rivers: the Narev, Vistula and San. This meant that Belorussia and the Ukraine would both be under Soviet control. Latvia, Estonia and Finland were assigned to the Soviet Union, whereas Lithuanian territory including Riga would go to Germany.[42]

Initially the Soviet Union did not get involved in Polish–German hostilities. On 17 September an official Soviet note was handed to the Poles explaining that in view of the collapse of state authority the Red Army was taking action to protect the population of Western Ukraine and Western Belorussia. The Polish

Ambassador to Moscow refused to accept the note. When the Soviet Army entered on to Polish territories they wished to be seen as liberators. This of course depended on the point of view. The oppressed Ukrainian and Belorussian minorities certainly hoped that the Soviet action would spell the end of Polish domination. To the indigenous Polish population this was naked aggression with little to distinguish it from German action in Western Poland.

It is not easy to understand what the driving motive was behind Soviet policy in the period between the German attack on Poland on 1 September 1939 and the German attack on the Soviet Union on 22 June 1941. Among a number of conflicting motives anxiety about Germany's strength and her future course of action stand out consistently. The difficulty facing the Soviet political leadership seems to have been the dilemma of how to deal with Germany. The desire to avoid conflict with the Nazis was not easy to square with a determination to improve the Soviet Union's strategic position and state of military preparedness. Soviet political and military leaders took it for granted that Germany would at some stage resume the military conquest of Eastern Europe.

In the immediate aftermath of German victories in Poland the future of the Polish state needed to be addressed. When Poland was occupied the government escaped to Romania where it was interned. On 3 October a Polish government-in-exile was formed in France. The Soviet leaders decided not to try and create a puppet government in occupied Poland. When this decision was eventually made remains unclear. Instead the Soviet Union consolidated its control over regions which were of relevance to Soviet security. Thus on 29 September the Soviet Union and Nazi Germany concluded an agreement whereby in return for Lithuania coming into the Soviet sphere of influence the provinces of Lublin and Warsaw were handed over to Germany.

The Poles, the Baltic people and the Romanians presumed that Soviet-German co-operation had freed the Soviet Union to pursue its old aims of re-conquering territories to which claims had been made since the end of the civil war. But it is debatable whether settling old scores was the Soviet Union's main priority. Anxiety about Germany's long-term ambitions in the east remained. The Soviet leadership believed that time gained through co-operation with the Germans was no more than a temporary postponement of the inevitable. Preparations for war continued unabated.

One of the Soviet Union's long-term aims had been to secure military bases which would improve the Soviet position in the Gulf of Finland. Experiences from the civil war suggested that a major threat to Leningrad could come from that direction. From the Finnish port of Petsamo an attack could be launched against Murmansk. The latter was of particular strategic significance to the Russians as the Gulf Stream prevented the port from freezing during the harsh northern winters. During the 1930s the Soviet Union warily observed Finnish contacts with Germany, which became stronger during 1939.[43] In October 1939 the Soviet military leadership returned to talks which had been taking place with the Finns since April 1938. In the new circumstances the Soviet demands were uncompromising: they asked for the right to site Soviet troops on the Finnish island of Hango. The islands of Suursaari and Koivisto were to be handed over to the Soviet Union. When the talks broke down on 30 November the Red Army launched an attack against Finland. Germany maintained neutrality, which did not change the fact that the war went disastrously wrong for the Russians. Soviet lack of understanding of internal politics was shown by their appointing of Otto Kuusinen, an ardent Stalinist and activist of the Comintern, as head of the so-called Democratic Republic of Finland. Kuusinen was never given a chance to try his hand at governing Finland, for the idea was suddenly dropped. In January armistice talks were opened only to break down and this in turn led to the resumption of the Soviet offensive on 1 February 1940.[44] This campaign was more successful and on 12 March armistice terms were dictated to the Finns.

The Finnish debacle exposed weaknesses in the Red Army. As a result major reforms were initiated, but it was realised that time was desperately needed for these to yield tangible results.[45] German occupation of Norway and then victory in France all continued to accentuate Soviet vulnerability. The French collapse confirmed the Soviet Union's isolation. In the circumstances the Soviet leadership was prepared to pay a heavy price to delay the German attack. The policy of consolidating the Soviet Union's strategic position in preparation for war proceeded irrespective of previous policies.

Soviet relations with the Baltic States show the same degree of inconsistency as had manifested itself in relations with Romania,

Finland and even occupied Polish territories. At the end of September 1939 the Soviet Union was content to use Latvia and Estonia for the purpose of siting military bases. Both states knew their territory could have been wholly occupied by the Red Army and therefore did not oppose Soviet demands. After the fall of Poland, Latvia and Estonia were each forced to sign Pacts of Mutual Assistance with the Soviet Union. This is striking, because the Soviet Union appears to have wanted to base relations with the two Baltic States on legal niceties. In view of the German commitment not to interfere in the Soviet sphere of influence such niceties could easily have been dispensed with. The Pact of Mutual Assistance with Lithuania was signed on 10 October and included a demand for the transfer of a strip of disputed land to Germany. In principle the sovereignty of the three Baltic States was maintained, even though Soviet troops had been stationed on their territories.[46] In mid-June 1940 previous policy was suddenly set aside and each of the Baltic States was presented with a demand to form a pro-Soviet government. Under duress they all obliged by 16 June. Then came a demand that general elections be called. Under Soviet supervision these returned pro-Soviet governments which then requested that the Baltic States be incorporated into the Soviet Union. The reason for such extraordinary lack of consistency was the fact that each of these initiatives were taken in response to a real or perceived German threat. In the summer of 1940 the Soviet military leaders believed that Germany was preparing to use the Baltic areas for anti-Soviet action.

On 26 June 1940, only a few days after the signing of a Romanian–German oil agreement which gave the Germans guaranteed access to the raw material essential to their war effort, the Soviet Union demanded Bessarabia and Northern Bukovina. Determined to protect the source of oil, the Germans advised the Romanian government to accept the Soviet demand.

Having turned their back on the Western Powers, the Russians no longer felt compelled to support the Romanian borders that had been decided by these powers twenty years earlier. Nor did the Russians believe in the usefulness of a strong Romania as a buffer state between their country and Germany. They opted for the acquisition of territory and the improvement of strategic position by moving their defence line first on the Pruth and then, if circumstances allowed, on the Carpathians.[47]

Soviet actions in relation to occupied territories and in particular in dealings with Germany suggested internal conflicts. The Soviet leadership was clearly unable to agree on an interpretation of German actions. Hitler was not to be provoked but at the same time Soviet interest in vital areas, most notably the Balkans, was restated. Nevertheless the Soviet role had now been reduced to that of responding to German initiatives and still security was not achieved. During 1941 preparations for the impending war with Germany proceeded hand in hand with attempts to reassure the Nazis of the Soviet commitment to co-operation. On 6 May Stalin became Chairman of the Sovnarkom, a post equivalent to that of Prime Minister, marking his assumption of direct control over the government.[48]

On 22 June 1941 Germany attacked the Soviet Union. For the Russians the war would be one of unimaginable brutality, in which approximately 30 million Soviet citizens died. To the Soviet leadership this confirmed Lenin's view that only Germany, if unhindered by hostilities in the West, had the capacity to destroy the Soviet Union. Unlike Britain and the United States, which could still choose their moment for entry into the European war, the Soviet Union faced a fight for survival and one from which it could not extricate itself unless and until Germany was finally and decisively defeated. This eventuality, more than any other, influenced the Soviet attitude towards the Western Powers during the abortive negotiations before the war and the more successful ones after it.

3 Czechoslovakia

Until 1918 the fate of Czechoslovakia had been almost entirely linked with that of Austro–Hungary. The collapse of the empire in the closing stages of the First World War made it possible for the Czechs and Slovaks to create the Czechoslovak Republic. Both national groups, while ethnically similar, brought into the union very different experiences. Hungarian policies towards Slovak territories on the one hand, and Austrian ones towards the historic lands of Bohemia and Moravia on the other, had been dissimilar. After the 1848 revolutions Hungary had dealt harshly with any signs of nationalist aspirations amongst minorities within its borders. The official policy of 'Magyarisation' had limited cultural developments and with that the evolution of a clear national consciousness among Slovaks. Slovakia's economic development had been further hampered by a policy of neglect, as investments had been channelled towards areas inhabited by Hungarian majorities. The little industrial and commercial development which had taken place in the Slovak territories was concentrated in Jewish and German hands. Universal male suffrage had not been introduced in Slovakia. Slovaks were excluded from policy making and had neither experience nor confidence in the parliamentary system. Slovak nationalism took an extreme form, frequently unrealistically focusing on unity between Russia and the Slavs of Central Europe, while the more populist form, like that propounded by the Catholic priest Andrej Hlinka, rejected association with Czechs and advocated the maintenance of the perceived Slovak distinctiveness.[1]

Czech lands had been incorporated into the Habsburg Empire during the Thirty Years War and over the centuries had benefited from Austria's more tolerant policies towards its minorities. While the Austrian Crown did not grant the Bohemian Kingdom the same independent status as Hungary enjoyed, Austrian investments in Bohemia had economically benefited the Czech people. As a result of reforms instigated in 1906 Czechs, in common with other national groups, were granted universal male suffrage.

72

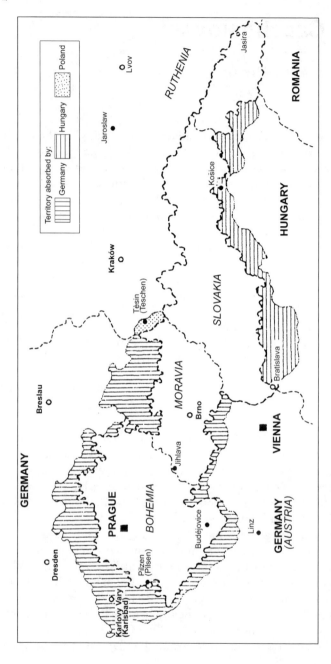

1 Czechoslovakia after Munich in 1938.

Czech representatives to the Vienna Reichsrat enjoyed all the privileges due to them as subjects of the Austrian Empire. The result was that Czech political parties developed a strong commitment to parliamentary democracy which was seen to offer them a real forum for involvement in the political life of the Empire. In addition to the widely supported Czech Social Democratic Party, at least two other Czech parties made their mark within the Reichsrat. These were the Young Czech Party and the Czech Realist Party. They concentrated on obtaining autonomy for the Czech lands. In the circumstances, independence for Czechoslovakia was not the only way forward. Since Austrian rule was not very oppressive, dissociation from the Empire was not elevated to the status of a universal solution to social and economic ills. In that respect Czechs differed from the Slovaks, who saw little merit in continuing Hungarian domination. At the time of the outbreak of the First World War Czech leaders still spoke of remaining within the Habsburg Empire.[2]

The 1910 census revealed that nearly 4 million Germans lived in the border regions of Bohemia, Moravia and Silesia. These were people indigenous to the region, usually living in self-contained population islands in the midst of ethnically Czech areas. Opposition to the granting of increased autonomy to national groups within the Austrian Empire focused the attention of both Germans and Czechs on these communities. Both believed that increased autonomy for one community would lead to the limiting of the rights of the other. Nevertheless until the emergence of the independent Czechoslovak Republic the problem remained an internal Austrian issue.[3]

At the time of the outbreak of the First World War the Czechs' national programme had not progressed beyond hoping that Austria could be persuaded to grant them increased autonomy within the Empire. A general, vaguely formulated assumption that Russia would act as a patron to the Slav people of Central Europe was stimulated by Russian military victories against the Austro–Hungarian armies during the first months of the war. Tsar Nicholas II fanned these hopes by making a declaration to a Czechoslovak delegation in August and the proclamation of a more general manifesto to the 'people of Austro–Hungary' in September 1914. In Slovak and the Czech lands hopes were raised that Russia would defeat Austria and that this would automatically lead to the establishment of a Czechoslovak state.[4] Not all national leaders were entirely happy with such talk. Czech and Slovak Social Democrats had good reason to doubt that a Russian victory over Austria would lead to the liberation of oppressed people. Czech leaders questioned whether Russian tutelage would turn out to be less oppressive than the irksome, but nevertheless liberal, policies of the Austrian Empire. In any event Czech and Slovak leaders remained passive in the face of events unfolding around them, hoping that the fate of their people would be decided by the outcome of the Austrian–Russian conflict. In the meantime soundings were taken to ascertain what would be the attitude of the belligerents to the question of their self-determination.

France and Britain seemed to be remote and unlikely to exercise influence over the region. In May 1915 a major military setback at Gorliz signalled the beginning of a Russian retreat. Czech and Slovak leaders were forced to become more active. They decided to broaden their campaigns by appealing to other allies, not just Russia. Britain was disinclined to make any long-term commitments for the break-up of the Austrian Empire. Efforts to secure more public support by the Allied Powers for the creation of an independent Czechoslovak state only started in earnest in the autumn of 1915 in France. Three names were closely associated with the propaganda campaign to which the French government, and in due course also the French Military High Command, gave support. These were Tomáš Masaryk, Edvard Beneš and Milan Štefánik. All three belonged to the intellectual Czechoslovak elite. Unlike the first two, Štefánik was a Slovak. They had excellent professional contacts with French academics and made use of these to gain support for their case. In November 1915 a Czech Foreign Committee was formed in Paris. In 1916 it was transformed into a National Council of the Czech Lands. French willingness to support the Czechs was motivated by a desire to make use of Czech officers and soldiers, who as Austrian prisoners of war in Russia could be persuaded to assist the Allied side. In December 1916 an agreement was concluded between the French Government and the National Council of the Czech Lands for the formation of the Czechoslovak Army in France. The Czechs had undertaken to bring to France their compatriots from the Prisioner of War camps in Russia.[5] The Czechs harboured few illusions about support which had been given to them in the West. Until April 1918 the Allied Powers refused to make unambiguous commitments to the break-up of the Austrian Empire. As long as it was believed that Austria could be persuaded to abandon her German ally, open discussions on the subject of the future of the Austrian Empire were discouraged. Any prior and open commitment made to the national groups within the empire would have stood in the way of these negotiations. In January the US President Woodrow Wilson made a statement of war aims in which he alluded to the rights of the Czechoslovak people. Nevertheless Woodrow Wilson's Fourteen Points programme fell short of a commitment to the creation of an independent state.

Masaryk and his colleagues in Paris had not been the only self-appointed group to speak on behalf of the Czech and Slovak people. Karel Krámař, who before the war headed the Slav Council formed in 1908, reflected the pan-Slav and anti-German section of thinking amongst intellectuals. His ideas were almost entirely concerned with the concept of a Slav Federation under Russian leadership. During 1916 the Russians, faced with the collapse of their front with Germany and Austria–Hungary, sought the support of national groups within the Austrian Empire. Krámař, by then based in Petrograd, was given funds to build up a Czech Legion recruited from Austrian prisoners of war. With the agreement of the Russian Foreign Minister he set up a Czech National Council in Russia. The confusion of two opposing Czech exile authorities, one in Paris and the other in Petrograd, each representing different political orientations, was halted by the outbreak of the revolution in Russia in February 1917 and the US entry into the war. In May 1917 Masaryk decided to go to Russia in order to ascertain whether the Provisional Government would support the establishment of an independent Czechoslovak state. Unfortunately, by the time he actually arrived in Petrograd the Minister for Foreign Affairs Milyukov had been toppled by Kerensky. The latter was less sympathetic to Masaryk's ideas. In any case, having witnessed the revolutionary turmoil in Russia, Masaryk decided that Russia could no longer be counted upon to act as midwife to the new Czechoslovak state. He thus broke with the traditional view that the fate of the Czech and Slovak people would be linked to that of Russia. After he left Russia Masaryk decided to concentrate on obtaining the support of the Western Allied Powers for the dismemberment of Austria–Hungary.[6]

One of the important consequences of Masaryk's visit to Russia was that he established the authority of the Paris-based Czechoslovak National Council over the rival organisation which had earlier emerged in Petrograd. By 3 September the US government recognised the Paris-based Czechoslovak National Council as a belligerent government, mirroring earlier British and French recognition of the Council.

The Russian Revolution was the catalyst for numerous political and social organisations which had viewed the war as an opportunity to fulfil long-cherished hopes for independence. Even the passivity of the Czech delegates to the Austrian Reichsrat was broken. In all parts of the Austro–Hungarian Empire national leaders, sensing a new trend in the government's attitude towards the nationality issue, sought to establish some form of leadership. In the spring of 1918, when the military balance shifted in favour of the Allied Powers, provisional authorities spontaneously came into being in the Czech, Slovak and Balkan territories of the empire. Returning prisoners of war, affected by what they had witnessed in Russia, leaders of the Social Democratic Party, workers and trade unionists established workers' and soldiers' councils. In Prague a National Committee was formed in July 1918, while in Slovakia, where Hungarian repression continued, a National Committee emerged in October. In all cases Czechs and Slovaks made joint statements on behalf of both national groups, thus underlining their commitment to the creation of a Czechoslovak state.

On 27 October 1918 the Austrian Imperial High Command sued for peace. On 3 November an armistice was signed. The Austrian Army pulled out of Prague and left a vacuum into which the National Committee stepped.[7] In years to come, the manner in which the Czechs established their first government would reflect positively on the new state. On 31 October Krámař, the leader of the Prague National Committee, met representatives of the Paris National Committee and agreed on the distribution of ministries in the government. Masaryk became the first President of the newly established Czechoslovak Republic.

The installation of a central authority in Prague turned out to be the easiest part of the process of building a new state. Czechoslovakia still had to define its borders. During the next two years, while trying to map out new frontiers, more than once military force was used to overrule the wishes of local populations. In the coal-mining region of Teschen Czechoslovak determination to maintain a hold on the district brought it into conflict with the local Polish population. Similarly the new state acquired a minority which deeply resented being separated from Hungary when, as a result of a victorious military campaign against the Hungarian Soviet Republic, territories inhabited by ethnic Hungarians were incorporated into Czechoslovakia. The wishes of the Austrian Germans living in Bohemia were overridden to incorporate the region into the Czechoslovak Republic. Each of these events sowed proverbial dragon's teeth, for the grievances of each of the national minorities were in due course taken up by neighbouring states who were driven by a strong desire to challenge the territorial decisions made earlier. Poland, Hungary and Germany all claimed the right to defend their co-nationals living in Czechoslovakia.

For Czechoslovakia the most obvious and difficult problem to resolve was that of the Austrian German community living in the frontier areas of Bohemia, Moravia and Silesia. The incorrect, nevertheless widely used, collective name for these groups was 'Sudeten Germans'. In reality these were diverse German communities representing the wide spectrum of political ideas and parties which had proliferated in the Austrian Empire. Regions inhabited by the Germans tended to be more industrialised. The disintegration of the Austrian Empire evoked from the German Reichsrat deputies a joint programme. On 21 October 1918 they proclaimed that the German parts of Bohemia, Moravia and Silesia belonged to the German–Austrian state. The German deputies' proclamation reflected their wish to belong to Austria. Most of the areas inhabited by Austrian Germans whose incorporation into the new Czechoslovak state was being considered in 1918 had no geographical or direct economic links with Vienna. It would have been impossible for Vienna to administer these regions following the creation of a Czechoslovak state. The realistic choices were either for the regions to be incorporated into Czechoslovakia or for the whole of Bohemia, Moravia and Silesia to become part of Greater Germany. In November 1918 Czechs occupied the German-inhabited regions. For the time being the problem was shelved by ignoring the wishes of the local population.[8]

At the Versailles Conference the Czechoslovaks gave the impression of having modest territorial aspirations. They merely

sought approval for boundaries which had already been deli-
neated. Their case was made easier by the fact that, with the
exception of the dispute with the Poles over the region of Teschen,
all territorial disputes were with ex-enemy countries. The incorporation of the German-inhabited region into Czechoslovakia
was upheld.[9]

With the signing of the Treaty of Trianon on 4 June 1920 war
between Czechoslovakia and Hungary ended. Slovak and Ruthenian territories which had formerly been part of the Hungarian
Kingdom were included in the Czechoslovak Republic. In a brief
period of time between the collapse of the Central Powers and the
signing of the Trianon Treaty, Hungary and Czechoslovakia had
become embroiled in a military conflict. The events of that period
cast a long shadow over Czech–Hungarian relations as well as
affecting relations between Slovaks and Czechs. The military conflict between the Czechoslovak Republic and Hungary was caused
by the setting up of a revolutionary government in Hungary which
coincided with the mobilisation of some sections of radical revolutionary Slovak groups. With the tacit approval of the Western
Powers, and assisted by French military advisers, Romania, followed by Czechoslovakia, started a war of intervention against
the Hungarian regime. Foreign intervention contributed to the
further radicalisation of the Soviet Republic, which was able to
organise a Red Army to counterattack. By June 1919 the Hungarians had penetrated deep into Slovakia. The response of the local
population to the Hungarian victories was complex. Hungarians
in the region welcomed the Red Army's victories, as did the Slovak
communists and ex-POWs who had been impressed by what they
had witnessed in Russia and who believed the revolution would
spread to Europe. On 25 May 1919 a Slovak Soviet Republic was
proclaimed in the occupied areas. The Czech left-wing movement
did not follow the Slovaks' example and instead supported the
Masaryk Government. The Hungarian–Czechoslovak conflict
ended when, following military defeat, Béla Kun was forced to
accept international arbitration and Slovakia and Ruthenia were
incorporated in the Czechoslovak Republic. The Slovak Soviet
collapsed at the same time.

The consequences of this brief episode were to have an impact
on developments during the inter-war period. Hungary, where
the revolutionary government was replaced by a reactionary

government led by Admiral Horthy, would never accept the loss of territories to Romania and Czechoslovakia. Czechoslovakia was acutely aware of the constant level of enmity harboured by Hungary and sought to build up alliances against Hungarian revanchism. In Slovakia the suppression of the brief period of revolutionary activism stimulated anti-Czech feelings within left-wing groups. At the same time some sections of the Slovak intellectual community and those of gentry origin fondly looked back to the days when Slovakia had been part of Hungary.[10]

The Czechoslovak Constitution, adopted on 20 February 1920, was modelled on the French one. It provided for a two-tier legislature to which elections took place on the basis of universal suffrage. The President's authority was clearly defined and balanced by the well-regulated powers of the Cabinet. During Masaryk's lifetime the Presidency played a mediating role, partly due to the immense personal prestige he enjoyed.

During the 1920s and 1930s Czechoslovakia experienced several political crises, frequently caused by foreign policy dilemmas and economic problems. Nevertheless the remarkable feature of all political conflicts was the stability of political parties. The Social Democratic Party faced ideological rifts which led to the Marxist Left section breaking away and forming a Czechoslovak Communist Party in 1921. During the 1920 general elections the Social Democratic movement secured over 48 per cent of the vote. Doctrinaire internal conflicts combined with the party's divisions along nationality lines meant that while, during the 1920s, the left wing was strong, its influence on political life was considerably smaller than its electoral successes.

From the outset the key parties in the National Assembly decided to create a political union dedicated to upholding the democratic system. This was justified by the internal weakness of the largest party in the National Assembly, the Social Democrats. The so-called 'Five' consisted of the Agrarian Party, National Democrats, Social Democrats, National Socialists and the Populist Party. Leaders of these parties agreed amongst themselves to support agreed policies. While this process reduced the importance of the National Assembly, it also guaranteed political consensus for necessary economic and social reforms.[11] Successive governments tended to be appointed by the 'Five' to deal with specific tasks and ministers were seen as specialists capable of tackling them. In this way Beneš acted as Minister for Foreign Affairs until he became the President in 1935. Nominally he belonged to the National Socialist Party, though in reality it was the 'Five' who had agreed that he was the best person to head the ministry. In 1926 the Agrarian Party replaced the Social Democrats as the biggest group in the National Assembly. The result was a succession of Agrarian–Catholic bloc governments. The influence of the 'Five' decreased. But it continued to determine the outcome of most parliamentary discussions.

The 1935 general election showed a major swing in favour of the Sudeten German Party. The ruling coalition was mobilised to find new partners. After extensive behind-the-scene negotiations a decision was made not to invite the Slovak and Sudeten Party representatives to join in forming a new administration. Instead the government was shored up by the addition of the minor Tradesmen's Party. In December 1935, following Masaryk's decision to retire from politics, Beneš was elected as the new President. The elections revealed how strong had become the demands of the national minorities for a degree of autonomy. The Slovak and Sudeten German communities now posed the biggest threat to the stability of the republic. The new government led by Slovak Milan Hodža, mindful of the fact that any concessions to the Slovaks and Germans would have to be followed by similar ones to the Ruthenians and Hungarians, was reluctant to commit itself to granting autonomy to either of these communities. By the end of 1937 the government knew that Germany was going to use the German minority issue to discredit Czechoslovakia. Suspicions that Poland and Germany were financing anti-Czechoslovak activities among the Slovaks and Ruthenians were strengthened by evidence that the Sudeten Germans, in their dealings with the government, were acting on instructions from Berlin.[12]

Economic factors lay very much at the root of internal divisions. These were not problems which successive governments found easy to overcome. The Austro–Hungarian economy had always enjoyed a high degree of state involvement and was cushioned by a policy of protectionism. The result was that certain areas had been favoured and others neglected. The new Czechoslovak Republic emerged from the coming together of one of the most highly industrialised parts of Austria with the most neglected part of Hungary. In the Czech lands 42 per cent of the workforce was employed in industry. In addition to light and consumer industries the Bohemian and Moravian districts contained coal mines and steel plants. Czech sugar refineries supplied sugar to major European markets. Industrial labour was skilled and urban. Incomes in the Czech lands were on the same level as those in Austria and Germany. High literacy levels were matched by a high standard of living enjoyed by the urban and industrial workers. In Ruthenia and Slovakia industrialisation was negligible and what there was fared badly when faced with Czech competition. Those areas contained few natural resources and in spite of official policies aimed at maintaining and increasing investment in local industry, during the 1920s Slovak industries tended to close down in the face of Czech competition. In Slovakia and Ruthenia 75 per cent of the population derived its income from agriculture.

In the immediate post-war period the Czechoslovak government faced disruption in its trading patterns with other European states. Eastern European markets were replaced by West European ones, either because of regional conflicts or because of a lack of purchasing power. It has been emphasised that the Czechoslovak economy was heavily dependent on exports, which accounted for 40 per cent of output.[13] This successful reorientation of the new state's trade was a source of economic stability during the Depression, when commercial links with Eastern Europe dramatically fell by two thirds while those with the West decreased only by a third. In agriculture the government resorted to protectionist measures, partly motivated by the desire to maintain high prices for domestic produce, most notably grain. The fact that in the 1920s the Agrarian Party was a key member of the political group of 'Five' accounts for the policy of supporting agriculture. Nevertheless the peasants constituted the most obviously disaffected social stratum within the Czechoslovak Republic. Land reform had failed to satisfy their demands, and in the mid-1920s rural indebtedness further alienated the peasants from the government. The fact that large sections of Slovakia, Ruthenia and parts of German-inhabited Bohemia and Moravia were agrarian was a major contributory factor in the national minorities' alienation and consequent willingness to associate with extreme nationalist ideas. Unfortunately, in the mid-1930s international issues preoccupied the government. The economic crisis of the early 1930s had caused polarisation in Czechoslovak politics. Parties and communities which hitherto, in varying degrees, went along with the idea of government by specialists, became more sensitive to the demands of their electorate. This had the most dramatic consequences in Slovakia and within the German communities.

It was inevitable that the bringing together of areas with such divergent political and economic traditions would lead to doubts, recriminations and suggestions that the more politically experienced Czechs were taking advantage of the Slovaks. In the early 1920s the Slovak autonomist tendencies were fuelled by real and imaginary Czech mishandling of the Slovak issues. Czech industry was better developed and a policy of reducing state expenditure led to the shutting down unproductive and obsolete Slovak industries. The Slovak population lacked an educated middle and professional class. Therefore the rapid expansion of education in Slovak lands was pushed through by Czech bureaucrats and teachers brought in for that purpose. This in turn led to accusations that Czechs were destroying Slovak culture. Land reform when introduced in Slovakia in 1921 could not conceivably have satisfied land hunger. In the 1920 general elections the Slovak National Party won 17 per cent of the Slovak vote. By 1925, the Slovak People's Party, led by a Catholic priest Andrej Hlinka, secured 34 per cent of votes poled in Slovakia, thus becoming the most important representative of Slovak autonomist aspirations. Other political parties emerged at the same time in Slovakia, but with the exception of the Slovak People's Party and the Slovak National Party they either merged with or agreed to co-operate with their Czech counterparts.[14] Between 1925 and the next general elections the Slovak People's Party was bedevilled by internal divisions and constrained by state harassment. Two distinct factions emerged: the first led by Hlinka, who campaigned for autonomy within the Czechoslovak Republic, and second, the anti-Czech group headed by Vojtech Tuka which hoped that Slovakia could pull out of its union with the Czechs and open negotiations to join Hungary.[15] The latter policy evoked the Czechoslovak government's fear of the destruction of the republic and accounts for the decision to sanction firm action against Slovak nationalist leaders.

In 1933, emboldened by the success of the National Socialist Party in Germany, Hlinka's People's Party staged a number of demonstrations against the government. By then Slovak nationalists concentrated increasingly on attacking democracy and the

Czechoslovak republican government. While the Italian Fascist model was one which the Slovak Fascists most readily imitated, German willingness to aid the Hlinka movement consolidated the German hold over it. In the last parliamentary elections held in Czechoslovakia in May 1935 a number of national minorities jointly campaigned against the Czechoslovak Republic. This was the so-called Autonomist Bloc which included Poles, Ruthenians and Slovaks. Behind-the-scenes contact had been established between the Autonomists and Konrad Henlein's Sudeten German Party. But it was the electoral success of the Sudeten German Party which alerted government to the need to draw the Slovaks into government. Unfortunately this proved a fleeting thought. Not even the Slovak Prime Minister, Milan Hodža, during his brief tenure in office in 1936, showed enough commitment to Slovak representation in government successfully to persuade the Slovaks of the government commitment to overcoming differences with the Slovak community.[16] After the Austrian Anschluss, the Slovak People's Party felt it had finally gained an upper hand. At the very time when Hungary and Poland were coordinating action to put pressure on Czechoslovakia for territorial concessions, the Slovaks joined forces with the Sudeten Germans.

Autonomy for Slovakia was one of the demands put forward by the German delegation at the Munich Conference. Consequently on 7 October 1938 Slovakia was granted autonomous status within the republic. The attainment of the long-cherished ambition of having a separate Slovak assembly was achieved in circumstances which contradicted the euphoria of Slovak leaders. The Munich Conference decisions effectively sanctioned Germany's right to arbitrate in all territorial and political disputes in Central Europe. Though to the Slovak nationalists this looked like a high point of their long campaign for equal status within the Czechoslovak Republic, they had achieved autonomy by destroying Czechoslovakia. In the following months the fate of the Czechoslovak Republic was decided in Berlin. Until March 1939 it suited Germany that Slovakia should continue as part of the newly created Czecho-Slovakia.[17] Economically and militarily Slovakia became dependent on Nazi Germany. On 15 March Germany occupied Bohemia and Moravia. The Slovak assembly had voted for independence on the previous day and, two days later, on 16 March

1939, requested that Slovakia become the Third Reich's protectorate. Hitler agreed to the Slovak petition.[18]

In the study of the origins of the Second World War, the fate of the Sudeten Germans is linked with Hitler's major international victory in renegotiating the frontiers of Europe. The community played a key role in legitimising Hitler's successful campaign to destroy Czechoslovakia. Britain and France, when faced with Hitler's claims that Czechoslovakia was mistreating the German minority, faltered and ultimately were drawn into the farrago of mediation between the Sudeten Germans and the Czechoslovak government. There were no historic links between the German communities in Bohemia and Moravia and Germany, and the willingness of the communities to fall in with Nazi aims against Czechoslovakia cannot be viewed as evidence of their wish to be united with a state with which they had some historic affinity. In due course Hitler's skills at presenting himself as the defender of the interests of the German minority caused Britain and France to accept the claim that these regions should be broken away from Czechoslovakia and incorporated in Germany.

The National Census taken in 1930 revealed that of the total of 13 374 364 Czechoslovak citizens, 3 231 718 declared themselves to be German. In effect this amounted to 22.32 per cent of the population of the Czechoslovak Republic.[19] This fact on its own fuelled anxiety about the German minorities' loyalty to the new state. The German community from the outset was far from confident that it would have a place in Czechoslovakia. German leaders anticipated a negative response to their determination not to be absorbed into the newly created state. The German community sought to defend its identity, its language and cultural distinctiveness, but foremost, it doubted that it would enjoy the same level of political influence which had been accorded to it previously in the Austrian Empire. Thus before 1920, the German minority leaders vocally and publicly opposed the creation of the Czechoslovak state and declared their determination to resist inclusion in its borders. In the first general elections the German community was represented by a variety of parties, which sought to send representatives to the National Assembly. Notwithstanding the fact that the German community was opposed to the Czechoslovak state, their representatives to the legislative assembly proved themselves fully committed to the democratic system. The German Social

Democratic Party had the loyalty of the majority of German voters. During the 1920 elections it had secured the second largest vote. In addition, the German Agrarian Party and German Christian Socialists were active in Czechoslovak political life. Even though nationalists within the German community spoke of their opposition to the Czechoslovak Republic and of the community desire to become either part of Austria or Germany, in reality autonomy was the real goal. Even then it was not clear what that would have meant. Some spoke of administrative autonomy, others merely of cultural freedom.[20]

The German minority was concentrated in regions which had been industrialised. Hence the community enjoyed a higher standard of living than Czechs living in surrounding areas. The policy of the Czechoslovak government had been to encourage industrialisation in the backward areas. The Germans viewed this policy with distrust seeing it as an attempt to destroy them economically. Similarly, the process of imposing Czech bureaucrats and civil servants on to German inhabited areas was interpreted as a deliberate policy to reduce German language teaching. State legislation guaranteed the German minority its own schooling and libraries. These and other measures led to the general perception in West European capitals that Czechoslovakia was one of the most liberal and progressive states in Central Europe. However, the German minority in Czechoslovakia did not agree with this general assessment of Czechoslovakia's handling of its minorities. It has been pointed out that the root of the problem lay in the fact that 'the Germans did not regard themselves as a minority but as an independent collective entity.'[21]

Even though the Depression affected all of Europe, the Sudeten Germans believed that their economic difficulties were the result of governmental prejudice. In the early 1920s the region had experienced the consequences of post-war territorial adjustments, when changing boundaries disrupted previous patterns of trade and land redistribution dispossessed wealthy German landowners. In the 1930s light industries, which predominated in regions inhabited by the German minority, suffered once more. While the government may have failed to assist the region economically, it was not to blame for the Depression. To the Germans this made no difference, and the economic problems stirred up a rich pool of anti-Czech feelings.[22] By the 1935 elections the balance had tipped in favour of German parties which rejected the republic and campaigned for the German-inhabited areas to be incorporated into the Third Reich. In the general elections of that year over 60 per cent of German votes were cast in favour of the Sudeten German Party, which had already made itself known for its aggressive and uncompromising attitude towards the Czechoslovak state. With 44 deputies the Sudeten German Party became the second largest party in the Czechoslovak Assembly.

Why did the German community turn away from parties which had previously represented them, and which had until then worked within the framework of the Czechoslovak state? Economic problems only partly account for this process of radicalisation. Even though light and export-oriented industries in the German-inhabited areas had been affected by the economic recession of the early 1930s, the state was aware of the potential for disaffection and did channel relief into those regions. Nevertheless, unemployment within the German community continued to be high.[23] The German Nazis' capture of power in the 1933 elections to a large extent acted as an inspiration to the Germans in the Czechoslovak Republic. The mood of uncompromising nationalism was heightened and confrontation appeared to be more attractive.

Ultimately the decision to seek German assistance in what up until then had been a conflict with the Czechoslovak state was made not purely because relations between Prague and the Sudeten leadership had broken down in the 1930s. The roots of the Sudeten German policy of conflict with Czechoslovakia lay in the political culture which prevailed in the German community. Since 1920 numerous nationalist associations, some of them quasi military, had been active in the German community. One of those was the German Cultural Association which was committed to educational activities. The Bohemian Movement had similar aims, as had its successor, the youth 'Readiness' movement. What had started with 'folkish' ideas, designed to link the youth community with its ethnic origins, in time became tainted by radical and anti-Czechoslovak sentiments. In 1925 the German Agrarian and the Clerical Parties were invited to participate in the formation of a government coalition. German parties enjoyed not only full representation in the Assembly but were involved in the government.

These concessions did not satisfy the community aspirations for autonomy, and conditions in the early 1930s increased the appeal of extremist groups. Youth and sporting organisations came to imitate the German Nazi displays which finally caused the Czechoslovak government to ban the German Nationalist and Nazi Parties.[24] Funds from Berlin, which up till then had been available in the form of grants for cultural and sporting activities, in the late 1920s were increasingly channelled to German associations in Czechoslovakia with clearer political objectives. Prior to the 1935 elections the Sudeten German Party received the enormous sum of RM 330 000. Konrad Henlein, the leader of the Sudeten Germans who had always been opposed to the Czechoslovak state and condemned any co-operation with it, rapidly gained popularity. After the banning of the two German parties, the ranks of the Sudeten German Party were swelled by Nationalists and Nazis who increasingly hoped the Third Reich would destroy Czechoslovakia in a military conflict. Nevertheless, after its electoral victory in its home region, the Sudeten German Party chose to take its seats in the National Assembly. Masaryk and then Beneš, who succeeded him as President in 1935, saw the need to defuse nationalist tensions. An olive branch was held out to the German community in the form of assurances that their grievances would be heard out.[25] On 18 February 1937 the Czech leadership formally undertook to increase investment in German areas and to end all discrimination. Nevertheless no promises for autonomy were made. Although throughout the pre-war period the Third Reich continued to finance the propaganda activities of the Sudeten Germans, it was not until February 1938 that Hitler in a Reichstag speech made a direct reference to Germans who had been prevented from joining the Reich and gave an assurance that they would be brought into the fold soon. In reality Hitler was using the Sudeten German issue to destabilise the Czechoslovak Republic and to mount an international propaganda campaign. The Sudeten Germans had by then become willing pawns in Germany's policy against Czechoslovakia. They obligingly declared that their aspirations had been thwarted and that they needed Berlin's support. Thus the Sudeten Germans' grievances became a critical issue in German–Czechoslovak relations.[26] The scene was set for a major crisis into which both the French and British were sucked, believing themselves to be dealing with a potentially dangerous breakdown of relations between two states that was nevertheless simple in its origins. Czechoslovakia's foreign policy during the whole of the interwar years was the exclusive domain of one man, namely Edvard Beneš. This accounts for the continuity and consistency in the republic's foreign relations. Beneš' position was unique in a democratic state in that he was relatively untroubled by criticism or challenge from within the parliament or political parties. All parties generally agreed with his broad objectives. Although briefly he was associated with the National Socialist Party, in reality until 1935 he had been given ministerial responsibility as an appointed specialist. The paradox of this well-functioning and publicly supported democracy was that a form of paralysis affected debates at the highest level. In all matters relating to foreign policy and security, Beneš could count on the fact that he would not be toppled as long as the 'Five' key parties agreed to close ranks against his critics.[27]

During the 1920s Beneš' foreign policy steered Czechoslovakia towards co-operation with the European Big Powers, frequently to the detriment of regional agreements. The main thrust of his policies went towards supporting collective security, upholding the Versailles decisions and co-operating with the League of Nations. This policy was in his country's interest because, by the end of 1920, Czechoslovakia had incorporated in her borders all territories to which claims had been made earlier. The new state's main objective henceforth would be to uphold the status quo and to commit other powers to doing likewise.

Before this, in the immediate aftermath of the First World War, Czechoslovakia had sought to consolidate her territories. Nevertheless the Teschen region, which had been claimed from Poland, and Hungarian areas, grabbed during the war with the Béla Kun regime, created insurmountable barriers between Czechoslovakia and her two neighbours. Beneš' policy aimed at guaranteeing security through obtaining international consensus on the maintenance of the existing borders. At the same time he steered Czechoslovakia away from alliances which entailed commitments but added little to her own security. In the early 1920s Czechoslovakia needed peace to concentrate on internal consolidation. Beneš calculated that in the foreseeable future the army's role would be confined to defending Czechoslovakia's territories. There was no scope for making commitments to assisting neighbouring states in petty squabbles from which Czechoslovakia had little to gain.[28] Beneš hoped to obtain British and French support for his policies. Britain showed only a limited interest in that part of Europe. In due course her detached attitude towards Czechoslovakia led Beneš to concentrate on France. France became Czechoslovakia's main partner in Prague's security calculations.[29] The two states shared a commitment to upholding the Versailles Treaty decisions. They agreed on the need to maintain a weak but independent Austria and on preventing a Habsburg restoration in Hungary. In her contractual arrangements with France Czechoslovakia did not go beyond very general agreements. Beneš did not agree with the French attempt to create an Eastern Locarno. His dislike of Poland was too strong for him to go along with a French proposal that the two act in concert against Germany. On 24 January 1924 France and Czechoslovakia signed a Treaty of Alliance, followed in October 1925 by a Treaty of Mutual Assistance. The latter was a French attempt to reaffirm the validity of the eastern agreements after the signing of the Locarno Treaties. Still Czechoslovakia was satisfied with both, since they offered basic provisions against Austria and Hungary. Military conventions had not been sought by Beneš, who felt that Czechoslovakia had little to fear from Germany. In any case, the French military mission continued to operate in Prague until 1938 and relations between the two military establishments were cordial. The assurance that Czechoslovakia could depend on French assistance was willingly given and understood as such by the Czechs.

During the 1920s Czechoslovakia was preoccupied with the threat of Hungarian revisionism. Unfortunately, the Little Entente, the only regional agreement concluded in 1921 by countries situated between the Soviet Union and Germany, was of limited value. Romania, Yugoslavia and Czechoslovakia shared an anxiety about Hungary, hence their willingness to enter into a series of agreements collectively known as the Little Entente. In the early 1930s attempts were made by the three states to give the Little Entente a more formal structure. In 1933 the Romanian Minister for Foreign Affairs, Titulescu, tried to mobilise the Little Entente against the Soviet Union. Czechoslovakia opposed these initiatives. She had no common frontier and no territorial dispute with the Soviet Union. Moreover, Beneš was sympathetic towards French attempts to draw the Soviet Union into an anti-German agreement.[30]

Even though France and Czechoslovakia generally agreed on the policy of not isolating the Soviet Union, Czechoslovak–French co-operation had its limits. Whereas France sought agreements against Germany, Czechoslovakia had no territorial claims on Germany. In line with his belief that Czechoslovakia could only gain from a conciliatory foreign policy, Beneš had on several occasions shown himself willing to negotiate with Germany and even to approve certain of Germany's revisionist claims. This led to further estrangement between the Poles and the Czechs. The Polish leader Piłsudski suspected that Beneš and Masaryk had, in their contacts with the German Foreign Minister Stresemann, let it be known that they would not oppose the return of Danzig to Germany. The Poles believed that in return Czechoslovakia had sought German commitments to maintaining Austrian independence.[31] On two separate occasions, in 1930 and 1932, Masaryk was quoted as having stated that the Polish Corridor and Silesia should be German.[32] While little was gained from Germany, the Czechoslovaks incurred the implacable hostility of the Poles.

Beneš' determination to steer clear of any involvement with Poland was less an act of omission, than a calculated risk. There was little to bring the two countries together, while clearly a number of issues divided them. The Czechoslovak leadership had decided that they did not want the republic's standing in Europe diminished by association with a country which clearly was going to be the object of German revanchism. In 1919 a territorial dispute over Teschen created hostility between the two countries. Poland's friendship with Hungary and sympathy for Hungarian revisionist claims further complicated any dialogue. By the middle 1920s the two states were separated by the entirety of their respective foreign policies.

In the early 1930s the international situation changed. The Eastern European states realised that there was an overwhelming need to co-operate. Poland and Czechoslovakia appeared to be facing the most obvious danger. In March 1933 Mussolini suggested the signing of the Pact of Four, the aim of which would have been to draw together the four dominant European states: Italy, Germany, France and Britain. It proposed a policy of settling territorial grievances by consensus between the four powers.

Poland and Czechoslovakia saw the Pact of Four as an attempt to legitimise Germany's claims in the east. Beneš briefly showed signs of anxiety and sought talks with the Poles. Once France gave assurances that the pact would not be ratified, Beneš once more distanced Prague from the impending Polish–German conflict.[33] The Little Entente, which had collectively expressed anxiety about the Pact of Four, was dissuaded by Beneš from proceeding with discussions on the matter further.

In January 1934 Poland and Germany signed a Pact of Non-Aggression. At a stroke the Poles rendered void regional attempts at a joint response to Germany's regional policies. Emboldened by her diplomatic success Poland would henceforth seek to resolve all problems by means of direct negotiations with Germany. For Czechoslovakia Poland's commitment to Germany could not have come at a more inauspicious time. The French, who had been negotiating a pact with the Soviet Union which would have included Czechoslovakia, changed their minds. Instead in 1935 two bilateral treaties were signed, the Franco–Soviet and the Czechoslovak–Soviet Treaties of Mutual Assistance. In effect the Czechs were assured of Soviet aid against Germany only if in the first place France had made the first move to defend them. Since the Soviet Union and Czechoslovakia did not share a border, the military value of these treaties was dubious. As to their political value, the French were the first to suggest that their agreement with the Soviet Union should not close doors on continuing talks with Germany. After the Anschluss Czechoslovakia's situation became particularly difficult. Internally divided and isolated from friends and allies in Eastern Europe, the Czech government was willing to accept assistance in the form of international mediation which, it was hoped, would limit German demands.

Before 1938 Nazi Germany's relations with Czechoslovakia appear to have been ambiguous and inconsistent. Policies towards the Sudeten Germans were also confused. Both facts helped to disguise the true extent of aggressive intentions towards Czechoslovakia. Although the incorporation of German-inhabited regions into the Third Reich was Hitler's professed aim, in implementing this plan he had to take into account the international situation and Germany's military and economic capabilities. Thus in the first years after coming to power, Hitler's public pronouncements concerning Czechoslovakia appeared to be predictable and within acceptable norms. Until 5 November 1937, when Hitler informed his military leaders that the Czechoslovak question would be resolved by force, diplomatic contacts between the two states moved in the direction of resolving all outstanding issues. In 1933 and 1936 proposals for a pact of non-aggression were put to the Czechs by Germany. Czechoslovakia, though keen to avoid any conflict with its powerful neighbour, felt that entering into so formal an agreement might upset the delicate balance of relations within the Little Entente, as well as irritating France and the Soviet Union. It was therefore Beneš who declined to consider a pact, while at the same time reaffirming Czechoslovakia's commitment to the Arbitration Treaty of 1925 and the Kellogg Pact of 1928.[34] However by the end of 1936 Hitler lost interest in talks with Czechoslovakia and the proposals were not referred to again.

Military preparations give a clearer picture of Germany's long-term aims. Since 1933 plans for aggression against Czechoslovakia had been discussed, though they formed part of a larger plan for the incorporation of Austria into the Reich. In 1937 more precise proposals were formulated. In November of that year Hitler authorised 'Operation Green', the planned attack against Czechoslovakia.[35] The destruction of the hated state became Hitler's main aim, though the right moment and methods were still to be decided.

Before 1933 contacts between the German states and Germans living in other countries lacked precision and were not co-ordinated. The Ministry for Foreign Affairs thought in terms of encouraging and facilitating the retention of German national consciousness and culture among the *Auslandsdeutsche*. When the Nazi Party came to power it set itself the goal of nazifying the German communities. The vigilance of the neighbouring states thwarted these plans, although rivalries between various Nazi organisations and leaders were just as important in precluding unity among the German diaspora. Not until 1938 did the German communities abroad come under Nazi control.[36] This allowed the Third Reich to coordinate the activities of the Sudeten German population with the propaganda war unleashed against Czechoslovakia.

Although the Czechoslovak government's policies towards the German minority were essentially an internal matter, the issue was never free of treasonable connotations. The government's handling of the German minority suggested that it was always alert to the fact that in any conflict, in particular with Germany, the Sudeten Germans would be a source of military weakness. Beneš put a brake on any attempts to grant the German minority a degree of autonomy. In the autumn of 1937 the German government made an indirect request for all Reich Germans living abroad to be compulsorily enrolled in Nazi organisations. The willingness of the Czechs even to discuss the idea suggests that they had already come to terms with the fact that relations with the minority had become a factor in their relations with the Third Reich.[37]

In the months which followed, various groups within the Sudeten German Party vied for Hitler's support. Henlein's requests for interviews with Hitler were turned down and he was given no clear instructions, even though he had decided to request international arbitration on the grounds that the Czech state was not acting in accordance with the Minority Protection Treaty, of which it was a signatory. On 20 February 1938 Hitler made an aggressive speech in the Reichstag in which he took up the case of Germans living in adjoining countries, who according to the Chancellor had been prevented from joining the Reich. On the night of 11–12 March German troops occupied Austria. In Czechoslovakia the impact of these events was immediate. Beneš had no doubt that Germany meant to destroy Czechoslovakia and that it would use the minority issue as a pretext to destabilise the country and to discredit it in the international arena. Prime Minister Hodža now urgently sought a means of conciliating the German minority. Certain categories of political prisoners were released and talks were opened on a number of German grievances. Henceforth Henlein was treated in Berlin and Prague as the spokesman for the whole German community. Inadvertently this willingness to accept the authority of the Sudeten German leadership led to the weakening of the remaining non-Nazi German organisations. All now hastened to join the Nazi Sudeten German Party.

The basis of negotiations between Henlein and the Czechoslovak government was the so-called Karlsbad Program which was publicised by Henlein in April. If conceded it would have granted the German community autonomy within the Czechoslovak state. Not surprisingly the Czechs felt that while they were willing to discuss specific grievances, they were still not able to concede full autonomy, which would effectively destroy the principle upon which the republic was built. In any case the Sudeten Germans were instructed by Berlin not to agree to the Czech proposals. In reality Hitler did not want the conflict resolved. He wanted it to fester, allowing the Germans to discredit Czechoslovakia and to offer an excuse for Germany to become involved more directly.

Britain's role in the crisis which unfolded between March and September 1938 is central to the understanding of the way in which Czechoslovakia was subjugated by Germany. Several factors combined to draw Britain into what was still at this stage an internal Czechoslovak matter. A successful and relentless German propaganda campaign, which disseminated false information about atrocities being committed by Czechs against Germans, was very important in swaying British politicians. It became irrelevant whether these were indeed occurring. Reports from British representatives in Prague were set aside in favour of information gleaned from German newspapers, radio and Nazi propaganda. The British Ambassador to Berlin, Nevile Henderson, enjoyed direct access to the Prime Minister. His suggestions and analysis, which clearly supported the German side of the argument, were heeded and formed the basis of Cabinet discussions.[38] But the most important consideration which involved Britain in the very midst of the problem was anxiety that a minor territorial dispute might precipitate a German attack which, by virtue of existing international agreements, would draw France and then the Soviet Union into a military conflict with Germany. Therefore during the period from February until September 1938 British efforts went in the direction of preventing this crisis from becoming anything more than a local difficulty.

The way Chamberlain chose to deal with the dangerous problem proved disingenuous. Using the obvious Czechoslovak dependence on Western support, the British Prime Minister in the first place persuaded the Czechs to accept Henlein as an equal partner in talks. After a crisis in May 1938, when rumours of an impending German attack on Czechoslovakia seemed to bring France to the brink of war with Germany, British involvement became more bullying. Beneš was instructed to issue a request for British official mediation. A colleague of Chamberlain's, the Industrial Advisor to the Government Viscount Runciman, was dispatched to Czechoslovakia in August. The pretext for his appointment was a statement that his mission was independent of the British government. No one was fooled, least of all the Czechs, who realised that they had no choice but to try to persuade Britain to aid them. The new French government had since May signalled its anxiety to avoid war at all costs. In the circumstances the Czechoslovak government could not assume that France would honour its obligations.[39] The Soviet Union, on the other hand, let it be known that it would honour its commitment to Czechoslovakia, but only if France took action first. Such a formulation was of little comfort to Beneš.

The sense of isolation felt by the Czechoslovak government, and its growing dependence on Britain and France, was compounded by Polish and Hungarian actions. In 1931 Marshal Piłsudski and the future Minister for Foreign Affairs, Colonel Josef Beck, prepared a basic outline of policy towards Czechoslovakia. After Piłsudski's death in 1935 Beck would treat this as an article of faith and guide Polish policies accordingly. While, in principle, the Poles merely sought to recapture the Teschen region, in reality their objectives were far-ranging. By encouraging the Slovaks to seek increased autonomy within the Czechoslovak Republic, Beck aimed to establish Polish influence in the region. Furthermore Poland wanted the incorporation of the extreme eastern part of Czechoslovakia, a region which was usually referred to as Sub-Carpatho Ruthenia, into Hungary. These territorial readjustments would have created a Polish–Hungarian border. The Poles worked on the assumption that a strong Czechoslovakia was a threat to their own ambitions in that part of Europe. They sought to counteract Czechoslovakia's influence by co-operation with Hungary.[40]

The Czech leadership was sufficiently worried about Polish–Hungarian co-operation to make a move in the direction of conciliating the Poles. President Beneš assumed direct control over border talks aimed at removing the main obstacle towards closer co-operation with Poland and Hungary. In May 1938 Poland's Minister for Foreign Affairs decided to stall on further negotiations with Czechoslovakia. German claims to Czechoslovakia, which were likely to weaken the country, seemed to offer more opportunity for Poland to increase her influence in the region. Beck informed his government that Poland was to concentrate on relations with Germany.[41] Cooperation in the destruction of Czechoslovakia was thus a foregone conclusion.

British and French attempts to defuse German–Czechoslovak tensions and the ensuing international initiatives were observed by the Poles with a mounting sense of excitement. Czechoslovakia was left in no doubt about Poland's proposed course of action. The leader of the Polish minority in Czechoslovakia, on Warsaw's instructions, coordinated his anti-Czech campaign with Henlein and Father Jozef Tiso, the Catholic leader of the Slovak community. In the meantime the Polish Ambassador in Berlin, Josef Lipski, probed Goering about German territorial aims towards Czechoslovakia. By August 1938 the Poles knew that in the event of Germany taking diplomatic or military action against Czechoslovakia, they would be assured of the Teschen region.[42]

The success of Germany's propaganda campaign against Czechoslovakia can be gauged by the willingness of the British Prime Minister to travel to Germany to meet Hitler with the explicit aim of finding a way out of the impending crisis. During the Berchtesgaden meeting on 15 September Hitler demanded the 'return' of the Sudeten region to Germany. Ominously he also referred to the Polish, Hungarian and Slovak claims. During the next meeting in Godesberg, Chamberlain was told that German demands and the final settlement were conditional on the satisfaction of Hungarian and Polish demands. Faced with the threat of immediate German action, Chamberlain believed that he had saved the situation by agreeing to the principle of territorial revision.

The Czechoslovak government realised that the coordinated actions of the national minorities would effectively lead to the destruction of the state. Far from being passive in the face of the impending crisis, the Czechs tried to address that main problem. Beneš took further initiatives to assure the Sudeten leadership that all their demands would be met. Unfortunately, by the end of August he could do nothing to reverse the momentum of events. British and French diplomacy combined to put pressure on the Czechoslovaks to accept the right of the Sudeten Germans to self-determination. Runciman's recommendations, heavily tainted by information obtained from Germany and Henlein, supported this point. In these circumstances Beneš' policies of dealing piecemeal with each of the minorities' grievances and only on the basis of increasing autonomy within the Czechoslovak state, were swiftly overtaken by new developments. On 21 September Prague informed London that it was bowing to British–French pressure and accepted that the German-inhabited regions were to be incorporated in the Third Reich. On 29 September a Four Power conference took place in Munich, attended by France, Germany, Italy and Britain. The only issue still to be agreed was the method for defining territories to be incorporated into Germany. France's commitment to Czechoslovakia was to be replaced by a joint Four Power guarantee of its frontiers. This was to come into force once frontiers had been stabilised. Poland and Hungary were still to lay claim to contested areas.

The Czechoslovak government had been brutally realistic in its ultimate decision to bow to international pressure. The German Anschluss with Austria had exposed Czechoslovakia's southern border and would have permitted the German army to proceed north from Austria into the industrial heartland of Bohemia. Not expecting a conflict with Austria, Czechoslovakia had concentrated on building her military fortifications on the western border with Germany. Furthermore she had based her security considerations on the assumption that France would be her closest ally. In the autumn of 1938 Czechoslovakia found herself isolated. Her immediate neighbours waited in anticipation, hoping to benefit from any signs of weakness. As France vacillated, swayed by the British determination not to allow a conflict to spread, so the key axiom of Czechoslovakia's diplomacy collapsed. The Soviet Union did inform Beneš on 21 September that, in accordance with the agreement, it would honour its commitment to the defence of Czech security. Unfortunately, France was obliged to take action first. The extent of Soviet willingness to assist the Czechoslovaks could not be gauged from this official statement. Czechoslovakia had no border with the Soviet Union, and had the Soviet Army crossed into Poland or Romania on its way to assist Czechoslovakia, both countries would have viewed this as an act of aggression. Nor did they permit the Soviet Airforce to overfly their territories. In any case Beneš recoiled from asking for aid, no doubt fearful of the full implications of events which he would have set in motion. The Czechoslovak military leadership was willing to fight Germany and during the key period in September had informed the politicians of their determination to do so. Few doubted that Germany would win. The politicians, led by Beneš, chose to negotiate, precisely because they could not cope with the unbearable responsibility of starting a war.[43] On 30 September the Czechoslovak government reluctantly accepted the decisions of the Munich Conference to which they had not been invited. As a result one-fifth of Czechoslovak territory was incorporated into Germany. On 5 October Beneš resigned and left his country.

The jackals gathered to complete the task. Last-minute attempts to forestall Polish action failed. Written assurance, from Beneš to Beck that no Polish demands, including territorial adjustments, would be opposed, failed to forestall military action. Beck, insulted at not being invited to the Munich Conference and anxious about the growth of German influence in Eastern Europe, belatedly desired to do something to limit this process. His method was to issue an ultimatum to the Czechoslovak government on 30 October. His demand was for the immediate return of the Teschen region to Poland. The Czechs accepted the Polish ultimatum. In addition to the contested town of Teschen, Polish troops occupied the strategically important railway junction in Bohumin. Anxiety about Germany now became the dominant motive in Polish actions against the now renamed state of Czecho-Slovakia.

The Polish Minister for Foreign Affairs, Beck, had associated high hopes with Hungary. His dream was for a bloc of Central European countries capable of holding the balance between the Soviet Union and Germany. In reality, unable effectively to mediate between the disunited states of the region, Poland sought to strengthen her own role. The weakening of Czechoslovakia was seen as a way of resolving some of these conflicts. If Hungary could regain territories which she had lost to Czechoslovakia after the First World War, she was more likely to become a dependable ally in Poland's grand design.[44] The precondition for this plan was Poland's ability to deliver the Sub-Carpatho-Ruthenian region to Hungary. During the course of the international mediation concerning Czechoslovakia and the Sudeten Germans, the Hungarian government realised what the Poles had singularly failed to note, that by obtaining the Western Powers' agreement to the break-up of Czechoslovakia, Germany had became the arbiter of all territorial disputes in the region. On 1 October Hungary asked Germany, rather than Poland, for assistance in dealing with Czechoslovakia. The Czechoslovak government tried to stave off the Hungarian problem by opening up direct talks but was only prepared to make minor concessions. As in the Polish case, Germany supported the principle of Hungary gaining territories from Czecho-Slovakia, but was not willing to make prior commitments. Fortunately for the Hungarians, Italy was prepared to assume a more direct role in the ongoing conflict. The pretext which continued to be used to justify the continuing piecemeal destruction of Czecho-Slovakia was arbitration. On 2 November Hungary and Czechoslovakia submitted their territorial dispute to Germany and Italy for arbitration and as a result of the so-called Vienna Award Hungary was granted Czechoslovak territories. Most of the Hungarian claims had been satisfied but Germany did not agree with the Polish claim that Ruthenia should go to Hungary. This would have created a Polish–Hungarian border and placed the volatile Ukrainian population under joint Polish and Hungarian control. The strengthening of those countries was something Germany now wished to avoid.[45] On 12 March 1939, when Hitler had made the final decision to destroy what remained of the Czechoslovak state, he allowed the Hungarians to occupy Ruthenia.

Throughout, Czecho-Slovakia had no choice but to comply. The Munich Agreement had stipulated that an international commission consisting of the Munich Powers and including the Czechoslovaks was to define more precisely territories which were to be ceded to Germany. In reality, France and Britain lost interest in the conflict once its potential for precipitating an international war had been defused. Thus Czecho-Slovakia had to bow to German demands and in due course to Hungarian and Polish ones too. She had lost a third of her previous territories. On 15 March the Czecho-Slovak President, Emil Hácha, was forced by Hitler to accept the occupation of Bohemia and Moravia. The Czechoslovak state ceased to exist.

4 Romania

During the Second World War Romania was Germany's ally. As a consequence it was occupied. Initially an Allied Control Commission took over responsibility for running the country. With the passage of time the exact nature of Romania's relations with Nazi Germany became less of an issue. Post-war treatment of Romania, and in particular the Soviet occupation of the country, has led us to view that country, like the rest of Eastern Europe, as a victim rather than a participant in the events leading to the war. In reality Romania was not a victim of developments beyond its control. The country, like all those which were not obvious targets of German aggression, adjusted to the circumstances and looked to benefit from the general turmoil.

Independent Romania emerged in stages from the diplomatic conflicts of the Crimean War. In 1856 the right of Romanians, in effect of the country's landowners, to decide their fate was accepted by the European Powers. Although initially Romania came under the suzerainty of the Ottoman Porte, in 1877 it declared independence. The squabbles of the country's ruling circles blocked social and political reforms and led to a peasant revolt in 1907. When this was bloodily put down the two rival ruling political groups, the Liberals and the Conservatives, still refused to consider land and social reform. Instead they concentrated on conquest and aggrandisement as a means of consolidating their power. The quest for 'Greater Romania' became their major objective.[1] Initially the territory of Romania included the principalities of Moldavia and Wallachia. Romanians in Austria–Hungary inhabited mainly the region of Transylvania. They were slow to associate with the aspirations of their co-nationals in the Romanian Kingdom. Immediately before the First World War, territorial conflicts with Bulgaria and hostility towards the latter's supporter, Russia, caused Romania to associate with the Triple Alliance countries. With Germany Romania was linked by dynastic ties, though rivalry with Austria–Hungary over Transylvania and Austrian influence in the Balkans limited any co-operation.[2]

Romania was not involved in the First Balkan War (1910–12) but took advantage of Bulgaria's military preoccupation with Greece and Serbia during the Second Balkan War in 1913. When Bulgaria was defeated by Serbia, Greece and Romania, Dobrudja was incorporated into the Romanian Kingdom. Romania had acted against Austro–Hungarian advice and the natural consequence of her incursion into Dobrudja was a cooling of relations. This led the Romanian government to consider the advantages to be gained from supporting France and Britain in their conflict with the Habsburg Empire.[3] Romanians in the Austro–Hungarian Empire, frustrated by limited autonomy, also started to campaign for union with the Kingdom.

The outbreak of the First World War gave rise to hopes that, once the prevailing balance of power was upset, the Balkan states would gain new territories and consolidate their frontiers. The European Powers let it be known that they were willing to reward the neutral states not merely for their direct assistance, but even for continuing to remain neutral. This led to a frenzy of intrigues and negotiations. Serbia and Romania, both keen to see the destruction of the Austro–Hungarian Empire, wanted to be party to talks dealing with the future of that state. The picture was complicated by the fact that while both were united in their dislike of Austria–Hungary, they were equally strongly divided by their joint claim to the territory of Bánát. The Central Powers had little to offer Romania other than promises of minor territorial readjustments. But association with the Allies was nevertheless problematic, as Romania expected the return of Bessarabia, which had been incorporated into the Russian Empire in 1812.

Generally, Serbia and Romania laid claim to Austro–Hungarian territory on ethnic grounds. Nevertheless in most cases the application of this principle stretched credulity. The distribution of population had always been uneven and patchy. Historically national groups lived in pockets and enclaves in which at best a given national group made up 50 per cent of the population. While hostilities lasted, the Big Powers were willing to turn a blind eye to the dubious nature of some of the claims made. At the end of the war and during the peace talks, the issue of promises made earlier became an embarrassment and a source of future conflicts between Eastern European states and the victorious powers.

Dynastic links between Romania and the protagonists in the First World War made the decision to join either side only more confusing. King Ferdinand belonged to the Hohenzollern family, so that his loyalties were with the Central Powers. His wife Queen Elizabeth was Queen Victoria's granddaughter. Her background and education were thoroughly English and her views were anglophile. In the event regional developments, rather than the wishes of the dominant European Powers, determined the timing of Romania's entry into the war. On 17 August 1916 Romania committed herself to declaring war on Austria–Hungary. The army was to take the military initiative on two fronts to coincide with Russian and Allied offensives in Galicia and Greece.[4] In return Romania demanded the Allies' commitment to Romania's extensive territorial demands. These included the regions of Transylvania, Bánát and Bukovina. At the time these territories belonged to Hungary.[5]

The French High Command was to learn that with friends like Romania, they were no longer in need of enemies. The Romanian war effort proved to be a drain on French resources. Corruption within the Romanian Army was on so vast a scale that it affected all military activities. In addition, the German and Austrian war effort proved to be unexpectedly superior. By the end of 1916 the withdrawal of Russian troops from fighting and the collapse of the Eastern Front left Romania encircled. Demoralised and believing itself to be abandoned by the Western European allies, the Romanian government decided to sign a truce with the Central Powers in December 1917. In May 1918 the signing of the Treaty of Bucharest concluded the disastrous Romanian war effort. Victorious Germany imposed punitive conditions upon the defeated state. One of the most important was that the strategically important oil fields should be leased to Germany. Not surprisingly the Romanians could not wait for an opportunity to back out of the treaty. In October 1918 the French, the British and the US signalled to King Ferdinand that the doors were still being held open for the ex-ally to rejoin. On 10 November the king authorised the re-opening of military activities against Germany. In reality war was finished and Romania was merely being guaranteed a place at the peace talks which were to follow.

The unification of Romanian-inhabited territories into a 'Greater Romania' was the pretext for staking claims to all disputed areas. Romania was not the only Balkan state to take the attitude that, when in doubt about the ethnic composition and the strategic importance of a given region, it was best to establish control over it lest your neighbours or enemies (in the Balkans interrelated concepts) got there before you did. In March 1918, taking advantage of the political turmoil in Russia, Bessarabia was claimed by Romania. In November 1918 Transylvania, formerly Austrian territory, was added to Romania. Bánát, Crişana and Marmareş were added soon after. Bánát thereby became a source of confrontation with the newly emerging South Slav Kingdom, in due course to be renamed Yugoslavia. Even before the war with the Central Powers was concluded, while making the most of Hungary's defeat, Romania was heading towards conflict with her war-time allies, Russia and Serbia. In March 1919 a revolutionary regime was established in Budapest. Romania and Yugoslavia took military action against Hungary. Their initiative received the blessing of the Big Four, who were meeting in Paris. Further occupation of Hungarian territories followed, only adding to the intense hatred which, in the ensuing years, Hungary would harbour for Romania. In most cases, the Paris Conference decisions upheld and legitimised Romanian territorial acquisitions, in particular those secured at the expense of the defeated states. The US delegation did try to maintain the principle of national self-determination but this proved very difficult to apply in the ethnically confused areas of the Balkans. In the end the Central Territorial Commission, set up during the Paris Conference to discuss disputed territories, and the Council of Foreign Ministers, which assumed responsibility for arbitration, were kind to Romania. Her control of Bessarabia and Bukovina was confirmed. Bánát was divided between Romania and Yugoslavia. When a decision was made to return a portion of Transylvania to Hungary, Romania responded by occupying the disputed region and refusing to relinquish it. The vicious circle of consolidating territorial conflicts rather than resolving them was completed with a settlement in Dobrudja that was favourable to Romania. This area, contested by Bulgaria, reaffirmed the enmity between the two countries.

Hungary was clearly going to be the most obvious future source of instability in the region. By 1920 it was generally hoped that frontiers had been settled and that they would henceforth be accepted by all involved. Thus in June Hungary and the Allied Powers jointly signed the Treaty of Trianon which recognised Hungary's frontiers with her neighbours. The state which emerged from the war proudly calling itself Greater Romania had increased its territory from 130 903 square kilometres to 295 049 square kilometres. Its inhabitants consisted of 71.9 per cent Romanians in addition to 7.9 per cent Hungarians, 4.4 per cent Germans, 4 per cent Jews, and smaller groups of Ukrainians, Ruthenians, Russians, Serbs and Croats. These national minorities tended to live in enclaves where they made up a majority, which only fanned strong nationalist sentiments and opposition to the Romanian state.[6] Nationalism, so clearly heightened throughout the course of the war by the hopes and ambitions associated with the eventual peace settlement, made an internally disruptive force when confronted by an intolerant and politically troubled state. Throughout the inter-war years Romania remained preoccupied with regional politics, in which Hungary was a permanent source of anxiety. Her response to the policies of the larger states was determined in the first place by the question of how these would help Romania in her dealings with her neighbours. Poverty and agrarian problems bedevilled attempts to introduce political stability in Romania. These internal problems were never overcome and contributed to the growth of radical nationalist sentiments which in turn stood in the way of regional unity and co-operation.

During the inter-war period the majority of Romania's population lived in the countryside and was employed in agriculture. The failure to alleviate peasant poverty, and indeed a trend towards further pauperisation, destabilised the Romanian economy and had serious implication for the politics of the country. In spite of land reforms which had taken place in the immediate post-war period, 52 per cent of farms consisted of less than 3 hectares of land and in effect the majority of Romanian peasant holdings remained at a subsistence level. It has been argued that land reform, which benefited mostly landless and small peasants, destroyed the great surplus-producing estates and created a patchwork of inefficient smallholdings. During the inter-war period increases in village populations and the inability of agriculture to absorb surplus labour contributed to the further subdivision of small farms.[7] It has further been suggested that excessive concentration on land reform as a panacea for all rural problems led the Romanian government to overlook the need for measures to promote the consolidation of plots, and laws forbidding the subdivision of small farms.

Not all peasant problems can be directly traced to the failure of the land reforms. Industrial development, which was seen as the obvious antidote for social poverty, had indirectly contributed to the worsening of the peasant's lot. The government policy of favouring rapid industrial growth led to the agricultural sector being financially neglected. Protective tariffs facilitated the growth of cartels maintaining high prices for industrial goods and kept down agricultural prices.[8] The result was the growing pauperisation of the village.

As a weak and unstable Balkan state, with few natural resources and a backward agriculture, Romania was of little strategic importance to the Big European Powers. She nevertheless had one resource, the importance of which increased during the inter-war period, namely oil. The First World War and the political crises of the late 1930s offered the Romanian ruling elites unique opportunities. The First World War had created circumstances in which neutrals could and did bid for territory as a reward for remaining neutral or joining the war. During the inter-war period the retention of territorial acquisitions became difficult. When Nazi Germany embarked on an ambitious rearmament programme, Romania briefly sought to exploit politically its complementary oil resources in order to strengthen its negotiating position. While remaining a poor and politically unstable country, Romania came to play a pivotal role in a number of regional conflicts. Germany, Britain and France all sought access to Romanian oil. But Romania's pivotal role in the late 1930s was not a reflection of its own military or political power. It was an outcome of wider European conflicts. As these reached their climax during the crucial years of 1938 to 1941, so Romania's apparently strong negotiating position evaporated.

Romania's most important natural wealth was oil and that proved to be a mixed blessing. At the end of the First World War all European Powers had an enhanced appreciation of the importance of oil supplies. Romania, which possessed the richest oil wells in Europe, became the object of attention motivated in equal

degrees by the desire to establish control over that militarily
important resource and a wish to deny it to other states

> For France ... Romania was not just a source from which,
> through investments and contracts, regular supplies of oil
> could be assured, but was part of the arrangements for contain-
> ing Germany from the east that were developed as a substitute
> for the transfer of the left bank of the Rhine, which the Peace
> Conference did not allow.[9]

British investment in the Romanian oil industry though substan-
tial, was motivated by economic rather than political factors.

In common with other Successor States which universally
declared their commitment to upholding the democratic system,
the political institutions of Greater Romania were defined by an
apparently democratic constitution. In 1923 Romania became a
constitutional monarchy. A national assembly was to be elected
by universal male franchise. Incorporated in the constitution
were guarantees of personal freedom and freedom of expression.
The reality turned out to be very different. King Ferdinand did
not like the assembly, therefore the monarch's extensive powers
to call the assembly, to dissolve it and to appoint ministers were
used to establish a royal dictatorship. The security of the state provided justification for action against strikers, peasants and political opponents. The rights of national minorities were set aside and
limited in law.[10]

The Romanian monarchy was the source of salacious gossip
throughout the inter-war period. The heir to the throne, Crown
Prince Carol, neglected his wife and developed a long-lasting relationship with Maria Lupescu, a Jewish woman. In December 1925
Carol renounced his claim to the throne and departed with Mrs
Lupescu for Paris. In July 1927 King Ferdinand died. Since
Carol's son was an infant, a Regency Council was appointed. But
in June 1930 Carol decided to return with Mrs Lupescu to Romania, and to resume his royal responsibilities. These and other scan-
dalous events were the source of titillation and amusement in
European capitals; they did nothing to enhance Romania's standing and undermined any attempt at political stability. Carol
remained in Romania until 1940, during which period he worked
to weaken the few democratic institutions which seemed to work

and to destroy existing parties. In 1937 he instituted a paternalist royal dictatorship. By then the biggest threat to his power came from the Fascist Iron Guard.

Nevertheless neither Ferdinand nor his son Carol were entirely responsible for destroying democracy in Romania during the inter-war period. It is debatable whether the liberal model was ever likely to take any other than tenuous roots in the Balkans. Political parties did emerge and seemingly held sway in the assembly. During the period 1922–8 the Liberals dominated the political scene. The National Peasant Party came to power next. But even this picture is not entirely correct, for a political party in Romania was often no more than the creature of a powerful patron. Conflicts between personalities and small sections of the ruling elites affected political life to a larger extent than ideology and political programmes. The bulk of Romania's population had no democratic way of bringing issues of concern to them to the attention of the state and its political institutions. Elections and party politics had little effect on policy.

In the early 1930s a new force emerged to challenge the existing institutions. The Iron Guard, created by Corneliu Codreanu went beyond attacking Jews and Communists, both common objects of hostility in the Eastern European politics of the 1930s. With the 1930s' economic crisis depressing the condition of the peasants, the Iron Guard appealed to the population by attacking capitalism and striking moral anti-corruption and Christian attitudes. The clash with the King was not a conflict between democratic and anti-democratic forces but between royal paternalism and a modern authoritarian patriotic ideology. The Iron Guard looked to Italy as an example. Initially it received relatively little encouragement from Berlin. While some training and military equipment was provided by the German Nazis, this was done to destabilise Carol's dictatorship rather than to put the Iron Guard in power.[11] During the crisis years of the late 1930s the Nazi German government continued negotiating with King Carol and his government rather than working through the local Fascist organisations.

Germany's economic policy towards South Eastern Europe was given an impetus in 1931 when the German Ministry for Foreign Affairs and the Economic Ministry tried to use direct trade and financial treaty negotiations to weaken the Little Entente.

Agreements were signed with Yugoslavia, Hungary and Romania although at this stage these did not amount to a comprehensive plan for the weakening of French influence. The possibility of using the Eastern European countries' economic dependence on Germany as a means of destroying France's eastern policy was considered by Germany at this time. Romanian oil was an exception, since its potential military importance attracted international attention. Even so, before 1935 most German commercial treaties with South Eastern Europe were motivated by economic considerations. After 1935 Germany's expansionist policies became a driving force in economic talks with states in the region.[12] Even then Germany conducted a cautious investment policy. Political considerations played an important role in Germany's Balkan policy but they never became the sole or even the most important factor determining investments and trade deals. Thus any willingness to offer the South East European states preferential treatment invariably depended on what Germany needed from those countries. Romania was in a unique position to benefit from the change in German policies and as a result petroleum exports to Germany rose by 50 per cent.[13] By 1937 Germany was increasingly prepared to humour Romania in order to secure a monopoly on its oil supplies. Nevertheless Romania's unpredictability and political instability inhibited German involvement in the country's economy.[14] The biggest change in Germany's attitude towards Romania came after the Munich Agreement, when it was recognised that progress in the production of synthetic oil products was not going to satisfy Germany's needs. This led directly to a further increase in imports of Romanian oil. By then German negotiators were pleased to see that the Romanian side was just as keen to secure agreements with Germany.[15] Thus oil played a crucial role in Germany's bid for Romania's favour. For their part, the Romanians saw oil as giving them the freedom to consider all options and in the circumstances association with Germany did have its attractions.

In the years immediately after the Depression and until 1937, when Germany embarked on a determined policy of becoming the sole market for Romanian oil exports, the Romanian government was unwilling to allow Germany to establish any monopoly over the country's foreign trade. Several factors contributed to this. The economic Depression, the King's return to Romania and the gradual disintegration of the political parties, a process in which the King actively took part, did not create an atmosphere conducive to the rational evaluation of the German option. The growth of radical national sentiments favoured opposition to increasing foreign involvement in Romania's economy. But, notwithstanding nationalist sentiments, financial considerations played an important role in the debates. At the time the state sought to raise its revenue by establishing closer control over the internal market, and introduced laws limiting the influence of foreign investors in joint venture companies. Since this legislation was almost entirely confined to the petroleum industry, the battle for state influence over the economy was fought around that sector.[16] These factors affected the Romanian government's negotiations with the French and British companies as well as German companies. In the case of Germany, Romania was also reluctant to increase its surplus holdings of Reichsmarks, which it had accrued as a result of earlier agreements.

In December 1937 the governing Liberal Party lost power and the King moved to complete the destruction of the last vestiges of democracy in Romania. He first appointed a government led by Octavian Goga of the extreme anti-Semitic National Christian Party. He then dismissed it to replace it by a Government of National Union, in reality a fig leaf for the royal dictatorship which followed. On 14 April 1938 all political parties were dissolved. The new constitution reaffirmed the right of the state to the nation's mineral wealth. This enabled the King, through the Ministry of National Economy, to reorganise the oil and military industries. Henceforth there would be no obstacles to the King determining the nature of commercial deals to coincide with whatever foreign policy initiative he at that moment favoured.

On 10 December 1938 Romania and Germany signed an economic agreement. Since this had been preceded by King Carol's visit to Berlin it clearly had political as well as economic implications. Germany undertook to increase imports from Romania and to supply the Romanian Army. The importance of this agreement, the first of a number that followed, lay in the fact that Carol had sought German co-operation in the restructuring of the Romanian economy.[17] Romanian–German economic relations dramatically improved during 1939. These were momentarily affected by the so-called Tilea affair, during which the Romanian Ambassador to London reported to the British Foreign Office that Germany had issued an ultimatum demanding the subordination of the Romanian economy to German needs. This disclosure led to the British government guaranteeing Romanian security, but it did not prevent the Romanian government from signing a new economic treaty with Germany on 23 March. Tilea's report had merely drawn attention to the existence of conflicts within the groups associated with the Royal Household and the army on the subject of co-operation with Germany.

Following the German occupation of Prague in March 1939 the Romanian government received approaches, more earnest than hitherto, from the British government seeking to limit the growth of German control over Romania's petroleum industry. But these did not get in the way of the Romanian government continuing to build its economic links with Germany. By the early summer of 1939 these included enhanced German commitments to the supply of arms.[18] Cynically the Romanian government expected the Germans to increase arms supplies after the occupation of Czechoslovakia. On the eve of the German defeat of Poland Romania sought a German commitment to share with Romania the ammunition the German army was expected to obtain from the defeated Poles. The agreement concerning the division of Polish arms was made at a time when Poland and Romania were still allies. Warsaw was assured of Romanian assistance, if and when the Polish government decided to flee to Romania.

Romania's economic relations were closely mirrored by her foreign relations. What made it a special case was the fact that oil became so important an issue in her foreign policy, determining Romania's foreign alliances. Romania moved to the German camp because other alliances could not protect her territorial acquisitions. The result was that Germany gained a virtual monopoly of Romania's oil exports.

Romania's attitude towards the other Great Powers was equally functional. France's support was sought in the hope that she would assist Romania financially and because of her encouragement of the Little Entente. But Romanian politicians were willing to consider co-operating with Italy and in due course also Germany, both countries likely to threaten French security. The most startling example of diplomatic pragmatism came briefly during the mid-1930s when Romania reached an accommodation with the Soviet Union. In 1934 Romania established diplomatic relations with the Soviet Union. In return the latter dropped all references to Bessarabia. These gestures enabled both sides to get down to the more serious issue of negotiating a mutual aid treaty which both sides needed. In the event the fall of the Romanian Foreign Minister Nicolae Titulescu, the main architect of the policy of rapprochement with the Soviet Union, destroyed the little that had been achieved between the two.[19] On the whole regional issues tended to determine foreign policy choices. The forging of long-term relations with the European Powers only mattered in so far as they strengthened Romania in her dealings with her hostile neighbours.

In these circumstances Romania's attitude towards the League of Nations was supportive. The League's commitment to upholding post-war peace treaties and to collective security was beneficial as the state clearly had enriched itself at the expense of its neighbours, had neglected to rectify its military weaknesses, and was therefore in need of all the support it could obtain. At the same time Romania tried to ensure that neither Hungary nor Bulgaria could use the League's support to reclaim lost territories. An amendment put forward by Romania to the Geneva Convention would have excluded disputes over national borders from the League's jurisdiction. Likewise, while Romania supported disarmament talks, her delegation insisted that restrictions should be calculated on the basis of the state's economy. While supporting the League's sanctions against Italy, following the invasion of Abyssinia, Romania also expected that the wealthy states would compensate her for loss of trade with Italy. Such blatant opportunism, from no position of strength, made little impact in Geneva.

Romania's relations with her smaller neighbours were complicated by territorial disputes. It was inevitable that at the end of the First World War Romania's neighbours looked for any opportunity to snatch back what they believed had been taken from them. Without a strong army to hold on to its acquisitions Romania sought the protection of the Great European Powers. The task was bound to be a difficult one. After the First World War Romania had doubled in size with territories acquired from Russia, Hungary and Bulgaria. None of her neighbours accepted this situation and as a result Romania lived in fear of her own weakness and of the revanchism of neighbouring states. On the whole, alliances were sought with states which shared an anxiety about common enemies: Poland, for example, with whom Romania shared a dislike of and anxiety about the Soviet Union. An alternative basis for co-operation was to identify areas where compromises could be made in order to scale down the degree of tension and then to agree on joint action against a common enemy. In the case of Yugoslavia Romanian politicians were prepared to go to great lengths to discuss the contested Bánát region. The aim was to close ranks against Hungary, whose revisionist policies both states were determined to oppose. Unfortunately blatant opportunism did not lead to lasting or durable agreements. Commitments signed were at best transient and liable to be repudiated if better ones were offered.

In 1921 Romania initiated a regional system of alliances which drew together states with shared anxieties. Thus fear of the Soviet Union, opposition to the Habsburg restoration in Hungary and anxiety about Hungarian revisionism were the basis of a plan put forward by the Romanian Minister for Foreign Affairs, Take Ionescu. Yugoslavia, Romania and Czechoslovakia signed the agreements, which came to be known as the Little Entente. Poland refused to be drawn into it. While sympathetic to the main objectives of the Little Entente, Poland harboured a strong loyalty towards the Hungarians.[20] In years to come, co-operation within the Little Entente was forged primarily on the basis of opposition to Hungary. Nevertheless the Little Entente did create a degree of regional unity which in turn led to the resolution of problems between Romania and Yugoslavia over Yugoslav Macedonia and Romanian Bukovina. Likewise Romania and Czechoslovakia negotiated all frontier disputes in order to reach an agreement on assisting each other in the event of an attack from Hungary. Until their agreement with the Soviet Union in 1934 the Romanians were left in no doubt that their conflict with the Soviet Union over Bessarabia was a long-term obstacle to Yugoslavia and France increasing their involvement in the Little Entente. The Serbs traditionally sided with Russia in international conflicts and in spite of the Communist regime they remained unwilling to side with Russia's enemy. The Little Entente's desire for the resolution of the Soviet–Romanian conflict over Bessarabia generally facilitated negotiations which took place

between 1932 and 1936, briefly stabilising an otherwise very volatile situation.

Mindful of her own security needs, France encouraged regional
pacts. Notwithstanding France's generally very supportive attitude towards the Little Entente the member states were left in no
doubt that France considered her involvement in Eastern and
South Eastern Europe subordinate to her desire to obtain
German, Soviet and Italian co-operation in the maintenance of
the European balance of power. France initially supported regional agreements in the Balkans but when it was realised in Paris
that these would bring France into direct conflict with Italy,
public support for these decreased. Likewise during the course of
the negotiations for a Franco–Romanian alliance France let it be
known that she wished to see the Romanians resolve their difficulties with the Soviet Union, a focal point of French political
debates. In June 1926, following the signing of the Locarno Treaties, France concluded a Treaty of Friendship with Romania. The
military convention which accompanied it gave the Romanians
little security, merely providing for consultations between the
General Staffs of the two countries. It has been suggested that the
main reason for the signing of this agreement was the fear of the
growth of Italian influence in Romania, following the appointment of the pro-Italian government of General Alexandru
Averescu.[21]

In 1933 the international situation was dramatically altered by
the Nazis coming to power in Germany. Italy and France showed
signs of wanting to reach an accommodation with Germany. This
in turn caused a reaction in Bucharest. Romania was particularly
vulnerable because of the unresolved disputes with the Soviet
Union and Hungary, and because of her internal weaknesses
which the Depression had exposed. The second half of the 1930s
marks a stage when Romania acted independently but still
showed a willingness to consider French proposals. Sensing that
its interests could become the object of negotiations between
France on the one hand and Italy and Germany on the other, the
Romanian government tried to disentangle itself from previous
arrangements and to negotiate independently. A greater willingness to oblige Germany and the resolution of the territorial conflicts with the Soviet Union marked a break with previous
policies. France was not entirely happy about these developments.

While the Soviet Union's acceptance of the inclusion of Bessarabia into Romania was a welcome development as it generally facilitated France's Eastern Locarno initiative, the improvement in Romania's relations with Germany caused alarm in Paris. The French view was that by acquiring access to Romania's oil resources Germany would gain a strategic advantage which could in turn weaken France's security. If France felt free to improve relations with Germany, Romania's freedom to do likewise was not seen as a positive move.

In Romania, foreign policy was subject to internal political fluctuations. Foreign policy making was the outcome of influence at the court and complex intrigues between various cliques. The winner of the ministerial portfolio briefly gained the freedom to pursue his own vision. When a minister was dismissed, this was usually not because of his failure to pursue an agreed policy, but because another clique had gained the King's support. Thus the policy of rapprochement with the Soviet Union is closely associated with Nicolae Titulescu, Romanian Foreign Minister from 1932 to 1936. His unique position of strength was due to the fact that he accepted responsibility for the conduct of foreign relations on the condition that only the King could dismiss him. He was thus beyond the reach of both the assembly and the government of the time. His weakness lay in the fact that when King Carol, his mistress and the coterie gathered around them decided that Romania's foreign policy was due for a change, Titulescu was summarily dismissed. Titulescu's distinctive contribution to foreign policy was his conviction that Romania needed France. Even if relations between the two states were unequal, and Romania had to pay a heavy price, Titulescu believed that long-term considerations justified the alliance. The price which France demanded in 1934 was that Romania resolve her differences with the Soviet Union. This was in line with the French hope that her agreement with the Soviet Union would be complemented by similar treaties with the Little Entente states.[22] In June 1934 Romania and the Soviet Union, by means of a so-called gentlemen's agreement, refrained from making any references to the contentious issue of Bessarabia. Titulescu had hoped that this amounted to a *de facto* recognition of Romanian control of the region. In return Romania was expected not to pursue a foreign policy unfriendly to the Soviet Union.[23]

Unfortunately the French hope that their own negotiations with the Soviet Union could be backed by parallel agreements with France's other allies in Eastern Europe were never realised. Poland and Yugoslavia refused to be drawn into the French scheme. To the Poles Titulescu's policy of making the Soviet Union a partner in the region's conflicts posed a threat to their own aspirations to dominate the region. They therefore unleashed an attack on Titulescu and put pressure on King Carol to dismiss him. Unfortunately for Titulescu, by 1936 the King had resolved some of the internal problems and concentrated on consolidating his position. As a result of German and Polish pressure, and egged on by pro-German elements in his entourage, Carol dismissed the francophile Titulescu. Titulescu's own achievements in negotiating successfully with the Soviet Union were undeniably weakened by growing Soviet belligerence over Bessarabia. The path to the improvement in Romania's relations with Germany was made easier by the fact that Germany was already the purchaser of Romanian surplus wheat and petroleum products.[24]

Germany's policy of obtaining monopoly control of the Balkan economy was part of the general preparation for war. The main concern was to secure access to raw materials and foodstuffs which would be vital to the conduct of war. In the event of war breaking out, Germany would be prevented from obtaining these from outside markets by the inevitable blockade which would be imposed by the belligerent states. In particular, if Romania was to embark on a policy of limiting her dependence on Germany, the latter was willing to consider using direct and indirect means to change this policy.[25] This was not necessary, for although anti-German sentiments were occasionally voiced within the court, these diminished, and powerful sections within the political elite actively sought closer co-operation with Germany. King Carol hoped that he could increase purchases of military material from Germany. Romania's preference would have been to offset her growing dependence on Germany by increasing economic contacts with France and Britain. While both countries were sympathetic, neither considered Romania to be an attractive economic market.[26] It was understood that Romania's growing dependence on Germany would inevitably be translated into political dependence, and possibly even estrangement from the Western democracies.[27]

In his conviction that he could control German influence in Romania Carol had to tackle two issues, namely the growing political power of the Iron Guard and the Nazi penetration of the German minority in Romania, which comprised 4.32 per cent of the whole population of Greater Romania. Of the two the first was more difficult. Having destroyed the Peasant and the Liberal Parties Carol certainly did not intend to share power with the Iron Guard. In November 1938 Corneliu Codreanu, the leader of the Iron Guard, and a number of his close associates were killed by the police, allegedly while trying to escape. The murder marked the high point of the King's backlash against an organisation which he viewed as posing a threat to his own authority. In the elections of 1937 the Iron Guard commanded nearly 16 per cent of the vote. Carol also feared that the Iron Guard was Germany's 'Fifth Column'. In reality by outlawing the organisation, the King forced the Iron Guard into Germany's arms. During the next two years Germany offered sanctuary to the young members of the Iron Guard. In Germany they received military training and funding. This programme was controlled by the Nazi Party. In spite of this, support for the Iron Guard never became Germany's main policy towards Romania. What is notable is that direct negotiations between the King and the German government continued. All rumours about a German-sponsored putsch by the Iron Guard were immediately denied at the highest level.[28]

The German minority in Romania, the Swabian and Saxon Germans of Bánát and Bácska who settled in the region in the nineteenth century, had not been adversely affected by the political turmoil and the growth of extreme nationalism in Romania. King Carol's keenness to use the minority to retain German goodwill became a feature of Romanian–German relations. Germans in Romania enjoyed extensive autonomy and benefited from agreements between the two states. Even in spring 1939, when Romanian security was guaranteed by Britain and France, Carol made sure that the German community was not made to feel insecure.[29]

After Titulescu's dismissal the King assumed closer responsibility for the country's foreign relations. While German determination to challenge the post-war order polarised countries, Romania sought to keep out of the impending conflict. This policy depended upon Romania's abilities to improve her international standing and on strengthening the country's defence. Before the Anschluss it was believed that by confirming links with the Little Entente, the Balkan League and the Soviet Union Romania's neutrality would be safeguarded.[30] In 1937, pressed by a number of pro-German generals in the army, King Carol was willing to consider improving relations with Poland. Several high-ranking visits to Warsaw briefly signalled the possibility that Romania might loosen her relations with the Little Entente and France, which were opposed by Poland.[31] Faced with choices which went against previous policies King Carol floundered and made no decisions.

After the Anschluss anxiety about Romania's security became more pressing. The issue of what were Germany's long-term aims became a matter of immediate concern. During the mounting international tension over the Sudeten issue, the King and his advisers continued to dither between pacifying Germany or improving relations with Britain and France.[32] Romanian assessments of the Western democracies' ability to stem German aggression in Eastern Europe were given a severe jolt in 1938. After the Anschluss the Romanians were irritated by inconclusive talks concerning supplies from France. Failure to obtain ammunition from France drove the Romanians further into German arms and in the process sharpened the debate on what options were open to Romania in view of the seemingly inevitable war. Doubt about British and French capacity to confront Germany was mirrored by an equal anxiety about Soviet intentions. In September 1938 King Carol travelled through Europe hoping to obtain a clearer idea of the likely responses to continuing German aggression. The picture was bleak. Western Europe seemed disunited and the likelihood of any assistance being given to any East European victim of German aggression was very small. Carol's conclusions were to confirm his predisposition to remain passive. In view of Germany's generally conciliatory attitude towards Romania, fear of the Soviet Union became a more frequent feature of all internal discussions.[33]

In March 1939 the pace of developments caught most European politicians ill-prepared to make clear decisions. German occupation first of the Baltic port of Memel, followed by the entry of German troops into Prague, the creation and incorporation into the Reich of the Slovak Protectorate and finally German consent to the Hungarian entry into Ruthenia, altered earlier assessments of German intentions. The Romanian government continued to be divided on how to respond to the new situation, and West European governments became unwitting players in the internal conflicts which beset the Romanian government.

On 17 March, by means of a calculated indiscretion, the Romanian Ambassador to London, Viorel Tilea, set in motion a train of events which ultimately resulted in Britain granting a guarantee to Romania. On 10 March the German government had requested that the output of key Romanian industries should be coordinated with German economic needs. Tilea, who represented a group opposed to Romania's further subordination to Germany, informed the British Foreign Office of this and furthermore claimed that this demand was presented in the form of an ultimatum. This may not have been the case, as the German request was in line with the substance of negotiations which had been taking place for some time. It is likely that a number of influential persons within the Romanian elite decided to use the German demand to reverse the pro-German trend in Romania's foreign policy. German unwillingness to guarantee Romania's borders, combined with evidence of German–Hungarian co-operation, had caused anxiety.

The response of the Western Powers to information provided by Tilea was initially slow. Neither France nor Britain had been willing to become involved in Romanian–German relations. They both had some idea of the substance of German–Romanian economic talks. But Tilea's calculated leak came in the wake of the German entry into Prague, followed by rumours of an impending German occupation of Danzig. In these circumstances both the Foreign Office in London and the Quai d'Orsay changed their attitude. At precisely the moment when the pro-Western Romanian Ambassador was trying to play his own game and suggest that the Germans were more belligerent than they had been hitherto, the British were searching for a way of warning Germany not to proceed with aggression in Eastern Europe. Thus Tilea's communication to the Foreign Office fell on fertile ground. By 20 March the Romanian King and his advisers, responding to British probing, decided that they could not risk joining the Western Powers in any anti-German block. But, taking advantage of the Western willingness to help the Romanian government, they counter-suggested that Britain and France should guarantee the security of Romanian borders.[34] The Romanian leadership, like

the Poles at the same time, sought to make the most of the situation
and used the British initiative to strengthen their hand in negotiations with Germany. Simultaneously with these exchanges, economic negotiations with Germany were resumed. On 23 March
an Agreement for the Promotion of Economic Relations between
the German Reich and the Kingdom of Romania was concluded.
As a result Romanian industry and agriculture were closely tied in
with Germany's economic needs.[35]

Although Romania was being drawn into the German orbit, it
attempted to keep open the British option. Unfortunately, during
the weeks following the German occupation of Prague, the Chamberlain Government was overwhelmed by a number of anxieties.
In making decisions to oppose Germany, the advice of the military
leaders was sought. During the two weeks following the occupation of Prague Chamberlain modified his original ideas. What
had started as a suggestion to consult in the event of a German
threat evolved into a proposal for building a bloc of countries
determined to oppose Germany. By the end of March Chamberlain was investigating means whereby Eastern European states
could be induced to aid each other. The Romanian–Polish agreement seemed to have been the model upon which Chamberlain's
mind locked. As it turned out neither Poland nor Romania wanted
to extend its scope, which was directed against the Soviet Union.
In that respect the Romanians and the Poles were in agreement.
They did not wish to be involved in any arrangement which
included the Soviet Union on their side, nor did they seek to join
an overtly anti-German bloc. Direct, bilateral agreements with
Britain, which both favoured, had the advantage of giving some
guarantee of security without precluding the possibility of continuing talks with Germany.

At the beginning of April the Romanians faced a confrontation
with Hungary which, emboldened by German support, mobilised
its forces on the Romanian border. Assurances of assistance for
Romania from Britain and France helped in defusing that crisis
without bringing Romania into direct conflict with Germany.
Once more the Romanians were lucky in their timing. The Italian
occupation of Albania on 7 April renewed anxieties about British
interests in the Eastern Mediterranean. The French government
took the initiative and threatened to enter into an agreement
with Romania without Britain. Open differences between France

and Britain would have weakened the two countries' policies towards German aggression. Therefore, on 13 April the British and French governments pledged jointly to uphold the security of Greece and Romania.[36] The commitment was intended to protect Romania against German aggression only.

In the following months the hollowness of these guarantees became fully apparent. The British military leaders made it clear that they were neither willing nor able to assist Romania in the event of an attack. This did not prevent them from expecting that, in the event of a German attack, the Romanian armed forces would put up armed resistance and that those armed forces would also aid any victim of a similar German attack. Britain had moved on from discussing a local Romanian–German conflict to considering Mediterranean security. The position of Turkey and schemes for the defence of the Balkans became a priority. Romania was expected to play a subordinate role in those plans. The security of Romania's borders was, on its own account, of no consequence to the British or the French.[37]

The Romanians refused to play the role of bolstering opposition to Germany, proposed to them by the British and French. In the first place they refused to discuss the possibility of drawing Bulgaria into the Balkan Entente. Unless Bulgaria was assured of the return of the Dobrudja district, regional unity could not be built. At the same time the Romanian Minister for Foreign Affairs, Grigore Gafencu, feared that any attempt to strengthen the Balkan Entente would provoke Germany. When Britain and France embarked on a tortuous course of talks with the Soviet leadership the Romanians became even more obdurate. They suspected that, as a concession, the Soviet Union would be offered Bessarabia. Therefore they refused to be drawn into any discussions. The maintenance of an equilibrium between the two potential enemies, the Soviet Union and Germany, became the sole aim of Romanian foreign policy after spring 1939. This policy was favoured by the group surrounding the King, which rightly pointed out that Germany was not putting pressure on Romania. Although there was irritation at Germany lagging behind with arms supplies, the overall state of economic relations boded well for the future.[38]

Romania's international situation was altered irrevocably with the signing of the Soviet–German Pact on 23 August. Earlier Britain and France had initiated diplomatic talks with Moscow.

Though these, if successful, would have had to address the issue of Soviet claims to Bessarabia, neither London nor Paris felt it necessary to inform King Carol of their substance. In Bucharest insecurity dominated all political talks. When the British–French–Soviet talks stalled and finally collapsed with the official announcement of the Soviet–German Pact, Rumania was further tormented. Though the substance of the Secret Protocol accompanying the agreement was not known officially, it was not difficult to assume that Soviet neutrality had been purchased by Germany making some concessions. In fact Article 3 of the Protocol explicitly recognised the Soviet claim to Bessarabia, while Germany declared its 'total political disinterest in this territory'.[39] The King and his advisers derived a crumb of comfort from the new situation by persuading themselves that Germany would henceforth seek to moderate Soviet aims towards Romania. As undesirable as it was for Germany and the Soviet Union to come together, it appeared to them that Germany would have the final say in any territorial demands made on Romania.

When Germany attacked Poland in the early hours of 1 September, the Poles knew that Romania would remain neutral. They preferred this state of affairs to Romania aiding them. In their plans for a war against Germany the Poles had hoped Romania would be a transit route for arms supplies to Poland and an eventual exit route for the government and army, in the event of a defeat. On 6 September the Romanian Crown Council met to discuss the outbreak of war. Within this hand picked group, as expected, full approval was given to King Carol's decision to declare neutrality, though a lingering desire to retain proper relations with Moscow remained. In all official statements hostile comments about the Soviet Union were studiously avoided and through its contacts with Turkey the Romanian government reaffirmed its desire to continue talks over all disputed issues with Moscow.[40] In order to strengthen the message a new Romanian minister was sent to Moscow with the stated objective of 'strengthening relations with the USSR'.[41] The British and French welcomed the decision of neutrality. It was optimistically believed that Britain would obtain Romanian assistance in denying Germany oil. By purchasing future production and chartering barges which would otherwise be used for the transport of that oil, it was calculated that Germany could be starved of that vital resource.

By the end of 1939 the British oil company executives had to admit that the scheme had become a farce due to Romanian co-operation with Germany. Earlier Romania had requested that Britain extend her already granted guarantee against German aggression to cover the eventuality of Soviet attack.[42] This the British government had not been prepared to consider.

The German attack on Poland caused anxiety in all the Balkan states. Nevertheless the signing of the German–Soviet agreements was of more immediate concern. Belatedly the Balkan countries sought to find strength in building a bloc of neutral states. This idea was considered by Romania, Yugoslavia, Hungary, Bulgaria and Turkey. The belligerent states quickly let it be known that they disapproved of this initiative. Germany feared that this arrangement would extend Turkish influence, whereas France suspected that the neutral states would come under Italian domination. The idea was abandoned by the end of October 1939.[43] In their search for reassurance the Romanians also looked to Turkey. They had hoped that the shared desire to prevent Soviet power in the Black Sea from extending into the Straits would act as a common bond. But Turkey, though sympathetic to Romanian anxieties, was not willing to support it. During his visit to Moscow in late October 1939 the Turkish Minister for Foreign Affairs noted that Molotov declared his support for Bulgarian claims to Romania. Turkey in her desire to continue talks with Moscow effectively refused to support Bucharest.[44]

In December 1939 Italy became the object of intense Romanian diplomatic efforts. Enquiries were directed to Rome with the explicit aim of finding out what Mussolini would do in the event of a Soviet attack on Romania. Mussolini's response was to give an assurance that he would support Romania, but also that he would ensure that Hungary, with which Rome had particularly good relations, would not press her territorial demands. This reassuring message was at odds with the tone of articles which had appeared in the Italian press. In these a less supportive attitude towards Romania had manifested itself. While Italian military support was not something Romania could count on, it had been hoped Italy would restrain Hungary. What Romania had not been told was that from his contacts with Csáky, the Hungarian Minister for Foreign Affairs, Ciano had concluded that were the

Soviet Union to take action to reclaim Bessarabia, Hungary would also present her demands to Romania.[45] The final stage in Romania's slide into the German camp was precipitated by the growth of Soviet belligerence. The King, wrongly as he ultimately found out, assumed that in the event of a Romanian–Soviet Union dispute, Germany would aid Romania. Instead Germany exploited Romanian anxiety to win further concessions in the country. After the fall of France Romania agreed to supply Germany with further quantities of oil. This failed to elicit any German commitment to aid Romania in the event of Soviet threats. On 27 June 1940, having been first assured of German acquiescence, the Soviet Union issued a twenty-four-hour ultimatum to Romania demanding Bessarabia and Bukovina. King Carol's attempts to obtain German support failed. Instead he was advised to comply with the Soviet demand. Germany used Romania's distress to further Hungarian and Bulgarian demands. Romania was assured that Germany would agree to guarantee her security but only after their territorial claims were satisfied. In August Bulgaria laid claim to Southern Dobrudja. Hungary followed with a demand for the return of Transylvania. On 30 August, as a result of the so-called Vienna Arbitration, Hitler awarded 40 per cent of Romanian Transylvania to Hungary. An interesting point has been made that the result of the arbitration was that Hungary's demands were not entirely satisfied and Romania was substantially reduced. The object of the exercise seems to have been to whet Hungarian territorial appetites, and thus to retain the country's loyalty, and to subdue Romania, while still holding out to the latter the hope that the award could be reversed. Romania lost one third of her pre-war territories. King Carol renounced the British guarantee and in its place accepted a German guarantee of the new frontiers.[46]

During the months which followed, King Carol's popularity plummeted while the Iron Guard became increasingly confident. The King's solution was to appoint General Ion Antonescu as Prime Minister. Antonescu was well known for his sympathies with the Iron Guard. By then the Germans had lost interest in the King and moved to negotiate with Antonescu. On 6 October King Carol was forced to abdicate in favour of his son and left Romania. Antonescu, aided and advised by the Germans, first gave the Iron Guard a free hand which they made full use of to instigate a reign of indiscriminate terror. In January 1941, again with German approval, the Iron Guard was put down. Antonescu became 'Leader of the Nation' (Conducator), but the regime over which he presided was military rather than Fascist. After the destruction of the Iron Guard the army, retrained and re-equipped by Germany, assumed total control.[47]

Notwithstanding Antonescu's co-operation with Germany, Romania still paid heed to regional issues. On 6 April 1941 Germany attacked Yugoslavia and Greece. Romania did not participate in military action and, unusually, even refused to take advantage of the German victories to reclaim Southern Bánát, the area which had been the source of friction between Romania and Yugoslavia throughout the inter-war period. The territorial redivision of Yugoslavia was decided by Germany and Italy.[48] Impotent to affect the course of developments, Antonescu allowed the passage of German troops through Romania. When Germany attacked the Soviet Union the regime was not so reticent. On 22 June 1941, in the wake of the German attack on the Soviet Union, Antonescu pitched Romania into the affray. Declaring a 'Holy War', Romanian troops joined Germany. In reality the objectives were territorial. Romania reclaimed Bessarabia and Northern Bukovina, which had been lost only a year earlier to the Soviet Union. This act more than many others confirmed Romania's preoccupation with regional politics and score settling. Neither ideological affinity with Nazi Germany, nor co-operation with the Western democracies, were sufficient attractions on their own, unless they held out a promise of stealing the march on Romania's neighbours. The issue of Romania's unwillingness to co-operate more closely with Britain and France on the eve of the Second World War can only be judged in the light of the whole course of its inter-war history rather than of its willingness to ally with Germany at the end of that period.[49]

5 Poland

Poland emerged at the end of the First World War as a result of the collapse of the three Central European Powers. The Polish Kingdom had ceased to exist in 1793 with the last of the three partitions, in effect the break-up of the territory of Poland between its three neighbours, the Russian and Austrian Empires and the Prussian Kingdom. In spite of this, Polish national consciousness endured and indeed matured during the nineteenth century. In August 1914 the European conflict in which the Russian Empire was pitched against its two previous allies, Germany and Austro-Hungary, was viewed by Polish national leaders as an opportunity to enter into the affray both militarily and diplomatically with the obvious intention of re-establishing an independent Polish state. From the beginning of the war Poles living in Polish territories, as well as those in political exile, believed that by offering their assistance to either the Central or to the Allied Powers they would obtain support for the Polish cause. After years of foreign domination, Polish aspirations were not modest. Fierce nationalism had enabled Poles to retain their identity and culture, but had also led them to over-estimate the importance of the Polish question in European politics. Poles everywhere were determined to ensure that they would never again be bullied by their neighbours. The national leaders believed that, whoever won the war, Russia, Germany and Austria would be weakened so that, in addition to regaining independence after the war, Poland would become the dominant power in Eastern Europe and would henceforth act as a pivotal point between the west and east, between the democratic traditions of 'civilised' Europe and 'Asiatic' Russia, and finally between the industrial parts of the world and the economically backward frontiers of the east. Clearly, plans for the reconstruction of Poland went well beyond hopes for the establishment of an industrialised, territorially integrated, democratic state.

History thus created a burden of expectations which was bound to bring Poland into conflict with neighbours, potential allies, the powerful states of Europe and, not least of all, previous foes.

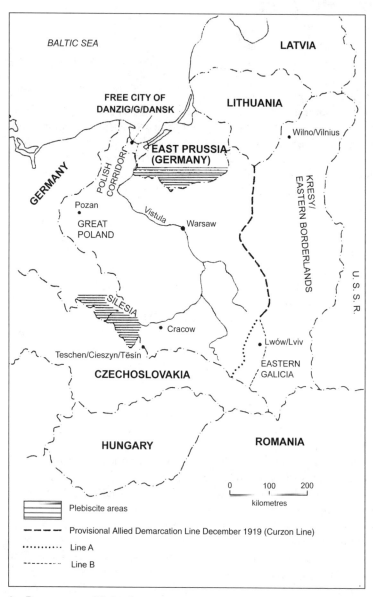

2   Reconstructed Poland

Fanned by its evident success in reconstructing a Polish state, nationalism became immoderate and intolerant of the aspirations of other nationalities. From its inception, Poland was on a collision course with the world and with itself. During the inter-war period the European powers were not prepared to accord Poland the respect and consideration which its government felt was due to its pivotal status in the region. The policies of the West European states turned out to be motivated by self-interest, and this made the politicians of the Successor States truculent and suspicious. Poles, rightly as it turned out, came to believe that they could not depend on the West European states to defend their interests. Their suspicion that, to the French and British, European stability would ultimately mean drawing Germany and possibly even the Soviet Union into an exclusive decision-making group, were repeatedly confirmed in the years preceding the outbreak of the Second World War.

The first test of strength in the battle for an independent Poland after the First World War took place even before the Paris Peace Treaty. Polish leaders in Poland and those abroad, on the Western and the Eastern Fronts, were waging publicity campaigns for an independent Poland. Since these activities were badly coordinated there was little consensus between individuals who claimed to represent Poland. Ideas put forward by a number of prominent leaders varied on the question of which European states were sympathetic and which hostile to the patriotic cause.

The belligerent powers were loath to spend too much time on analysing representations made by various self-appointed Polish national leaders. When the issue was addressed it was invariably because it was felt that it would be useful in resolving an immediate military problem. This was the reason why German and Austrian leaders made promises to the Poles. Without committing themselves, Britain and France used the issue to discredit the Central powers by accusing them of being the oppressors of the independent peoples of Europe. In 1915 the Austrian Prime Minister went a step further and made a promise that the rights of the Polish nation would be recognised. He promised that the Polish Kingdom would have an independent status within the Habsburg Empire, in the same way that Hungarian national aspirations had been honoured. In 1916 Germany formulated its own policies on the Polish question by suggesting publicly that at the end of the war an independent Polish Kingdom would be created. In reality, motivated by military and economic considerations, the German High Command planned to create a puppet state. The Russians who had been the first publicly to air their plans concerning the Poles had made similar promises. All the Tsarist government was prepared to concede in a declaration in August 1914 was a commitment that the Polish state would have an independent status within the Russian Empire.[1]

The Polish national elite, most notably the landed gentry, were at odds as to how to take advantage of the unfolding European conflict. The two most influential groups which emerged were, firstly, the National Democrats led by Roman Dmowski, who believed that Germany was Poland's biggest enemy. He advocated that Poles should look to Russia. The second main protagonist was Józef Piłsudski who advocated co-operation with the Austrians. Neither was successful in obtaining any long-term commitment to the creation of an independent Poland. As a result Dmowski went to France and worked on obtaining French support while Piłsudski sought to persuade Poles under Russian control to accept his leadership. The first authority actually to proclaim its commitment to the creation of an independent Poland was the Russian Provisional Government which emerged after the February Revolution in 1917. Only in 1918 did the Polish question become more than a peripheral issue in allied war-time planning. The Western Allies were motivated by pragmatic considerations and sought a means of breaking the military stalemate with Germany. Having toyed with the idea of an independent Polish Kingdom, Germany and Austria accepted Piłsudski as the only leader of sufficient stature to head a provisional government. In November 1918 German troops were withdrawn from Warsaw to continue fighting in the east. This created a power vacuum into which Piłsudski readily entered.

Piłsudski's success in the territory of the Kingdom of Poland was mirrored by a similar process which was taking place in the west. The battle to obtain Allied support for the Polish cause yielded results when in November 1918 the Dmowski-led Polish National Committee was recognised by France as the *defacto* government of Poland. This apparent diplomatic success turned out to be illusory, as neither France nor Britain were in a position to influence the course of developments in Polish territories. The Poles still had to resolve their differences and to learn to speak with one voice, in particular if they hoped to succeed in influencing decisions at the forthcoming peace talks.[2] In Poland, Piłsudski was able to reduce the influence of the left-wing parties, whose earlier attempt to form a revolutionary government in Lublin had collapsed by November 1918. The more difficult and immediate task was to bring the Paris-based National Committee to heel. The famous Polish pianist Ignacy Paderewski acted as mediator and succeeded in obtaining a compromise between Piłsudski's authority in Warsaw and Dmowski in Paris. The result was that while Piłsudski acted as Head of State in Warsaw, Dmowski's Committee was, not entirely convincingly, transformed into a Polish delegation to the Paris Peace Talks. It has been argued that the consequences of this compromise were very damaging to the Polish cause, since the two sides continued to hold firmly to their own respective ideas concerning the future of Poland. For Western diplomats, anxious to see the Polish question resolved and to move on the more weighty issues of the future of Germany, the squabbles within the Polish delegation and its well-publicised differences with the authorities in Warsaw acted as a warning about the potentially disruptive effect the Poles would have in the future.

In Poland the first elections resulted in an uneasy stalemate between the right-wing parties which polled 37 per cent of the vote, and the left which polled 34 per cent. The need to knit together territories which had been administered during the past 100 years by entirely different authorities, and which had experienced varying degrees of industrial development and agricultural progress, was a formidable task which awaited the first freely elected Polish government. Although foreign policy remained a priority, internal difficulties constrained the government, with the result that it was constantly juggling the need to define still-fluid frontiers against the need to proceed with administrative and economic consolidation of Polish territories. The settlement of the frontiers of Poland was complicated because the western frontier was dependent on Western Powers' decisions relating to the future of Germany. In the south the border with Czechoslovakia remained undefined due to a number of territorial disputes between the newly emerging administrations in Poland and Czechoslovakia. In the east and south-east the Russian Civil War continued and the Poles were obliged to consider the national aspirations of the Baltic people and the Ukrainian and Belorussian communities.

The role of the army in internal politics was to remain very important. Military leaders took upon themselves the responsibility not only of defending Polish sovereignty, but also of securing for the newly independent Poland towns and districts which were considered to be historically Polish. Since other nationalities were also grabbing territories, this process was essentially won by the use of force and audacity. Poles were generally dismissive of the claims of the Ukrainian, Belorussian and Lithuanian nationalities to statehood. The debate which ensued during this formative period in 1919 and subsequently was not whether Poland had rights to those territories, but about the way in which they were to be linked with the newly independent Poland. In the face of the collapse of the Russian Empire, Piłsudski advocated a Polish state into which the East European people would be incorporated on a federal basis. This scheme was at odds with Dmowski's deeply nationalist, even anti-Semitic, concept of an ethnically compact but strong state prepared to fight Germany.

During 1919 Piłsudski, acting as Commander-in-Chief of the Polish Army, led a number of military campaigns aimed at consolidating Poland's eastern borders and implicitly subjugating the eastern national groups to Polish domination. In April the Poles occupied the town of Vilnius, held by the Lithuanians. While militarily successful the campaign inspired a lasting hatred of the Poles in Lithuania. Simultaneously war was being waged against the Ukrainian People's Republic of Semen Petrula. At issue were the Ukrainian-inhabited East Galician territories around the Polish-inhabited city of Lvov. While this conflict ended in a truce in August, Ukrainian nationalism was to have a serious destabilising influence on Polish politics in subsequent years.

On 25 April 1920 the Polish Army started a campaign against the Red Army. Having under-estimated its military abilities, and displaying total disdain for the aspirations of the people inhabiting the regions over which hostilities ensued, the Polish Army sowed proverbial 'dragon's teeth' which would be the cause of future short- and long-term problems. In the first place the Red Army successfully pushed the Poles back into Poland and in August threatened Warsaw. The Poles appealed to the Allied Powers to assist in opening negotiations with the Soviet Union, while at the same time successfully mounting a counter-offensive. The latter was successful in pushing the Red Army out of Poland. Covertly Piłsudski authorised one of his generals Lucjan Żeligowski, to retake Vilnius, which had been returned to Lithuania earlier. When Żeligowski handed the city back to Poland and this was approved by its government, British and French suspicions about Polish opportunism were confirmed. On 18 March 1921 a Treaty of Peace was signed by Poland and the Soviet Union at Riga. In the eastern territories acquired by the Poles, and those which had been temporarily occupied by the Polish Army, the memory of gratuitous violence against Ukrainian peasants and most obviously against the Jewish community would linger.[3] Lithuania never accepted the loss of Vilnius either.

The Poles were hopeful that they would receive a good hearing at the Versailles Conference. The United States had earlier recognised the importance of the Polish issue, incorporating a commitment to the creation of Poland with access to the sea into Woodrow Wilson's 14-point declaration. The surprise which the Poles had not anticipated was British opposition to their vision of a new Poland. In the course of the debates on the subject of Poland's border with Germany, Lloyd George, the British Prime Minister, had become distrustful of French support for an enlarged Poland. British opposition to the incorporation of Upper Silesia and of the Danzig port into Poland was not a reflection of a consistently thought-out British policy towards that state, but of an evolving distrust and hostility towards the growth of French influence in the Continent.[4] In addition, Dmowski's prejudice against Jews raised anxieties and ultimately influenced decisions made at Versailles. The result was that while the Polish right to enjoy access to the sea was recognised, the city of Danzig, which lay strategically at the outlet of Poland's main navigable river the Vistula, was denied the Poles. Danzig, with its adjoining territories, became a Free City, whose status was to be regulated and defended by the League of Nations. East Prussia remained in German hands. The fate of Upper Silesia was decided by a plebiscite in 1921. This turned out in favour of Germany. Nevertheless the local Polish population staged a series of uprisings and the area, rich in coal deposits, was divided between Poland and Germany.[5]

The manner in which the Polish borders were defined left a lasting impression on the national psychology. The prevailing attitude was one of distrust of Big-Power politics combined with an over-estimation of Poland's capacity and freedom to act as she chose. Quick foreign policy successes were a useful ploy in rallying support at times of economic stagnation. The cultivation of long-term friends and allies, a process requiring consistent effort and never guaranteed to succeed, was neglected. In-fighting between parties of marginal popularity and lack of political stability made it difficult for any government to pursue any potentially unpopular foreign policy, however prudent. By the late 1930s Poland's rulers were in need of quick and easily recognisable diplomatic successes in order to distract attention from repressive policies pursued after Piłsudski's *coup d'état* in May 1926. Economic disasters further undermined the government's claim to have broken with the stagnation of the earlier period. The great hopes which had been associated with the re-emergence of an independent Poland had not been fulfilled. By the mid-1930s Poland, in common with other predominantly agricultural areas of Eastern Europe, was experiencing an economic crisis which undermined the little industrial progress which had been achieved since the end of the First World War. Equally worrying was the fact that the Depression of the early 1930s exacerbated the economic disparities between industry and agriculture, and between the economically advanced areas of central and western Poland and the backward eastern and southern regions. At the same time as industrial areas were stagnating, agriculture was barely affected by independent Poland's economic policies.

In 1920, when a unified currency was finally introduced in Poland, industrial production was still below the pre-war levels, as war-time activities had severely disrupted industry. Polish territory had been first the battle zone between Austria and Russia and later between Germany and Russia. All sides had exploited the industrial capacity of territories under their control without concern for any future serviceability. Both Germany and Russia had evacuated whole or parts of factories out of the fighting zones. Reconstruction took a long time but aspirations had been raised that Poland, once rid of its oppressors, would become rich. Among its national aspirations was the hope that Poland could break with poverty by introducing an ambitious programme of industrialisation, which in turn would consolidate Poland's role in the region strategically and politically. Unfortunately successive governments were not able to build a strong industrial infrastructure. The Poles cannot be held wholly responsible for the failure of their economic hopes. The international situation was not favourable. Before the First World War industrial expansion in the Polish territories, where it had occurred, namely in the Łódź district and in Silesia, was largely state encouraged, and facilitated by protective-tariff policies. These policies of the partitioning powers were frequently politically motivated. The creation of an independent state of Poland meant that these industries were cut off from the markets in which they had developed, and which had been the basis of their past success. The industries in central Poland had been established to trade with the Russian Empire, where their markets were protected by high-tariff policies against imports from the west. The collapse of the Russian market meant that Polish industry had to re-orientate itself to western markets, where it could not compete with European producers. In some cases Polish industry was inhibited from competing on international markets by the policies of the neighbouring states. Thus coal and steel industries suffered in the mid-1920s from the German tariff war against Poland.[6]

One of the biggest obstacles to a rapid industrial take-off was the shortage of indigenous capital. Industrial development in independent Poland was characterised by state involvement and foreign investment. A successful entrepreneurial ethos failed to emerge, and the domination of landed gentry in politics was a reflection of that problem. This was made worse by the tendency of indigenous capital to mirror foreign investors' reluctance to commit long-term finance to projects in Poland. Foreign capital tended to be short-term. During the mid-1930s, as a result of the Depression, this capital was the first to be pulled out. At the same time Poles were left in little doubt that bad relations with Germany and the prospect of German revanchism undermined any prospects for long-term investment. Poland was simply too risky a proposition for foreign banks and investors.

And so by the time of the outbreak of the Second World War the new state had failed to establish the economic foundation for a modern industrial state. In some key industries even by 1938 pre-war standards of production had not been attained. This was the case with zinc and lead ore exploitation. Mining and textiles production remained at pre-war levels, while cement, electricity and fertiliser manufacture had advanced. Poland's exports tended to be confined to basic industrial items and to agricultural produce. By the 1930s Poland was subsidising the export of some of its industrial goods.[7]

Agriculture, which continued to employ the majority of the labour force, did not improve either. The characteristic feature of Eastern European farming has always been the absence of middle peasants and the predominance of small and dwarf peasant holdings. As a result few village households produced a marketable surplus of food and in most cases families augmented their income by hiring themselves out for seasonal work and by emigrating to industrial areas or to North America. In spite of emigration overpopulation increased. In the 1920s emigration to the US was limited by strict controls. At times of economic stagnation in Poland, most notably in the 1930s, opportunities for employment in industry dried up. Prices paid for agricultural produce fell, while prices of industrial goods rose. Land hunger and poverty were endemic in Polish villages. Nevertheless successive governments balked at implementing long-overdue land reform, in part because the large farms, in particular those in the eastern parts of Poland, were producers of surplus foodstuffs. In any case neither Piłsudski, nor the colonels who assumed power after his death in 1935, wanted a confrontation with the powerful landed gentry which continued to oppose the break-up of estates. In the 1930s limited land reform was reluctantly implemented. But this was never decisive enough to make a difference to the bulk of Polish peasantry or to the village economy.[8]

The political life of Poland was transformed in May 1926 by a military coup staged by Piłsudski, who had ostensibly retired from political life in 1923. One of the more interesting aspects of this event was the fact that his coup took place with the tacit acquiescence of the President and with the obvious approval of most political parties. This was largely due to the political *impasse* in the elected assembly, where small parties and vested interests were obviously blocking measures to deal with the political and economic problems of the time. Piłsudski had cultivated the image of an elder statesman, unsullied by politics and singularly committed to exposing corruption, mismanagement and venality. He exploited popular discontent and addressed one of the most potent sentiments of the time, namely disappointment with the failure of independence to resolve Polish political and economic problems, in order to change the political system in Poland. The *coup d'état* received the support of some trade unions, sections of the Socialist movement and of the centre and even right-wing parties. Within the army there were individuals who felt that it was wrong to attack a government to which an oath of loyalty had been given. But most Poles (including the Communist Party) believed that the coup was necessary in order to prevent the extreme right National Democrats from capturing power. After the coup Piłsudski surrounded himself with a coterie of military men with whom he shared the experiences of the Legions, which he had formed in 1914 to fight for Austria. This group had no political programme to solve Poland's problems. Piłsudski's most obvious aim was to strengthen the executive, namely the Presidency, and to diminish the power of the assembly, the Sejm. From 1926 until 1935 the parliamentary system continued to function in accordance with the earlier constitution but in reality the Parliament was forced into subservience to the military regime. In 1935 a new constitution completed the process of strengthening the role of the executive and the Presidency, and diminishing the power and prerogatives of the assembly.[9] The army took over ministries, key administrative posts and industries associated with military production. The militarisation of civilian life was accompanied by attacks on opponents of Piłsudski and the army. Frequent stage-managed fracas in the Sejm, during which army officers rendered debate impossible, were accompanied by physical intimidation and by beatings of those who dared to object to attacks on democratic institutions.

Piłsudski, who initially was seen as the non-partisan saviour of the nation, was to realise quickly the importance of building a power base beyond the army. He distrusted the nationalist right and refused to associate with his pre-war allies, the Socialists. In 1927 he publicly made peace with large landowners and as a result land reform was slowed. In the run-up to general elections in November 1927, anticipating a successful challenge from a coalition of centre- and left-wing parties, the Minister of the Interior ordered the arrest of Socialist and Christian Democratic leaders. This was followed by imprisonment of trade unionists, leaders of national minorities, journalists and critics of the government.

Some were incarcerated in the notorious fortress of Brześć, others in the concentration camp of Bereza-Kartuska. Torture and humiliation were routinely used against the prisoners.

Internal repression was also used to deal with national minorities. As many as 30 per cent of Poland's population defined itself as not ethnically Polish. The most numerous and politically active was the Ukrainian community, numbering approximately 6 million, followed closely by the Jewish one of 3 million. Mistreatment of Jews during the 1919–20 eastern campaigns had already put Poles in a bad light. The League of Nations was deeply critical of Poland's minority policy. During the second half of the 1920s the Army was used in punitive campaigns against the non-Polish population of eastern Poland. This made the Ukrainian population more susceptible to outside influence, notably from Czechoslovakia and Germany. Both these countries sought to destabilise Poland. The military regime failed to appreciate the need for a consistent nationality policy, and ignored its implications for Poland's security. In the 1930s Czechoslovakia encouraged anti-Polish sentiments by providing military training for Ukrainian nationalists. This, combined with a dispute over the Teschen region, eventually led the Polish Minister for Foreign Affairs, Josef Beck, to conclude that the break-up of Czechoslovakia and the creation of a rump Slovak state would be advantageous to Polish security. The Poles believed that Hungary was Poland's best potential ally, and not one to tolerate the anti-Polish activities of the Ukrainian community. The incorporation of the extreme eastern part of Czechoslovakia, the so-called Ruthenian region, into Hungary and the creation of a Polish–Hungarian border were supposed to decrease foreign interference in the affairs of the Ukrainian community inhabiting Ruthenia and south-eastern Poland. After the signing of the Munich Agreement in 1938, a general survey of issues affecting Polish–German relations inspired Poland's military rulers to attempt to persuade Germany to stop fomenting Ukrainian nationalism. Germany denied supporting the Ukrainians, but in fact continued to do so precisely because Germany did not want Poland to become unduly strong in the Central European region.

In spite of progressive militarisation, which affected all aspects of civilian life even before the introduction of the new constitution in 1935, Poland's military capability decreased after 1926. In the early 1920s Piłsudski set out basic military principles for any future war. In view of his personal prestige and the patronage system upon which his regime was built, these ideas went unchallenged. Indeed, in the 1930s, when the threat to Polish security became a reality, his views continued to be accepted as absolute dogma. Piłsudski believed that the highly mobile warfare, dominated by cavalry manoeuvres, which had been so successful during battles against the Red Army in 1920, was going to be the style of wars to come. The development of the airforce was neglected, and anti-aircraft guns, a common defence against aerial attack in the west and in Britain, were rare in Poland. Cavalry units were the most important and prestigious units. Coordination between the artillery and the infantry, which had featured in the Austrian conflict with the Russian Army as well as on the Western Front, was ignored by the Polish High Command. Piłsudski persuaded himself that the Soviet Union was the only likely aggressor and his successors continued military planning on the assumption that the only possible future military confrontation was going to be in the east. Only in 1936 were plans considered for a war against Germany, and even then actual preparations for war in the west were not commenced until the autumn of 1938.[10]

By the time of Piłsudski's death his trusted war-time colleagues had assumed control of ministerial and military posts. Of those the best-known is Colonel Josef Beck, who in 1932 became Minister for Foreign Affairs. Unhampered by the need to obtain parliamentary approval for his policies, Beck was able to proceed to implement what he believed to be Piłsudski's directives. Military matters were the domain of another of Piłsudski's men, Marshal Rydz-Śmigły, Inspector General to the Army and Commander-in-Chief designate. The rules of the game were such that neither interfered in the other's fiefdom. Thus the unthinkable occurred: namely, in what was a military regime the Minister for Foreign Affairs had no clear idea of Poland's military strength and conducted foreign relations separately from important questions of Poland's offensive and defensive capabilities. Conversely, the Commander-in-Chief respected his colleague's control over his ministry and did not attempt to influence him in order to minimise the likelihood of defeat, or to increase the number of allies, in the forthcoming war.

Inevitably the economic situation had a considerable bearing on Poland's foreign policy and military capabilities. The consequences of economic constraints upon Polish policies cannot be analysed in simple terms. Polish politicians, in particular those who came to power after the Piłsudski coup in 1926, were well aware of the possibility of Poland being economically strangled by Germany. What did they, and indeed, what could they do about it? Piłsudski apparently attached little importance to economic matters. During the Depression of the early 1930s successive ministers chose merely to follow conventional policies of maintaining balanced budgets and upholding the convertibility of the Polish currency. These policies were based on the assumption that the economic collapse was a short-term phenomenon. Economic planning was pursued in a haphazard manner, though anxiety over security tended to be a strong motivating factor in the government's deliberations. Hence repeated requests were made to France to increase its investments in Poland and efforts were made to decrease the trade deficit with Germany. In 1936 the government initiated the development of the Central Industrial District, the aim of which was to expand the modern industrial base. At the same time it was admitted that there was a need to concentrate production away from the militarily vulnerable frontier areas. Even though the initiative was a success, it was hampered by a shortage of capital and finally was cut short by the outbreak of the war.

Poland's international standing was very weak from the outset. In 1919 the unwillingness of European powers to make unconditional commitments to the new state manifested itself clearly. Successive Polish politicians suspected that anxiety about the future of Germany was the single most important factor in determining British and French policy towards Poland. And it was with France that Polish statesmen were to experience the most obvious disappointments. From 1919 they had assumed that their shared anxiety about Germany would lead France to commit herself to the military and economic build-up of Poland as the pivotal partner in the east. This did not happen. Within French political and military circles a number of ideas were considered. Ultimately commitment to Poland was not sustained even by those who were considered to be polonophiles. Initially, when the outcome of the Russian Civil War was unclear, the French hesitated. The Poles did not want to see the White Russians win because the latter wanted to restore Russia to its pre-1914 boundaries. But as the situation in Russia clarified itself with the Bolsheviks' victory, the Poles became aware that the French commitment to Poland was far from guaranteed.

On 19 February 1921 a Political Agreement was signed by France and Poland. This was supported by a Military Convention which stated that France would aid Poland in the event of an attack from Germany. The Poles were to realise quickly the hollowness of the French commitment. Ambiguities of phrasing meant that even though France guaranteed to assist Poland in the event of a German attack, it was not made clear what form this assistance would take. Investments and military co-operation, which were necessary if Poland was to assume the weighty responsibility of being France's key East European ally, were not forthcoming. While all political groupings in Poland supported co-operation with France, in France major differences prevailed. Marshal Foch was known to share with other military leaders the view that Poland would only be of use if she were part of an eastern bloc. But neither Poland, nor Czechoslovakia, France's other eastern ally, wanted to co-operate with each other. Both preferred bilateral relations with France. Any attempt by France to base her East European policy on the Little Entente conflicted with Poland's regional policy, which assumed close ties with Hungary, against whom the Entente was directed.[11]

France's lack of commitment was a crucial weakness for Poland. The new Polish state needed the support of strong allies. Poland had re-emerged because of the collapse of the three dominant Central European Powers. During the inter-war period the key question was whether it could retain its hard-won independence in the face of the growth of German and Russian positions in European politics. But at stake was not merely Poland's precarious independence. Far more worrying was the fact that frontiers had been consolidated at the time when Germany was defeated. Even a moderate recovery of Germany's economy and political fortunes spelled disaster to the Poles. At the same time the attitude of the European Powers towards the Soviet Union continued to be characterised by hesitation, which gave rise to the hope that they would not support the Soviet Union in any frontier disputes with Poland. In the case of Germany, the Poles were to witness an initially gradual, and then rapidly escalating, process of drawing the ex-enemy into European politics. After the politically damaging occupation of the Ruhr even France showed signs of wanting to re-establish a dialogue with German politicians. Unfortunately for the Poles this did not increase German willingness to accept the border with Poland. Poland's position was made more difficult by her being in conflict with all her small neighbours. When in the 1930s Beck embarked on the policy of building a Central European bloc of states which would form a counterweight to the Soviet Union and Germany, regional rivalries precluded such co-operation.

After 1923, when Gustav Stresemann became Chancellor of Germany and then Minister for Foreign Affairs, Poles wearily observed his apparent success in re-establishing relations with France. In May 1924 the socialist-dominated Cartel des Gauches government was elected in France. The left was critical of Polish foreign policies. In Britain the Ramsay MacDonald Government had openly declared its commitment to improving relations with Germany. The Poles knew that any policy of drawing Germany into European politics could only take place at their expense, as Stresemann had reaffirmed Germany's commitment to the revision of the border with Poland. In October 1924 the French government recognised the Soviet Union, and thus added to the picture one more reason for playing down France's commitment to Poland. Henceforth in Paris successive governments would seek to underpin France's policy towards Germany by maintaining and possibly strengthening relations with the Soviet Union. The hope was that in due course a strong Russian ally would replace the fragmented eastern bloc of Poland and the Little Entente states.

In Poland, the signing of the Locarno Treaties in October 1925 confirmed doubts about France's commitment to Poland.[12] Of the agreements signed at that time the Treaty of Mutual Guarantee was the most important, as it related to Franco–German and Belgian–German frontiers. The three states undertook not to violate each others' frontiers. Additionally Britain and Italy, as the guaranteeing powers, undertook to take as yet unspecified action against the aggressor. One of the other Locarno Treaties was the Arbitration Treaty with Poland and Czechoslovakia. This was not covered by the Treaty of Mutual Guarantee, thus allowing

Germany to challenge the eastern borders with impunity. But the Poles noted that the Locarno Treaties contradicted their agreements with France. France's commitment to aid Poland, which arose from the Franco–Polish Political Agreement of 1921, was not included in the Locarno Agreement, thus making it effectively impossible for France to honour the spirit of her undertaking to Poland, as such action would be viewed by Italy and Britain as aggression. Anxieties raised by the Locarno Treaties led to 1925 becoming a watershed in Poland's foreign policy. When Germany and later the Soviet Union were admitted to the League of Nations this confirmed Polish suspicions that Polish borders would be the object of future debates. Piłsudski's answer in 1926 was to strengthen Poland's position by reaching an accommodation with Germany and the Soviet Union, while at the same time building a strong Central European regional bloc. He did not propose to reject Poland's previous pro-French policy. Piłsudski was nevertheless determined to respond to the ominous signs of the preceding years. Henceforth, distrustful of France and Britain, Poland would feel free to investigate all possible means of guaranteeing its own security.

The most obvious success was scored in 1934, when in January Poland and Germany signed a Declaration of Non-Aggression. Valid in the first place for a period of ten years, the agreement was an undertaking not to use force and to seek peaceful means of resolving all disputes. There were several reasons why this treaty was noteworthy. Up till then successive German governments had refused to enter into any agreements with Poland and had reaffirmed their commitment to the revision of the Polish–German border. The Nazi government, in spite of its ideological commitment to expansion eastward, broke with the previous policy. The Danzig issue, which had been the bone of contention between the two, was, by agreement, set aside and joint efforts were made to keep it off the agenda.

In Poland the Polish–German agreement was seen as a major diplomatic coup, confirming Poland's Big-Power status in Europe. Immediate benefits were gained by the revival of international trade and the decrease of tension in the Free City of Danzig. It has also been suggested that Piłsudski hoped that the agreement would lead to joint plans for a war against the Soviet Union. Thus in 1934 the Poles became convinced of German non-belligerence towards Poland. Henceforth, Polish foreign policy inclined towards condoning German revisionist claims in Eastern Europe without securing for Poland compensation either in strategic or political terms.

One of the more persistent myths relating to this period is the suggestion that Polish–German relations were adversely affected by the unresolved issue of Danzig. The truth is that while both sides firmly believed that decisions made at the end of the First World War were unjust, neither looked at the city in isolation from the whole relationship between the two states. Indeed, when Polish–German relations were good, the Danzig issue was set aside and its implications were played down. On the other hand, when doubts were voiced about each other's intentions, Danzig was put under scrutiny for signs of goodwill or evidence of its breakdown. It is for that reason that the issue deserves to be looked at in greater detail.

At the Paris Peace Conference in 1919 the Polish right of access to the Baltic Sea was recognised. What Poland did not gain was the city of Danzig. On the 15 November 1920 the League of Nations, which briefly assumed control over the city, declared the town and the surrounding area of 1892 square kilometres a Free City. Henceforth it was governed by an elected Senate. Economically the city was totally dependent on Poland. Nevertheless the predominantly German population resented the prerogatives which the Polish state had in the area, namely control of the port facilities, the Post Office and customs. The artificiality of the situation was compounded by the fact that the city was separated by a narrow strip of Polish-controlled land from German West Prussia. The status of the city was guaranteed by the League of Nations, but it was never clear what that entailed. As the key members of the League commission dealing with Danzig, France and Britain, moved towards seeking rapprochement with Germany, so the League's commitment to upholding the status of the city was put in doubt.

During the early 1920s the Poles were ambivalent about the use they could make of their newly acquired access to the sea. Germany and the Successor States were Poland's main trading partners. But Polish prestige and military planning were tied to the idea of access to the sea. When Poland looked to France as a military partner in any future war, the sea seemed the most secure

means of obtaining material aid. In 1925, as a result of anxieties
about a German trade war against Poland, plans for the new and
strategically better-placed port of Gdynia were laid down.
   The Poles resented the League's intrusion into Danzig affairs
and rarely co-operated with it. Developments taking place in the
city on their own account rarely merited serious consideration by
Polish governments. Thus in 1933, when Josef Beck embarked on a
policy of rapprochement with Germany, the election of a Nazi
Senate in Danzig in May 1933 was regarded with equanimity.
The Polish government showed no interest in requests made by
Danzig Social Democrats to support them. Since the real object
of Polish foreign policy initiatives was the establishment of direct
lines of communication with the Nazis in Berlin, the nazification of
the Free City was, on its own account, not a source of anxiety. Beck
believed that the Berlin Nazis would exercise control over the
volatile Danzig Nazi movement, if only to prevent them from casting a shadow over the ongoing negotiations for the Declaration of
Non-Aggression which were taking place at that time.[13] As it
turned out, the Poles were right in believing that Danzig was the
touchstone of Polish–German relations. After the signing of the
Declaration of Non-Aggression in 1934, in spite of the continuation of conflicts between the Polish and German communities in
the city, Danzig was not seen as an insurmountable problem by
the two governments. In the first half of 1938, when Germany
was coordinating an international campaign against Czechoslovakia with which the Poles fully concurred and from which they
hoped to benefit, the two governments remained in agreement on
the subject of the desirability of terminating the League authority
over the city. The change came after the Munich Agreement when
Hitler, perceiving that Britain and France would not oppose his
policy of extending influence into Eastern Europe, assumed a
dominant role in Germany's relationship with Poland.
   Not until 21 March 1939 would the Nazi officials restate their
demand for the return of Danzig to the Reich, but by then the
Poles were debating the weightier issue of what it was that Germany sought to obtain from her growing influence in Eastern
Europe. After March 1939, Beck still maintained that Germany
was a reliable, if difficult, partner. Nevertheless as a precaution
he entered into direct negotiations with Britain and sought to
reconfirm France's commitments to Poland.

Up to October 1938 Polish leaders viewed the expansion of German influence in Eastern Europe with equanimity because they believed that Poland's sphere of influence was not being challenged. During the German occupation of Austria, Poland took advantage of the fact that international attention was focused on that crisis to deliver to the Lithuanian government an ultimatum demanding the restoration of diplomatic relations. This somewhat idiosyncratic manner of re-establishing contacts between the two states masked no more than a Polish attempt to consolidate its influence in the Baltic States. Following German actions against Austria, Poland and Germany co-operated in the destruction of Czechoslovakia. Beck persuaded himself that neither Britain nor France would interfere. He wanted not merely to obtain satisfaction for the Polish claims to Teschen lost to Czechoslovakia during the turbulent period after the war, but also to use the Czechoslovak crisis to assert for Poland a dominant role in the region. The Poles hoped to see the break-up of Czechoslovakia and the end of its influence in the Ukrainian region and Ruthenia. If the Czechoslovak state could be broken-up into the Czech lands and a weak Slovak state, under Polish influence, then, as Beck reasoned, Poland could satisfy the Hungarian claim to eastern parts of Slovakia and thereby obtain a border with Hungary, as well as extending the Polish border with Romania. These demands were presented to the German leadership before Chamberlain's personal diplomacy opened up new possibilities for resolving the Czechoslovak issue. When Hitler pressed the British Prime Minister to accept the principle of the cession of the Sudeten region to Germany, he was confident that the Poles and the Hungarians would also lay claims to other parts of Czechoslovakia.[14]

As the Czechoslovak crisis unfolded Poland was unexpectedly sidelined. On 18 September the Czechoslovak government yielded to British and French pressure to accept mediation over the Sudeten crisis. When on 30 September 1938 the Munich Conference completed the process, Polish claims to the Czech region of Teschen were not included on the agenda and therefore did not figure in the final agreement. Germany had not invited Poland to participate in the international conference which dealt with the Czechoslovak crisis. On 10 October, to forestall any decisions by the Munich Powers on Poland's claims to Czech territory, Beck took direct action and issued an ultimatum to Beneš, threatening the use of force unless Czechoslovakia returned to Poland the town of Teschen and adjoining territory which had been captured from Poland in 1919. The Czechoslovak government bowed to Polish demands and Beneš was forced to accept the principle of further plebiscites to determine the future of areas inhabited by a majority Polish population, which would then also be ceded to Poland. In taking this action Beck had two aims in mind. In the first place he felt bold enough to recapture territories which had been bones of contention between the two states since 1919. In the second place he wished to establish for Poland a better strategic situation. Germany's actions during and immediately after the Munich Conference suggested that Hitler would not tolerate the extension of Polish influence in the region. Hungary, hitherto Poland's ally in her anti-Czechoslovak plans, seemed to waver and showed signs of timorousness. If Poland wished to lay claim to Eastern and South-Eastern Europe as her sphere of influence, then she needed to be seen exercising that role. Thus Beck's highly opportunistic move against an already-defeated Czechoslovakia was meant to increase Poland's standing in the region, precisely at the time when Britain and France were giving in to German demands.[15]

Beck's actions, preceded by a propaganda campaign against Czechoslovakia and accompanied by appeals to national senti-ments, was greeted in Poland as a victory and a diplomatic success. Within the government and High Command a certain degree of disquiet prevailed, as the consequences of the break-up of Czecho-slovakia appeared to be still unclear. These were brushed aside by Beck who, though unsure about the implications of the changing balance of power in Central Europe, was confident that Poland and Hungary would dominate that region, and that problems with Germany would be cleared up by direct talks between Lipski and the Nazi leadership.

On 24 October 1938 Josef Lipski, the Polish Ambassador to Berlin, had an interview with Ribbentrop. The former had sought a meeting with the explicit purpose of clarifying a few diffi-cult issues which were casting a shadow over otherwise good rela-tions between the two states. Ribbentrop explained that Danzig would have to revert to Germany and in return Germany would promise to be sympathetic to Polish colonial aspirations, to plans for the removal of Polish Jews and in any future war with the Soviet Union.[16] Although Ribbentrop's statement was slightly re-phrased during the following days, it had clearly come at a particularly vulnerable time for Poland. Having incurred the anger of the British and French for having connived with Germany in pressurising Czechoslovakia to accept German demands, Beck was in need of reassurance that Germany would not exploit her newly acquired position of strength to settle the Danzig issue. This he was not to get from Berlin in October. The apparent reasonableness of demands made by Ribbentrop to Lipski on 24 October 1938 marked the end of any Polish–German collaboration based, as Beck had assumed, on equality between the two countries. Germany changed her style and the content of negotiations with the Poles. The German proposal clearly and unambiguously transgressed upon an issue which both the Poles and the Germans appreciated to be an extremely delicate one, namely the question of Danzig. Earlier German commitments to respect the status of the city were seen by the Poles as a sign of Germany's determination to maintain good relations with Poland. In November 1937 and January 1938 Hitler had made repeated commitments to respect Polish rights in the Free City.[17] In October 1938 Lipski heard for the first time that Germany expected Danzig to be returned to Germany. What the Poles would obtain in return was assurances relating to the status quo, to the continuation of the German–Polish Agreement and finally that Germany would support Poland in any future plans. Thus real territory was to be traded in for mere promises. Not surprisingly, exchanges between the German leadership and the Polish Ambassador to Berlin confused the Poles.

A prominent Polish historian has pointed out that Beck's main mistake was that he had failed to comprehend fully the implications of Poland's failure to build a Polish–Czechoslovak barrier against German expansion into Central and Eastern Europe. In the autumn of 1938 the Czechoslovak Army was well equipped. It was backed by a modern and efficient armaments industry which was able to provide spares and to maintain production in the event of war. Poland had a large army but it lacked equipment and was short of modern armaments. The combination of the two could have formed a credible deterrent. Unfortunately neither the Poles nor the Czechs accepted the need to build regional pacts. Instead Czechoslovakia looked to France which, in 1938, was wavering in its conviction that an Eastern Front was the way to

keep Germany at bay. Poland had earlier come to doubt France's
reliability and in 1938 confidently looked forward to resolving all
difficulties through direct negotiations with Germany. A regional
pact was not a real possibility.[18]

British and French entry into the German–Czechoslovak conflict spelled the end of Polish importance in German calculations
concerning Eastern Europe. Polish acquiescence in the break-up
of Czechoslovakia had become irrelevant as Hitler had secured
not merely Western acquiescence to his plans but also their active
co-operation in breaking up Czechoslovakia. In the wake of the
Munich Conference, Polish attempts to consolidate a sphere of
influence in the region became a nuisance and a threat to
German plans. In any case, by the end of 1938 both Hungary and
Romania realised that they had more to gain from going along
with German economic and political ambitions. Romania entered
into extensive long-term trading agreements with Germany, with
the latter investing extensively in the exploitation of Romanian
oil. Romania had felt uneasy about the collapse of Czechoslovakia
but turned to Germany for reassurances against the Soviet Union.
Hungary too appeared to act out of step with Polish plans. Instead
of turning to Poland for assistance in enforcing territorial claims to
Czechoslovakia, Hungary sought German and Italian arbitration, which resulted in the award of Ruthenia and parts of Slovakia to Hungary.

Against the background of these events came the crisis of March
1939. Poland was not merely discomforted by the suspicion that
growing tension in Danzig was a sign of more fundamental difficulties in Polish–German relations. Beck was tormented by suspicions that behind Hungarian and Romanian actions lay a German
determination to undermine Poland's standing in the region.
German influence in Eastern Europe was dramatically manifested
on 15 March, when German troops entered Prague, occupying
Bohemia and Moravia. Ominously, Ribbentrop had a conversa-
tion with Lipski on 21 March during which he announced that
the port of Danzig had to return to Germany. This was followed
on 23 March by the Lithuanian government handing the port of
Memel to Germany. On 18 March the British Government took
the initiative to build an alliance of countries opposed to German
aggression. In the face of rumours and counter-rumours and
spurred on by information about Germany taking over Romanian

oil production, Chamberlain made a declaration on 31 March of Britain's determination to defend Poland.[19] These diplomatic manoeuvres allowed Beck to activate an option which he had been considering since October 1938, namely, renewing his contacts with France and establishing closer contacts with Britain.[20]

In the early 1930s relations between Britain and Poland had gradually improved on the background of a progressive weakening of French commitments to her eastern allies. In 1935 the signing of the Franco–Soviet Treaty, followed by the completion of the Franco–Czechoslovak Treaty, caused fury in Poland. Even earlier, the Poles had been unwilling to back up the Locarno Treaties by agreeing to the French scheme for an Eastern Locarno. They rightly believed the proposed guarantees of the Polish–German border were not going to amount to a security pact, but would merely act as a preliminary step to the renegotiation of contentious territorial issues between Poland and Germany. As far as the Poles were concerned, they were not prepared to consider any adjustments of their border with Germany, and any arbitration would only serve as an excuse for France to slide out of her commitments to Poland. Their opposition to treaties involving Czechoslovakia continued. Equally undesirable to the Poles were agreements which would bring the Soviet Union into European politics. It was with surprise therefore that France received in March 1936 from the Polish Minister for Foreign Affairs a suggestion for a preventive war against Germany. Hitler had just authorised the stationing of troops in the demilitarised zone of the Rhine. French politicians did not treat the approach seriously, although some historians have since suggested that this was a missed historic moment when the Nazi regime could have been defeated at an early stage. The most likely explanation for their surprise offer is that the Poles, who were not prepared for war against Germany, sought to remind the French of the continuing need for co-operation and at the same time sought France's reaffirmation of her commitment to defend Poland.[21]

As is known, the French government did not at the time respond to the Polish challenge and indeed relations between the two states continued to develop in an inconsequential manner. The French dislike of Beck, encouraged to a large extent by the Ambassador to Warsaw Leon Noël, made trade and financial talks between the two states difficult. In August 1936 General Gamelin visited

Warsaw, and this was followed in September by a visit of Rydz-Śmigły to Paris. Trade talks were the main topic. But in reality both sides sought to investigate the possibility of reviving and possibly re-negotiating their alliance. The unanswered question of the precise extent of French military commitment to Polish defence was a subject which both the French and the Polish military leaders were only too willing to discuss.[22] The result was the granting of a 2 billion francs' loan to Poland to be paid over a period of four years. French politicians balked at cutting links with the eastern ally. They recognised that Poland's industrial infrastructure needed to be improved if Poland was to take upon herself the burden of building an Eastern Front. Thus the objective of the loan was to allow the Poles to purchase armaments in France, to improve their communication system and finally to finance contracts with major French firms. Ironically, in the years preceding the outbreak of the war, the loan, which was paid in instalments, became a focus of further Polish–French recriminations as French firms were unwilling and unable to satisfy Polish demands. Unfortunately each financial setback was viewed as a political slight and contributed to the further weakening of relations between the two.[23]

In spite of the inconclusiveness of their diplomacy, relations between the Polish military leaders and France were always characterised by intimacy, even if that did not automatically amount to friendliness. After the First World War the French had established a military academy in Poland. As a result most officers had either direct personal contacts with their French counterparts or had at least been trained in the French military doctrine. Within the Polish High Command debates about the desirability of strengthening ties with France raged constantly, and even Josef Beck, who expressed openly anti-French and pro-German sentiments, never sought to renounce entirely Poland's relations with the French. After the Munich Conference Beck did refuse to inform the French of the German demand for Danzig and consistently denied that Germany and Poland were discussing that contentious issue. His aim was clearly to keep the French out of the picture. This was motivated by an anxiety that the French government, in pursuit of a rapprochement with Germany, would refuse to support the Poles. But at the same time in January 1939 Beck made an ostensibly private trip to France. Still flushed from the apparent diplomatic success of having signed an agreement with Germany, French politicians did not take advantage of Beck's presence in their country to conduct informal talks. Instead Beck on his way back stopped in Berlin where he was reassured by Hitler that Germany would not press the Danzig issue.

During the crisis which unfolded in March 1939 and during the following months, France was no longer taking the lead in stemming the growth of German influence in Eastern Europe. Since the autumn of 1938 Britain had assumed that role. Neither during the crisis days of March, nor in their subsequent dealings with Poland and Romania, were the British to build on the diplomatic, economic and military contacts which France had developed with these states since the war. In March the fall of Prague and rumours concerning a German ultimatum to Romania caused Poland and Britain to search independently for a suitable response. The Chamberlain Government knew it could not militarily stop Germany, whereas Beck did not believe in the final breakdown of contacts with Germany. In these circumstances, when on 21 March Howard Kennard, the British ambassador to Warsaw, suggested to Beck that Poland join in a declaration to warn Germany, Beck seized on this, aiming to make full use of the favourable circumstances.[24] However he refused to make a joint declaration. He also rejected the British suggestion that Poland and Romania, and possibly also the Soviet Union, should issue a statement of intent to support each other against aggression. Beck's counter proposal, made on 21 March, was that Britain and Poland should conclude a bilateral agreement to aid each other against aggression. On 31 March Chamberlain announced in the House of Commons that Britain had undertaken to guarantee the security of Poland and that this commitment extended to the city of Danzig. The British guarantee, badly thought-out and issued in anticipation of an impending crisis in Danzig, was in essence a warning to Hitler, and not a commitment to fight for Poland.[25]

Poland's keenness to secure a British guarantee of Polish security was not a simple ploy to draw Britain into defending both Polish interests and the status of the Free City. Rather it should be seen as an attempt by Beck to transform the British offer to facilitate the building of an anti-German block into an insurance policy against the possible breakdown of his own negotiations with

Germany. Beck had hoped that Chamberlain's declaration to the House of Commons on 31 March to defend Poland would not be treated by Germany as a sign of Poland's final alienation from Germany. By leaving the Soviet Union out of the guarantee, Beck thought that Germany would view the British–Polish agreement as a political rather than a military gesture. As Beck realised, British policy towards Germany had hitherto been conciliatory. Chamberlain's House of Commons declaration, he felt, was unlikely to be seen by Hitler as aggressive in intent. In that respect both Beck and Chamberlain were mistaken. On 3 April a new directive was issued by Hitler to the German military leaders, instructing them to prepare for war against Poland. On 28 April Hitler made a speech to the Reichstag in which he renounced the German–Polish Non-Aggression Pact and the Anglo–German Naval Agreement. Henceforth the Poles found it impossible to gain access to Nazi leaders and policy makers. In Berlin and Warsaw all avenues for contact had closed.

On 3 April the Polish Minister for Foreign Affairs arrived in London for a visit which had been arranged before the March crisis. His demeanour, while in London and on his way back, suggested that he wished to strengthen ties with Britain. At the same time Beck rejected all attempts to draw Poland into broader regional agreements. In effect he did not wish to participate in the building of an anti-German alliance in Eastern Europe, hence his refusal to see the extension of the Anglo–Polish agreement to include Romania and the Soviet Union. At the same time, by means of diplomatic gestures such as a willingness to see the German Ambassador in Warsaw and messages conveyed through the Polish Ambassador in Berlin, Beck continued to indicate that he still hoped that talks with Germany would continue.[26]

By early summer the Polish leadership was coming to terms with the fact that war with Germany was a distinct possibility. Planning for the Western Front, in effect for war against German aggression, authorised in 1936, had been proceeding since the autumn of 1938. But by then the German occupation of Czechoslovakia and the creation of the Protectorate of Slovakia, the occupation of Memel and the growth of Nazi belligerence in Danzig had made the previous military plans obsolete. The industrial zone of central Poland, key communication routes and even military stockpiles were all within easy range of German bombers.

Moreover shortcomings in the command structure, in the training of officers, in rearmament, and finally in the preparation of military plans for all contingencies could not be overcome in a short space of time. Lack of imagination and the generally low quality of training continued to manifest themselves in the Polish Army. The Poles over-estimated their military prowess, under-estimated the German Army and finally ignored the possibility of Germany and the Soviet Union coming together. When anxiety was voiced about the inevitability of war breaking out, Polish military leaders comforted themselves with the conviction that neither Britain nor the west could afford to allow Poland to fall. Thus from spring 1939 efforts were made to clarify western military commitments to Poland and to obtain maximum financial and material support.[27]

Military talks with the British were conducted in Warsaw from 23 to 30 May. The Poles were to learn that the British Committee for Imperial Defence envisaged no military action in support of Poland. They in turn revealed their heavy dependence on Royal Air Force operational and material support in the event of a German attack. During the coming months they were also to find out that the RAF was not capable of reaching Germany's key industrial areas from Britain and that no plans for stationing British planes in Poland would be considered. In any case British policy governing aerial action was so narrowly defined as to prevent the RAF bombing German military industry and communication lines in the event of their attacking Poland.

Notwithstanding bad relations with the French, Polish military leaders always believed that were war with Germany to break out France's support could be counted on. At times when relations between Poland and Germany were peaceful, there was an inclination to ignore any advice from Paris. This is what had happened during the Czechoslovak crisis. Beck had rejected French attempts to stop the Poles from making claims to the Teschen region. Nevertheless when relations with Germany were less secure France and Poland tended to come together and restart talks on the subject of the Alliance and the still-undefined military commitments. Not suprisingly, therefore, at the end of April 1939 the Polish Ambassador to Paris initiated talks with Georges Bonnet, the French Minister for Foreign Affairs, with the aim of defining more closely France's commitment to Poland. At the same time a military delegation arrived in Paris to discuss joint action. In both cases the illusion of success was contradicted by lack of final approval. The Poles believed that Germany would in the first place use the full force of her military power against Poland and only then take action against France. They therefore demanded that, in the event of a German attack east, the French Army take offensive action against Germany. In this demand the Polish delegation seems to have been successful. On 19 May a military convention was signed which explicitly stated that in the event of a German attack against Poland France would use the bulk of her forces ('le gros de ses forces') to attack Germany. General Maurice Gamelin, the French Chief of Staff, appeared to be sympathetic to the Poles. Nevertheless the convention was made conditional on the ratification of the political talks which had been taking place at the same time as the military ones.[28] Neither Gamelin nor Bonnet were entirely clear about the role of the eastern ally in the rapidly changing international situation. As a result the political document was not signed and that meant that, in spite of written assurances given to the Polish High Command, legally France was not obliged to aid Poland. Both Gamelin and Bonnet toyed with the Poles, neither seeking to increase France's commitment to Poland nor wanting the Poles to yield to Germany. The Poles comforted themselves with the conviction that France would be forced to do all in her power to defend her eastern ally.[29]

Since it was known that in the event of war, it would be well-nigh impossible for Britain and France to resupply Poland, the Polish government expected to obtain military supplies and cash with which to purchase equipment in advance of any military confrontation. On 12 May the Polish Ambassador to London, Edward Raczyński, requested the opening of financial talks. The Poles sought credits amounting to £60 million, of which £24 million was to be in gold or convertible currencies. It was hoped that British aid would be used to purchase military supplies but also for the continuing programme of electrification and development of the Central Industrial Zone. What the Polish government did not realise was that their request was one of a number which the British had to consider carefully. The Treasury was unsympathetic to the Polish demand and the Chiefs of Staff considered Poland to be low on their list of priorities. The Foreign Office, on the other hand, advised that the Polish request be treated sympathetically.

The result was that Poland was offered a joint Franco–British credit amounting to £5 million and 600 million francs. Simultaneously a Military Mission arrived in Britain, with the aim of purchasing equipment and armaments. Beck's response to the limited financial package was to reject it as derisory. He and his advisers considered that they had been insulted by conditions which had been attached to the granting of the limited financial package. The Treasury had demanded that the Polish economy should be restructured and the currency devalued. Haughtily rejecting the British offer, Beck pointed out that when anticipating the outbreak of the war, the Polish government could not even consider long-term conditions in particular because, if implemented, they would weaken Poland's ability to make purchases abroad and prepare against aggression. The Polish Military Mission was equally shocked to learn that there was no sympathy for the Poles in London.[30] In plans for the future war imperial priorities took precedence over European considerations. Therefore the supplying of the Eastern Front was considered to be too wasteful to be considered seriously.

In the first days of August increased tension between the German community and Polish authorities in Danzig exposed the contradictory nature of British and French commitments to Poland. On 1 August the City Senate had informed the Polish government that it would no longer recognise Polish customs inspectors. Beck responded by refusing to accept the new measures. In his determination to stop the Danzig Senate eroding Polish rights in the City, he was prepared to resort to bombing. When the Senate withdrew its notice to the Polish government the crisis was temporarily defused. Nevertheless an uneasy state of anticipation continued to hang over the city. The fact that the Polish Minister for Foreign Affairs had not consulted his Western counterparts, even though the case of German action in Danzig was covered by the Chamberlain guarantee to Poland of 31 March, filled the British and French with profound unease. But Beck was quite deliberate in this. In the first place he had threatened the Danzig Senate with reprisals, because he suspected that Germany was behind the escalation of violence, and in the second place he did not trust either Britain or France to defend Polish interests in the Free City.[31] In spite of the continuing state of tension in Danzig, by the middle of August German actions in Europe were the object of fevered speculation. The unavoidable conclusion, drawn in the capital cities of Europe, was that war between Poland and Germany was inevitable.

One of the last opportunities the Poles had to influence the course of international negotiations was given to them in the context of Franco–British talks with the Soviet Union. These had started in May 1939, with the British looking for a means of obtaining a general Soviet commitment to oppose German aggression. The Soviet Union took an entirely different view from that presented by the British Foreign Office. On 3 May Maxim Litvinov, the architect of the Soviet collective security policy, was replaced as Commissar for Foreign Affairs by Vyacheslav Molotov. This change of personnel signalled an abandonment of the previous policy of co-operation with the Western Powers. Since March, when Stalin hinted at a willingness to enter into a dialogue with Germany, two alternative foreign policy options had been considered by the Soviet political leadership. Thus, unbeknown to the British and the French, the Soviet Union was at the same time conducting talks with the Germans.[32]

As the British–French talks with Molotov seemed to be leading nowhere, the Soviet side demanded that progress should be made with military talks. The Western delegation, when it arrived in Moscow at the beginning of August, was faced with a blunt enquiry as to how the Soviet Union was expected to oppose Germany without a right of entry onto Polish territory. The Poles, who had taken a detached view of the Anglo–French talks with the Soviet Union, made it clear that they would neither require nor welcome the Red Army's assistance in the event of a German attack.[33] Since the Soviet enquiry appeared to go beyond what British politicians had been prepared to consider, the military talks foundered ostensibly on the issue of the Polish unwillingness to allow the Soviet Union to help them. But it is worth noting that, prior to the opening of the military talks with the Soviet Union, the British Chiefs of Staff had not considered the question of the Eastern Front seriously enough to take into account the implications of the mutual Soviet–Polish hostility upon issues which were bound to crop up in their talks with the Soviet leadership. While the British and French delegations in Moscow frantically communicated with their governments and with military and embassy representatives in Warsaw with the object of obtaining from the

Poles a suitably non-committal agreement to accepting Soviet assistance, news came of a Soviet–German agreement. The Polish military leaders had considered the Soviet inquiry and had concluded that this was merely an attempt to sabotage the talks. They felt that they had no need for Soviet assistance and in any event if the Red Army were to enter onto Polish territory this would be followed by attempts to foment a revolution.[34] French attempts to extract from the Poles a positive response to the Soviet request were cut short when, on 24 August, it became known that Ribbentrop had flown to the Soviet Union to finalise the Soviet–German Pact of Non-Aggression. The Poles continued to be dismissive of the possible consequences of the two coming together. The military regime which ruled Poland had not considered seriously the possibility of concerted action by the two formidable neighbours, even though throughout the last months of peace the Poles had noted the Soviet and German delegations travelling across Poland. Polish indifference to the Soviet Union went further, for no efforts were made to secure Soviet goodwill even after Germany attacked Poland on 1 September. While it could be argued that these would not have been sucessful, the signal feature of the Poles' attitude towards the Communist regime was an inability to accept that it could have any role to play in the impending conflict. Thus the Soviet entry into Eastern Poland on 17 September caught the government by surprise.

As the German–Soviet Pact of Non-Aggression was made public, on 25 August, the Anglo–Polish Agreement of Mutual Assistance was signed in London after months of haggling. Talks had been dragging on since April, with the Poles determined to have Danzig included in the agreement, while Britain sought to have references to the possibility of German aggression against Holland and Belgium incorporated in the Polish commitment to Britain. The truth of the matter was that neither side wanted to see the agreement concluded as it had already served its purpose of persuading Germany of British and Polish determination to treat further German territorial demands in Eastern Europe as aggressive. The fact that Britain could not directly aid Poland had already been confirmed by earlier Staff and Financial talks. Nevertheless once Germany and the Soviet Union had reached an understanding, and it was generally assumed that this was at Poland's expense, the signing of the agreement became necessary, if only to create an impression that Poland was going to be assisted by the Western Powers.

When war broke out, German military action was swift and precise. On 1 September the German Airforce bombed clearly identified military objects and in the course of the first day of the war followed this up with bombing raids on major cities. Poland was ill-prepared for the ferocity and pace of the attack. Fighting continued until 17 September, when the entry of the Soviet Union onto Polish territory hastened the well-advanced flight of the government and High Command to Romania.[35]

Danzig, the issue upon which international attention had been focused earlier, was not the cause of the military conflict. On 23 August the Danzig Senate had voted to join the Third Reich. The Poles could do little to stop this. In any case they were by that time solely preoccupied with the impending war. Since Polish–German relations in their entirety had collapsed there was no reason to focus upon the Danzig manifestation of that collapse.

6 Hungary

The political character and foreign policy of inter-war Hungary were to a large extent determined by the dramatic events surrounding the Béla Kun's Hungarian Soviet Republic and the backlash which followed its overthrow in 1919. This distinguished Hungarians from other Eastern European and Balkan peoples who viewed the First World War as the most important and formative period in their recent history. The collapse of the Dual Monarchy marked an important point in the history of modern Hungary. But the events which followed traumatised its people and affected their attitudes towards the newly emerging state.

In 1867, following years of resentment and rebellion against Austrian tutelage, relations between the two kingdoms of the Dual Monarchy were formalised. While Hungary and Austria were joined by a common monarchy, complex constitutional agreements confirmed extensive freedoms enjoyed by the Hungarians in their own lands. Paradoxically it was this freedom which limited the extent of Habsburg interference in Hungarian lands. Most of the other territories in the empire had been changed by legislation aimed at modernising the state. In Hungary the nobility remained supreme and proved an obstacle to the development of constructive relations with other national minorities and to economic progress. Because the Hungarian magnates and nobility retained more of their privileges than the landed aristocracy in Austria, they came to stand in the way of a redistribution of land and economic progress which would support the development and growth of the middle class and urban strata of society.[1]

The nationality issue was always a source of tension within the Hungarian lands. Magyars made up less than 50 per cent of the population of the Hungarian part of the Dual Monarchy. Romanians, Serbs and Slovaks were the most numerous other national groups, though Jews, Ruthenians and Swabian Germans were just as important. The Hungarians did not intend to allow the other national groups to enjoy the same degree of autonomy that had been granted to them. To maintain stability, the nobility

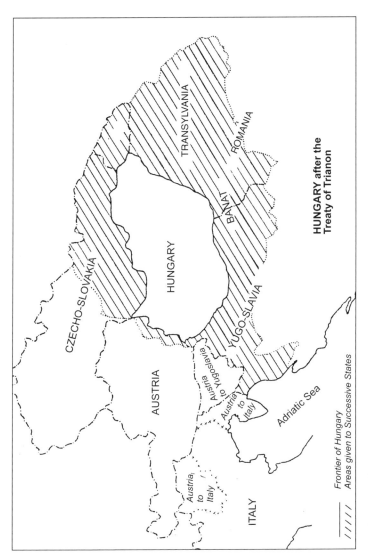

3   Hungary after the Treaty of Trianon

from other national groups was encouraged to ally itself with the Hungarian gentry, but all demands for a federal structure in the Kingdom were resisted.[2]

The Hungarians generally agreed that the Dual Monarchy placed them in an advantageous position. The 1867 settlement had allowed the Hungarians to establish a political system which was corrupt and subservient to one key objective, namely upholding the Hungarian domination in the kingdom. Revolutionary, democratic and liberal ideas were anathema, either because they were too strongly associated with the disasters of 1849, or because implicitly they suggested that the aspirations of other nationalities were of equal weight to those of the Hungarians.

When the First World War broke out Hungary was already experiencing internal strains caused primarily by pressure from its national minorities, and social tensions caused by conflict in the rural sector. No military activities took place on Hungarian territories, and the population was generally badly informed about the course of the war. Thus the defeat of the Dual Monarchy was greeted with surprise. The Allied Powers signed an armistice with Austria–Hungary in Padua on 3 November 1918. On 4 June 1920 the Treaty of Trianon defined conditions for the future peace. During the 18 months separating the two agreements Hungary experienced two revolutions, a foreign invasion and a counter-revolution. Furthermore, her size was reduced by two-thirds. Hungary's population was reduced from 18 to 7.6 million.

The break up of the Dual Monarchy had not been one of the war aims of the Allied Powers. In fact during the course of the war efforts were made to detach Austria–Hungary from Germany, only in order to weaken the Central Powers. To the Allied Powers the nationality issue was only important in so far as it destabilised the enemy and was a means of forcing Austria–Hungary to the negotiating table. When the Allied Powers did make commitments to national groups these were usually undertaken in order to tempt a neutral state to become involved in the war. The contradictory nature of these promises did not seem to be an issue at the time when they were given, as their purpose was primarily military. In August 1916 the Treaty of Bucharest, signed by France, Britain, Italy and Romania, brought Romania into the war. In return the Allied Powers accepted the Romanian demand for territories in the Hungarian Kingdom. Secret assurances were made that Romania could claim Bukovina, Transylvania, the eastern part of the Great Hungarian Plain and Bánát.[3] At the same time during secret negotiations and in major statements concerning their war objectives, the Allied Powers avoided calling for the end of the Austro–Hungarian Empire. The collapse of the Russian Empire and the US entry into the war forced the debate into the open. But it was the small states of the Balkan region and the national groups who were first to see the advantage of demanding that the rights of national groups to self-determination should be on the agenda of the increasingly open debate on war aims. As it turned out, military progress most obviously determined the course of developments. By 1918 the internal disintegration of the empire and the Allies' realisation that Austria would not withdraw from war caused a change in the nature of the debate. The end of the Dual Monarchy became a foregone conclusion.[4]

During the war Hungarians generally supported continuing co-operation with Germany. Even the opposition parties advocated this policy. One of the leaders of the opposition Independence Party came to disagree publicly and tried to steer Hungary in the direction of co-operation with the Allies. Mihály Károlyi had supported liberal ideas before the war. At the beginning of 1918 he was associated with the battle for parliamentary reform and genuinely representative governments. His natural allies were the Radical and Social Democratic Parties. Károlyi realised that it was impossible to defend the status quo in the face of the vocal Polish, Slovak, Czech, Serb and Croat calls for self-determination. Unfortunately for Hungary, the establishment of Polish and Czecho–Slovak provisional administrations acted as a warning that self-appointed leaders of each nation that was now emerging would aim to grab not merely its own territories but hope to establish control over other areas too. Serbs, Croats and Romanians were also preparing to assert themselves.[5] By October 1918 Károlyi seems to have realised that the appointment of a new Hungarian government might forestall some of the harsher conditions which the Allies might impose on the defeated country. He also feared the outbreak of a Soviet-style revolution.

On 25 October Károlyi became the president of the spontaneously formed Hungarian National Council. Within days it assumed the authority of a government. Its political programme included the introduction of democratic institutions and, most importantly, land reform. When addressing nationality issues it only partly dealt with what was swiftly becoming an uncontrollable tide for separation from Hungary. Whereas the Károlyi Government was willing to recognise the right of Poles, Czechs, and South Slavs to independence, it was reluctant to accept that the Croats and Slovaks should have the right to separate from Hungary.[6]

Nevertheless the biggest blow to Hungarian attempts to reform their own political and social system came from the Allied Powers, most notably from France. Austrian representatives signed armistice terms with the victorious powers on behalf of the Dual Monarchy. Károlyi's representations were rejected. But the armistice terms left many issues unresolved. In the month following the signing of the armistice specific demands made by Hungary's neighbours became mixed up with French military plans for the continuation of the war against Germany and for intervention in Russia. Serbs demanded that Austria–Hungary evacuate all Serb and Croat territories. Romanians wanted Transylvania while the Czechs expected that Slovakia would secede and join in forming a Czecho–Slovak state. France in the meantime sought to resume fighting against Germany and demanded the right to move troops across the Dual Monarchy's territories. French military leaders pressed the last point because they hoped to open a Southern Front against the Bolsheviks. The emergence of a government in Budapest complicated the picture by imposing a need for diplomacy and consultation.[7]

The Hungarian issue was one of many discussed at the Paris Conference. Unfortunately for Károlyi the period from the signing of the armistice onwards was one during which he faced continuing territorial demands from Hungary's neighbours. His own political supporters demanded that he not yield, though Hungary had no means of preventing neighbouring countries from grabbing Hungarian lands. Romania in particular was determined to gain control of Transylvania, while Beneš fought hard for Slovakia. France was not prepared to weaken her future influence in that region by opposing Romanian, Yugoslav and Czech demands on Hungary and therefore turned a blind eye to their determination to grab Hungarian lands. Faced with escalating territorial demands Károlyi resigned on 20 March 1919. His government

was succeeded by a radical left coalition led by the Communist
Béla Kun. The replacement of the Hungarian Republic with a
Hungarian Soviet Republic was a gift to Hungary's neighbours.
The spectre of a Soviet-style regime establishing itself in Central
Europe appeared to be the realisation of the worst French appre-
hensions. In the atmosphere of anxiety about the spread of the Bol-
shevik regime in Russia, events in Budapest offered Hungary's
neighbours a convenient pretext for taking direct military action.[8]

When the news about the revolution in Budapest reached Paris,
the Big Four generally accepted that Hungary had been treated
shabbily. The desire to keep Hungary out of the Soviet camp dictated moderation. Unfortunately negotiations which had been
tentatively opened between the Béla Kun regime and the Big
Four were overtaken by developments on Hungary's border.
Encouraged by Franchet d'Esperey, the Allied commander in the
east, Romania and the Czech Republic attacked Hungary. The
international reaction to this aggression was sufficiently ambivalent to encourage both states to believe that they could get away
with their territorial expansion and that France would not try to
reverse any redrawing of maps at which they might succeed. While
President Wilson condemned aggression and called for an end to
hostilities, Italian and French military assistance ensured further
Romanian and Czech advances into Hungarian territory. Romania understood that her troops could proceed as far as the river
Tisza, while Czechoslovakia aimed to occupy Ruthenia.[9] When
it appeared at the beginning of May that the intervention troops
would reach Budapest the French government decided not to
encourage the Romanian government any further. The reason
for this sudden moderation was the French realisation that exces-
sively punitive treatment of the Hungarians could have led to a
prolonged conflict which the French would have to police with
their own troops.[10] Another explanation for West European reluctance to encourage Romania was the fear that the revolutionary
government in Russia could be drawn into the conflict.
It has been suggested that a Soviet warning was issued to Romania
that the Red Army would take action against Bessarabia.[11]

The Hungarian revolutionaries believed that foreign intervention and international approval for Romanian and Czech actions
was politically motivated. In reality, as far as France was concerned the matter was a strategic issue. France wanted a viable

settlement which would offer France a base for any future action she might wish to take against Russia. Simmering conflicts in Eastern Europe would distract and weaken any French pressure on Russia. Nevertheless French motives were confused by assistance given by various sides to two Hungarian counter-revolutionary groupings which emerged outside Hungarian territory. One, led by Károlyi, called for a return to parliamentary democracy. The other to whom the Romanians chose to give their support were assorted pre-war politicians and noblemen whose abhorrence of the left was possibly their only unifying factor. Any hesitation about the wisdom of intervening in Hungary was dissipated in June when the Paris Peace Conference decisions were accepted by the German government. This freed the French to concentrate on settling the conflicts of their Eastern European protégés. By 3 August Romanian troops reached Budapest. In November the Big Four finally agreed to back Admiral Horthy who headed the anti-Communist *émigré* groups.

In November Hungary was invited to attend peace talks. The impetus towards completing all territorial settlements was provided by the fact that all three neighbouring states took advantage of Hungary's defeat to continue 'rectifying' their borders. The state of flux needed to be ended by the signing of an agreed and binding final settlement. On 4 June 1920 the Treaty of Trianon was intended to settle all matters relating to Hungary. It has been stated that the Treaty

> formed, once signed, a fixed point to which every subsequent act of Hungarian international policy was directly related, in attempts or preparations for attempts to secure revision of it, or merely, in debate whether it might not be wise to modify or abandon the claim for revision on certain points in the light of new considerations most of which also arose out of the Versailles Peace System.[12]

In understanding the deep sense of grievance which the Trianon Treaty restrictions created in Hungary, it is important to bear in mind that the treaty was not merely intended to end the war. It was also meant to prevent the rise of Hungarian revanchism. Thus Budapest's freedom to conduct foreign and defence policies was severely restricted. Hungary was made to abolish universal conscription. The army was to number no more than 35 000 men and their functions were to be restricted to internal security and border control. The manufacture and purchase of military equipment was forbidden. Hungary was not allowed to unite with Austria.[13] Reparations were to be paid to the Allied and Associated Powers. In due course Hungary would be admitted to the League of Nations.

The punitive nature of the Trianon Treaty and the potential it created for revisionism led the neighbouring states to presume, rightly of course, that Hungary would do everything in its power to challenge all conditions imposed by force. The response of the neighbouring states to Hungarian attempts to review the punitive provisions of the Trianon Treaty was swift and usually exaggerated. Every attempt to lift restrictions relating to the army caused immediate corrective action by the Little Entente. In 1927 the Hungarian government re-introduced conscription and that in turn caused the Little Entente to increase its conscription thresholds. In 1929 the Little Entente Powers made plans for joint military action against Hungary. This was in response to a Hungarian attempt to limit military inspections sanctions imposed at the end of the First World War. It has been estimated that by the beginning of the 1930s the Little Entente countries 'were 20 times stronger than Hungary, which made it possible for them to launch an immediate attack and to occupy the country unhindered, if Hungarian policy or the Hungarian army decided to make a threatening move towards them'.[14] By 1934 the Hungarian General Staff had concluded that the growth of Germany and Hitler's determination to challenge the post-Versailles order gave Hungary its own opportunity to challenge the armaments restrictions.[15] Aware of the Western Powers' muted response to German actions, they rightly presumed that they would not take retaliatory action against Hungary.

The events of 1918–19 not only estranged Hungary from her neighbours and alienated her from the European Powers. They also created deep and painful divisions within Hungarian society, exacerbating the social divisions which had already manifested themselves before the war. In future years the Béla Kun Republic and the White backlash which followed its collapse were used to justify the subsequent regime's anti-democratic legislation. This and the punitive and corrupt practices of the Horthy Regime precluded any national reconciliation.

The Béla Kun regime only lasted 133 days, to be precise from 21 March to 1 August 1919. Kun had been captured by the Russians during the war and during his spell in a prisoner-of-war camp came into contact with other Communists. He witnessed the Bolshevik Revolution. When he returned to Hungary it was with a mission to replicate the Bolshevik success in Hungary. Initially the Communists, together with the Social Democratic Party, supported Károlyi. In March Kun and other Communist leaders and the radical sections of the Social Democratic Party were arrested on suspicion of inciting strikes. When Károlyi resigned the imprisoned leaders found themselves the focal point of political attention. The Communists and the Social Democrats, by agreeing on a joint programme, formed the next government. At the time of the establishment of the Soviet Republic the Social Democrat–Communist alliance was the only one prepared to tackle long- and short-term social grievances voiced in the cities and in the countryside, where workers and returning soldiers demanded change.

The Béla Kun regime had to grapple with three main problems. One was that of its own identity and programme. Not unlike the Bolsheviks, the leaders of the Hungarian Soviet Republic were unsure as to whether to allow the revolution to take its own course or head a more controlled revolution. The workers' and soldiers' councils which sprang up everywhere did not always readily submit themselves to the authority of either of the parties. The second issue faced by the government was that of food production and distribution. In the countryside peasants called for the end of the feudal system and the redistribution of land. Lacking experience and unsure of its future course, the Béla Kun Government nationalised key industries but opposed the distribution of land to landless and poor peasants. Instead it was hoped that land could be held jointly in the form of co-operatives. Finally foreign intervention confronted the revolutionary government with an insoluble problem. Béla Kun favoured negotiations with the Entente Powers. Unfortunately Hungary's neighbours were less accommodating, seeing in the turmoil into which the country was slipping an opportunity to grab disputed land. The indecision of the Big Four at the Paris Conference seemed to indicate a certain ideological prejudice.[16]

When the Soviet Republic fell, power passed into the hands of a deeply hostile landed aristocracy and professional and middle classes who had been the target of 'Red Terror'. The peasants too remained deeply ambivalent about the Béla Kun period, which clearly failed to address their key grievances. Insensitive policies towards the peasants, combined with food requisitioning during the intervention, turned the villages against the towns. After the fall of the Soviet Republic, during the period of the so-called 'White Terror', those who had been involved with the Béla Kun Government were murdered and thousands of workers and peasants were arrested, tortured and executed. The reactionaries intended to set the clock back to 1914. The willingness of the Western Powers to turn a blind eye to their activities made it possible for the Horthy regime to ignore their own earlier assurances about the establishment of democratic institutions. The first legislative measures introduced in the summer of 1920 testified to that backward-looking programme. Although unity with Austria was abolished the question of the role of the Crown was left open, giving rise to hopes for a Habsburg restoration. While Hungary did not have a king, it continued to be a monarchy and Admiral Horthy, who was elected Head of State, assumed the title of Regent. The new government then pronounced all legislation which had been introduced during the Károlyi and Kun period invalid.

The new regime thus inherited all the social and economic problems of the pre-war period. Added to these were the specific economic difficulties caused by the Trianon Treaty. The pattern of landholding in Hungarian areas had been predominantly that of large estates. In non-Hungarian areas small farms coexisted with large ones. Trianon, by reducing the country's borders to ethnic Hungarian regions, increased the proportion of land under large estates. Most of the industry had also been concentrated in the Hungarian areas. While the retention of these by the post-Trianon state might have been economically advantageous, the state also inherited unresolved industrial conflicts while adding to the stock of grievances the frustrations and anger which came in the wake of the brief republican experience.[17] The ruling circles had, though, no intention of attempting to resolve these deep conflicts and merely looked forward to turning the clock back to a time when they had been able to rule corruptly and without challenge, either from Vienna or from any organised opposition within Hungary.

The Communist Party was the main object of repression after the fall of the Soviet Republic. As a result of the continuing activities of various 'patriotic leagues' and officers' detachments which the government tolerated, the Communist Party was destroyed. Its centre of gravity first moved to Vienna and then to Moscow. Béla Kun, after a brief period in the wilderness caused by the Comintern's censure, assumed the leadership of the exiled Hungarian Party. In Moscow the exiles succumbed to ideological infighting. Attempts to resume activities in Hungary were unsuccessful, partly due to the Horthy regime's repressive measures, but also because of differences which developed in the 1930s between the exile leadership, which reluctantly accepted the Popular Front policy, and underground Communist cadres in Hungary who rejected such compromises. The Hungarian Party was probably dissolved by the Comintern in 1936. In 1940 there was no party organisation in Hungary.[18]

The Communist Party's allies during the Béla Kun period, the Social Democrats, continued to be tolerated by the Horthy regime though their activities were so severely restricted as to render the party politically impotent. In 1921, in return for the right to association and having obtained assurances that confiscated party and trade union property would be returned to them, the Social Democrats committed themselves not to undermine the government. Furthermore the party undertook not to organise strikes and not to agitate among agricultural workers.

Although Hungary was, at least in name, a democracy throughout the inter-war period, it is important to distinguish between the exercise of democratic rights and the use of democratic symbols to maintain a group's grip on power. The latter was the case in Hungary. Elections took place regularly and candidates were free to put themselves forward for election. But elections were not secret and even independent candidates to the assembly knew they needed to secure the support of the influential local groups, usually the landowners. Networks of patronage regulated the results of elections and decision-making in the assembly. Party leaders whose authority was traditionally unquestioned determined who was nominated for elections. Elections, though conducted correctly, merely confirmed decisions made before polling.

After the 1920 general elections the Smallholders' Party became the largest single party in the assembly. Although this seemed like progress from the backward-looking political elites of the pre-war mould, in reality this majority was of little relevance. The electorate of the Smallholders' Party had, in spite of its name, tenuous roots in agrarian communities. It represented the anti-Habsburg and modernising sections of the community without actually having a clearly defined programme. The Smallholders' main rivals were the Christian Nationalists – as the name suggests, a conservative party. In 1921 Horthy entrusted the formation of the new government to Count Isván Bethlen, a Christian Nationalist. As has been aptly stated, until 1931,

> The country was ruled again on a very slightly modified rendition of its old system, in the interests of that system's old beneficiaries, from whom only the inescapable minimum of social and economic sacrifices had been exacted in the process.[19]

Bethlen's commitment to the old order manifested itself in the limitations of his social and economic programme. His basic creed was that the war, revolutions and peace treaties were responsible for economic difficulties and the ensuing social unrest. His priority was the restoration of the old order as a means of pacifying all political dissent. Until 1945 Admiral Horthy continued as Regent of Hungary. He believed absolutely in the right of the traditional ruling-class elites to govern Hungary. They combined to form a Government Party which changed little during the course of the inter-war period.[20]

In 1930 the economic crash hit Hungarian industry and agriculture. This destroyed a precariously achieved economic stability which had been largely fuelled by foreign credits. In 1932 Gyula Gömbos was appointed Minister President. He had already distinguished himself in racist and patriotic organisations which had proliferated before the Depression and which had been given an added impetus by difficulties experienced by state employees and the army. The civil service and the army had always been a haven for impoverished noblemen, providing sinecure posts for sons of the aristocracy. Restrictions of state expenditure limited employment opportunities for these social groups. Trade, commerce and industry were regarded as demeaning activities for graduates and those of noble origins. The economic difficulties caused these groups to move towards anti-Semitic and Nationalist groups which acted as custodians of national traditions. The Hungarian patriotic organisations modelled themselves on the Nazi example rather than the Italian one. The very proliferation of various groups and lack of a clear programme prevented them from establishing a dictatorship. Of these the Scythe Cross and the Arrow Cross were best organised and attracted the largest following.[21] Gömbos' aim was to establish a Fascist state in Hungary. With that in mind he in the first place tried to sideline the more patrician old elite and replace them with new men, conservative in outlook, and more directly dependent on him. His manoeuvres were blocked by the very complex balances which had until then prevented any radical changes in Hungary. Though anti-Semitic riots increased in frequency from the mid-1930s, the truth was that the Hungarian economy was largely dependent on the Jewish community and on foreign Jewish capital. To force the Hungarian Jews to leave Hungary, which is what Gömbos advocated, would have meant certain national bankruptcy. While anti-Semitic slogans and legislation limiting the rights of Jews won some popularity, consistent enforcement of these restrictions was neither possible nor desirable. In spite of complex wheeling and dealing with the Smallholders' Party, Gömbos could not secure total freedom of action. In 1936 Horthy made up his mind to get rid of him. The conflict had deep roots. The breaking point might have come when Gömbos tried to build up a power base in the army, which enjoyed an exceptional degree of independence. Horthy was also unhappy about the Minister President's support for land reform, an important point in the programme of the radical Arrow Cross and Scythe Cross movements. The conflict was resolved by Gömbos' death, from natural causes, in October 1936. Horthy was apparently invited to head a coup by the Arrow Cross, which he refused to do. Lacking a leader the Arrow Cross did not take action. The opportunity for the establishment of a Fascist regime in Hungary was lost and instead the political situation continued as before, with Horthy acting as custodian of the political balance of power between the Conservatives, the Fascists and the Smallholders' Party.

Frustrated nationalism and demands for the restoration of Greater Hungary were widely-held sentiments which the inter-war governments used to full advantage. Anger at the way Hungary had been treated after the signing of the armistice talks and the punitive nature of the Trianon Treaty made it possible to rally the Hungarian people behind a nationalist and anti-revolutionary programme. For Hungarians it was only too easy to point to the fact that their state had been forced to hand over to its neighbours not only areas inhabited by national minorities but that they had also lost wholly Hungarian-inhabited territories. The government's uncompromising commitment to the restoration of lost territories served to consolidate its position in the country. In no other European country, not even Germany, did foreign policy objectives so strongly serve the purpose of rallying the population behind the government's internal policy. The desire to divide Britain, France and Italy and to weaken Hungary's neighbours became the common purpose of all diplomatic endeavours, while the restoration of pre-war borders was the only long-term objective. These factors account for the apparent willingness of the Hungarian government to use occasional accommodations with neighbouring states in any consistent way.

Although France was regarded as the main architect of the Trianon Treaty, forming an anti-French bloc with Germany was not at first an obvious solution to Hungary's problems. The Hungarian governmental circles viewed the post-war territorial changes as temporary and believed these would be reversed in the nearest future. Their responses were therefore essentially short-sighted and impulsive. In the immediate aftermath of Trianon this attitude was perhaps justified. France still hoped to retain Hungarian goodwill, primarily because of the continuing policy of intervention in the Russian Civil War. The French government hoped to relieve the anti-Bolshevik Southern Front in the Ukraine and the Caucasus from Hungary. During the Polish–Russian war, Hungary saw an opportunity to gain international prestige by pledging support to Poland and allowing troops and supplies to be moved from Hungary to Poland. With the end of the Russian Civil War and the negotiated conclusion of the Polish–Soviet conflict French interest in Hungary waned.[22]

The biggest obstacle to Hungary's breaking out of international isolation was the Little Entente. On 14 August 1920 the signing of the alliance between Czechoslovakia and the Kingdom of Serbs, Croats and Slovenes, soon to be renamed Yugoslavia, laid the foundations of the Little Entente. It was aimed against unprovoked Hungarian attack. Over the next few months, Yugoslavia and Italy resolved their most important territorial conflicts. This robbed Hungary of a potential ally. Italy and Hungary shared an anxiety about Austria, with which both had territorial disputes.

The *cordon sanitaire* around Hungary was completed in March 1921 when Charles IV, the ex-Emperor of Austria and also King of Hungary, tried to press his claim to the throne in Budapest. Horthy had no interest in supporting him while the general attitude in Hungary towards a Habsburg restoration was ambivalent. Nevertheless Hungary's neighbours strongly protested and the coup was thwarted. In October another attempt was made to restore the Habsburgs to the Hungarian throne. Both events consolidated the neighbouring states' policies towards Hungary. On 23 April 1921 the Romanian–Czechoslovak Treaty was signed, providing for joint action in the event of Hungarian aggression. In June 1921 Yugoslavia was drawn closer into the anti-Hungarian regional agreements by an alliance with Romania which offered security against Bulgarian aggression.[23] Although the issue of Habsburg restoration would no longer be a real threat, it continued as an issue which tended to consolidate anti-Hungarian feelings in the region.

In the generally unsuccessful attempt to break out of isolation, Hungary derived a lot of comfort from her relations with Poland. Both countries had a sentimental regard for each other dating back to the fifteenth century when a Hungarian princess became the Queen of Poland. These ties had been strengthened at the time of the 1848–9 revolutions, when Polish revolutionaries fought in Hungary. In the immediate post-war period a more pragmatic desire to keep Czechoslovakia weak was added to traditional sentiments. Poland disapproved of the Little Entente, which was viewed in Warsaw as a French creation, and of Czechoslovakia's key role in it. Poland was still smarting after the loss of the Teschen region to Czechoslovakia during the war with the Soviet Union, while Hungary sought to reduce the effectiveness of the Little Entente as an anti-Hungarian alliance. While relations between the two did not lead to the signing of any joint treaty, Poland's unwillingness to approve policies which would have isolated Hungary was a source of hope. In August 1922 Poland championed Hungary's successful admission to the League of Nations.

During the inter-war period Hungary and Austria had surprisingly little in common. In Hungary there was little support for the return to the Dual Monarchy. Even those who supported it wanted union renegotiated to offer Hungary greater equality. Nevertheless, even with her ex-partner Hungary had a territorial dispute. As a result of the Treaty of Saint-Germain of September 1919, Hungary was expected to evacuate the district of Burgenland which had been awarded to Austria. The Hungarians tried to avoid this and, after prolonged negotiations and threats by the Allied, they eventually agreed to a plebiscite. As a result, Burgenland was again awarded to Austria. The possibility of an Anschluss between Austria and Germany was universally opposed by all Hungarians. They feared that a strong German bloc would further undermine Hungary's position in the region.

The country which was destined to play a major role in Hungary's foreign policy during the inter-war period was Italy. Until Mussolini captured power in October 1922, relations between the two were confined to sentimental references to common past experiences. Mussolini reversed this by launching a policy of direct involvement in Balkan affairs. In April 1927 the Hungarian Prime Minister Belthen and Mussolini signed a Treaty of Friendship and Co-operation. Both countries sought to destabilise Yugoslavia by supporting Croat nationalism. They were also committed to preventing Austria's Anschluss with Germany. Mussolini was willing to back up Italy's foreign policy with financial aid and credits to countries that co-operated. Thanks to this policy Hungary obtained credits from Italy and a market in Italy for wheat at a higher price than the world market one. As a result of complex deals involving Poland and Austria, Hungary was able to purchase Italian military supplies which should have been denied to her as part of the Trianon Treaty.

Nevertheless relations between Hungary and Italy did not become really close until Gömbos became Prime Minister. Until then Italy was only too willing to take Hungary's pro-Italian orientation for granted. In any case Britain and France continued to be more important to Italy. Hungarian government circles were strongly pro-French and pro-British.[24] The decision to orientate Hungary's foreign policy in the direction of Italy was only made in 1932. Internal policy considerations were probably decisive. The Social Democratic and the Liberal Parties supported a pro-French policy because they felt that France would help them bring about greater democracy in Hungary. Gömbos calculated that Mussolini would be interested in destroying French power in the Danube region and would support anti-democratic movements. His calculations proved right and Gömbos continued to emulate Italian Fascist trends. After his visit to Rome in April 1933 Italy increased economic and political assistance to Hungary, consolidating Rome's influence there.[25] The economic Depression of the early 1930s left Hungary with few options. Hungary and Italy were united by their shared desire to maintain an independent Austria. In January and February 1934 Italy, Austria and Hungary held meetings to keep Austria out of the German sphere of influence. The result was the signing of the Rome Protocol on 17 March 1934 which confirmed Hungarian and Italian commitments to maintaining the independence of Austria. But Italy and Hungary could not prevent an Anschluss without incurring German hostility, in particular because of Hungary's growing economic dependence on Germany and the limited commitment of the French and British to Austria.[26]

Whereas Gömbos had initially been pro-Italian, after Hitler came to power he deferred to Germany's growing strength and the importance of the Nazi movement. On 16 June 1933 Gömbos made a secret trip to meet Hitler in Berlin. In the course of this brief visit, Gömbos was left in no doubt that to Germany the Anschluss with Austria was a priority. The destruction of Czechoslovakia had also been decided upon. Hitler assured his visitor that Slovakia and Ruthenia could be taken by Hungary. In return, Hungary was to respect its borders with Yugoslavia and Romania.[27]

In October 1934 Gömbos visited Poland, which had recently signed a Declaration of Non-Aggression with Germany. In a letter to Piłsudski, Horthy let it be known that he believed that improvements in Polish–German relations created a possibility for Poland and Hungary to co-operate in destabilising Czechoslovakia. Furthermore Horthy expressed the hope that this would in turn lead to the creation of a joint border in Ruthenia. These ideas went beyond the hope that simple territorial rectifications could be imposed on Czechoslovakia. Horthy believed that were the two countries to support Germany in an anti-Soviet war they could reverse the post-war divisions and benefit territorially in the east.[28] Poland's aims in signing the pact with Germany had not extended as far as that. Piłsudski refused to be drawn into signing any agreements with Hungary, although he assured Gömbos that Poland would never take action against Hungary. In the meantime the Polish government stressed the need for Hungary

to reestablish good relations with her neighbours, primarily
Romania. Polish hegemonic plans for the region depended on
regional co-operation. If Hungary and Romania could be persuaded to set aside their differences this would create a climate
for progress towards a Polish-dominated 'Third Europe' in Central Europe.

Even though Poland was unwilling to become involved in planning for war against the Soviet Union, from a Hungarian point of
view the improvement in Polish–German relations was a positive
move. During the following months Hungary slipped irrevocably
into the German camp. The reasons were almost entirely economic. After coming to power, Hitler's economic policy towards
Central Europe and the Balkans was to depend increasingly on
systems of blocked accounts. As a result of a new trade agreement
in 1934 Hungary could only use its Reichsmark surpluses to buy
industrial goods in Germany. In exchange Germany spent its
Hungarian currency surpluses on Hungarian goods, mainly agricultural produce which Hungary could not sell in a European
market already saturated with cheap foodstuffs. It was inevitable
that political dependence followed in the wake of Hungary being
tied into the German economic bloc. In 1934, of the few mineral
resources which could be sold to Germany, Hungary and Yugoslavia supplied half of Germany's bauxite imports. But Hungary
was keen to sell cereal to Germany. By 1936 the situation was
slightly reversed in so far as Germany was short of foodstuffs and
was therefore more willing to sell arms in exchange for food. But
Hungary had by then come to the conclusion that it would gain
more by selling wheat on the world markets. An attempt was
therefore made to reduce the agreed sales quotas to Germany.
In June 1937 Hungary agreed to sell less than 10 per cent of
its annual surplus of corn and wheat in exchange for chrome
and manganese.[29]

Trade with the West European democracies was hampered by
the apparent lack of political guidelines. In the mid-1930s the British government devised clearing agreements whereby the Hungarian government agreed to retain a portion of sterling earnings
from exports to Britain. These could then be used to settle outstanding debts. It had already been noted in London that sterling
accounts tended to be spent in markets other than Britain.[30]
In 1936 the British government initiated a review of its trade with

east and south-eastern Europe. The Foreign Office had voiced anxiety about increased German trade with the region, which was leading to political dependence. In spite of the general agreement that this was an undesirable development, the government refused to change its fiscal policy to allow credits to the Balkans and Central European states for political reasons. The French were quicker to note the political implications of Germany's trade agreements with Hungary and Yugoslavia. Nevertheless France's commitment to the Little Entente meant that Yugoslavia and Romania were the real objects of France's economic assistance.

The Abyssinian conflict and the League of Nations' condemnation of Italy marked the point after which Italy moved more closely towards Germany. Italy's preoccupation with Africa reduced her interest in Central European affairs. As Italy became more dependent on Germany so her willingness to pursue policies which would bring Italy into conflict with Germany rapidly evaporated. The Spanish Civil War confirmed Italy's reliance on German supplies of vital resources, most obviously oil. Hungary gauged correctly that Italy's interest in upholding Austrian independence was fast vanishing. Previously the Hungarian government had hoped that a partnership could be developed with Italy and Germany. After 1936 Hungary found herself in the uncomfortable role of a state with no bargaining power in relation to Germany, and Italy was clearly reducing her previous policy of direct involvement in the Balkan and Danubian region.

Briefly in 1937 Hungary took an interest in the Little Entente states' attempts to improve relations in the region. Unfortunately none of the concessions suggested satisfied Hungary's demands. The Little Entente states were prepared to accept Hungary's right to rearm. Rightly calculating that the Little Entente was losing its cohesion, and posing less of a threat, Hungary showed only passing interest in these conciliatory gestures. At the end of 1937 the increasingly aggressive German foreign policy made clear to the Hungarian politicians that they should take heed of what was happening in Berlin. Budapest was only too keen to reassure Germany that Hungary would not oppose German actions abroad. During a visit to Berlin in November 1937 the Hungarian Prime Minister Kálmán Dáranyi and his Foreign Minister Kálmán de Kánya assured the Nazis that they would not oppose the Anschluss. When Hitler once more reaffirmed that he would take action against Czechoslovakia, the Hungarian politicians agreed to coordinate their campaign with Germany's attack on Czechoslovakia. Thus, even prior to the Anschluss, Germany was assured of Hungarian co-operation. In return Hitler undertook to mediate between Yugoslavia and Hungary. The Romanian issue remained the only one on which agreement was not reached. The Nazis wanted Hungary to set aside her territorial claims to Romania, something the Hungarians were not prepared to do.[31]

In 1938 Hitler's determination to destroy the Czechoslovak state brought to the fore the question of relations with Poland. The Hungarians wanted to secure Polish co-operation, even though the Poles were not willing to support them against Romania. This effectively set the limits of Polish–Hungarian friendship. The Poles continued in their unsuccessful attempts to mediate between Romania and Hungary. Hostility toward Czechoslovakia emerged as the only possible platform for joint action. But even here there was a potential for major differences. In February 1938, during his visit to Warsaw, Horthy made it clear that Hungary wanted Ruthenia and Slovakia. The Poles refused to be drawn on details of their plans for the break-up of Czechoslovakia because they had their own plans for Slovakia. Josef Beck, the Polish Minister for Foreign Affairs, was still not sure how he would proceed. He spoke of exploiting pro-Polish sentiments in Slovakia and he alluded to Slovakia being a Polish sphere of influence. Horthy wanted the outright incorporation of Slovakia into Hungarian territory.[32]

After the Anschluss, both Hungary and Poland were kept informed of Germany's plans and sought to coordinate their responses accordingly. Once more, while agreeing that Czechoslovakia should be partitioned, the two countries disagreed on how this should be done. Whereas Beck made belligerent noises, assuring his advisers that Poland would be prepared to take military action in pursuit of its claim to the Teschen region, Hungary hesitated, acutely aware of the Little Entente on its south-eastern borders. Bewilderingly only a few weeks before the Munich Conference Hungary ratified an arms limitations agreement with Yugoslavia, Romania and Czechoslovakia.[33] At the time it emerged that the only issue on which Hungary agreed with Poland was the creation of a joint border with Poland through the incorporation of Ruthenia into Hungary. Poland continued in her refusal to support Hungary's claim to Slovakia. The evolution of the Czechoslovak crisis gave the Hungarians no opportunity to take the initiative. Initially Budapest was anxious not to be seen overtly supporting the German claims, lest they incur the anger of the Little Entente and of Britain and France. Chamberlain's negotiations with Hitler which assurred Germany of the imminent satisfaction of her demands, made the Hungarian, appear over-cautious. On the eve of the Munich Conference the Hungarian Prime Minister, Béla Imredy, rushed to Berlin to obtain a German promise that the principle of self-determination would be applied not only to the Sudeten Germans but also to the Hungarian minority in Czechoslovakia. Hitler wanted the Hungarians to take military action against Czechoslovakia at the time of his talks with Chamberlain, but Imredy was still not prepared to participate in putting pressure on the British Prime Minister. Instead a war of notes was instigated with Prague. Rome was approached to secure its support. Mussolini assured the Hungarians that he would make sure that the Hungarian issue was treated on a par with the Sudeten one.

The Munich Conference results were a disappointment. Germany was granted the Sudeten region, whereas the Polish and Hungarian demands were left to future arbitration. But the very fact that the post-war order was being revised boded well for Hungary.[34] Disappointment, however, set in soon after. In the first place Hitler developed his own plans for Slovakia and Ruthenia. The Werhmacht was opposed to allowing the control of these key regions to slip out of German hands. Hitler discouraged talks on the future of Czechoslovak territories and instead nudged the Hungarians in the direction of the Czechs, advising them only to resolve claims concerning the Hungarian-inhabited regions. Mussolini, who had earlier been effusive in his support of the Hungarian claims, seemed to have lost interest during and after the Munich Conference. In fact the full implications of Hitler's victory caused the Italians a certain degree of discomfort. Thus Mussolini agreed to support the Hungarians but only by putting to Hitler a request for four-power arbitration.

On 27 October 1938, at a meeting in Vienna, Hungary, Czechoslovakia, Germany and Italy discussed the territories to which Hungary laid claim. In reality the German and Italian

governments made the decisions. As a result of the Vienna Award
Hungary regained the regions of Kassa, Ungvár and Munkács
with 1 100 000 Hungarian nationals.[35] To the Hungarians this
represented only a partial victory. They were determined to
obtain Ruthenia. Their aims were two-fold. The region was
inhabited by diverse ethnic groups, Poles, Slovaks, Hungarians,
Ukrainians and Jews. The Hungarian government wanted to
bring them together to form a united front and complete the
destruction, first of the new renamed Czecho-Slovak Republic,
and ultimately the Trianon agreement. The other aim was to
establish direct control over a region which contained a number of strategically important railway links and a transit route
from Central to Eastern Europe and from Northern Europe to
the south. It was already known that Germany was training
Ukrainian paramilitary organisations. Hungary and Poland separately financed and armed various irredentist groups in order to
destabilise the region. Joint Polish–Hungarian preparations were
made for an uprising. These were abandoned when Berlin let it be
known that it did not support Hungarian and Polish plans. Hungary was the first to realise that Germany would not tolerate interference in what had by the autumn of 1938 become a German
sphere of influence. The Hungarians abandoned plans for destabilising the region and decided to co-operate with Germany in the
final destruction of Czecho-Slovakia. Poland, furious at Hungary's timidity, withdrew from joint talks. Beck had grandiosely
planned to exclude Germany from the region. In the circumstances Hungarian leaders displayed better judgement.[36] After
the Vienna Award relations with Poland cooled.

Hungary finally reclaimed Ruthenia when German plans concerning Slovakia had become clearer. At the beginning of March
1939 Slovak leaders were invited to Berlin and encouraged to
declare independence from Prague. On 12 March a special envoy
flew from Berlin to Budapest and informed the Hungarians of
impending German plans for the occupation of Bohemia and Moravia. The Hungarians were told they could occupy Ruthenia.
In return the grateful Horthy committed himself to coordinate
Hungary's economy to satisfy Germany's needs, and to protect
German economic and communication interests on Hungarian
soil.[37] On 14 March the Slovak parliament declared independence. On 15 March the Wehrmacht marched into Prague. Once

the Slovak declaration was made public Hungary moved into action, demanding that Czecho–Slovak troops evacuate Ruthenia. The next day the Hungarian Army occupied the areas evacuated by the Czecho–Slovaks.

Having satisfied some of the territorial demands which, throughout the inter-war period, had been repeatedly put forward as being of the greatest importance to Hungarian pride and dignity, Horthy's regime took stock of the newly evolving balance of power in Europe. Not all Hungarian leaders approved of the role assumed by the country on the eve of what was known to be an impending European crisis. Co-operation with Nazi Germany had been a means of initiating the revision of the Trianon Treaty. It is doubtful whether the government had ever intended to tie Hungary to the German war effort. But they were aware that, while they no longer faced any challenge from the Left, either in the form of the Communist Party or organised labour, they now faced a threat from the Right. The Arrow Cross with its radical programme, which spoke of corporate economic policies and land reform, had replaced the routed Left as a threat to the old political order. In the general elections in May 1939 the Arrow Cross came second. The organisation had been receiving financial assistance from Berlin. It was widely suspected that they were armed with German weapons. As a counterweight to the growing dependence on Germany, the government tried once more to cultivate relations with Italy. Briefly in the late spring of 1939 Italy showed signs of disquiet at German interference in the Balkans, an area which the Italians considered to be their sphere of influence. This was a shot in the dark as Italy's involvement in the Spanish Civil War had confirmed her economic dependence on Germany.[38] But Mussolini's disappointment with Hitler was short-lived; Hungary quickly learned she could not depend on support from those quarters.

The full implications of the growth of German influence in the region and its aggressive intentions were faced by Hungary during the emerging Polish–German confrontation after March 1939. The Hungarian government wanted to avoid being drawn into Germany's wars. Nor did she seek involvement in a European war. Her aim had been to settle old grievances. Since by the spring a number of those had either been satisfied or were likely to be dealt with in the near future, Hungary sought a way out of becoming embroiled in Germany's wars. Neutrality seemed to guarantee that Hungary might not have to do any fighting, but would remain friends with both sides. Here the Hungarian military leaders looked back to their experiences in the First World War and considered ways of securing their position. They advised that the collapse of the army, as had happened in 1919, was to be avoided by keeping it intact. At the same time it was agreed that loss of control over internal developments and weakness in the face of rapacious neighbours had been Hungary's undoing. Thus plans were made to keep the army for the decisive battles at the end of the war. Opportunistically, it was hoped that a European war would allow the Hungarians to conduct their own local war against Romania.[39] The army, which had always occupied a role separate from the political leadership, thus devised its own response to the forthcoming war. Horthy was in conflict with the army, which he wanted to subordinate more fully to the government. He tried to curtail its interference in foreign policy. In effect the conflict between the army and the government paralysed policy making. If the rapid pace of international developments cautioned against excessive commitment to either side, the desire to continue the process of regaining territories lost at Trianon remained equally strong. During August, when it became apparent that war between Germany and Poland was inevitable, Poland was assured that in the event of a German attack, Hungary would remain neutral. At the same time preparations were made to recapture Transylvania from Romania, for it was calculated that the defeat of Poland would weaken Romania.[40]

On the eve of the outbreak of the war Mussolini and Hitler wished to bind Hungary more closely to the Axis. Italy in particular was able to put pressure on the Hungarians. The Italian army was helping in secret preparations for war against Romania. However, Hungary wished neither to commit herself to the Axis, nor to defy Germany. When Germany attacked Poland on 1 September the Hungarian government boldly declared that it would not permit the passage of German troops to Poland. As German troops gained control over Polish territory and subsequently when the Soviet Union entered into the conflict by occupying eastern Poland on 18 September, the Polish–Hungarian frontier remained open to allow Polish troops to escape into exile. Germany had tried to tempt the Hungarians to allow them the use of their railway lines by making veiled promises that the Romanian issue could be discussed in the future. They were unsuccessful, although it has been suggested that the reason for Hungarian steadfastness was the conviction that Italy, herself anxious about the implications of the German–Polish conflict on her relations with Britain, would back Hungary. There was also the comforting thought that Germany was unlikely to seek a conflict with a country with which it had good economic relations.[41]

In February 1939 Pál Teleki formed a government. His conviction that Hungary could 'stand aside' from the turmoil which engulfed Europe was as steadfast as was his determination that Hungary should fully exploit all opportunities to continue rectifying old grievances. These two guiding principles led Hungary into a cul-de-sac out of which by 1941 there was no escape.

For the Hungarian government the German attack on Poland was a serious issue, whereas the signing of the Ribbentrop–Molotov Pact was a watershed. Since hostility to the Soviet Union went hand in hand with repression of the Left in Hungary, the new-found relationship between Nazi Germany and Communist Soviet Union caused confusion and disorientation in Budapest. In the meantime Britain and France seemed to be pursuing thoroughly inconsistent policies. In principle Hungary sought to exploit any desire by the Western democracies to contain Germany. But since neither seemed to be either willing or able to take action against Germany, this policy did not yield results. The military leaders and the Arrow Cross demanded that the government make a commitment to Germany. It also looked as if the Transylvanian issue could be satisfactorily resolved with German co-operation. Since the beginning of 1940 the Hungarians had been aware of German plans for the occupation of Romania. Germany was worried that in the event of a conflict with Romania, the Soviet Union might occupy the oil fields, which were vital to Germany's war effort. Plans were put in place for a German pre-emptive entry into Romania.[42] In the circumstances Hungary would be forced to allow the Wehrmacht right of passage to the Romanian border, which would strain Hungary's neutrality. Appeals to Mussolini elicited a clear statement that Italy was bound to Germany. In the circumstances the Hungarian government accepted that when faced with German demands it would have to comply.[43]

The Hungarian desire to benefit fully from the crisis which was engulfing Europe manifested itself most clearly in relation to Transylvania. After the fall of Poland Hungarian leaders disseminated rumours which were meant to convey the impression that Hungary was preparing to take military action against Romania. German anxiety about Soviet plans towards Romania were used as a pretext. But the Hungarian leaders shrewdly concluded that Germany would go to great lengths to stabilise the Balkans, in particular because of German preoccupation with Western Europe and the Soviet Union. When on 26 June 1940 the Soviet Union demanded that Romania return Bessarabia, the Hungarian government exacerbated the crisis by repeating its demands for Transylvania. The problem faced by the Hungarian government was that it could not take military action against Romania. Without either Italian or German assistance Hungary was militarily too weak. In the meantime Romania complied with Berlin's request to cede Bessarabia to the Soviet Union. Henceforth Romania's stock would rise in Berlin. King Carol had committed himself to guaranteeing Germany's oil supplies. In return he expected Berlin to hold back the Hungarians. The Romanian oil deal was of sufficient importance to Hitler to warrant his intervention in the conflict. On 29 August 1940 a conference was convened in Vienna to deal with the issue. With Mussolini's agreement Ribbentrop imposed a settlement on Romania and Hungary. Half of Transylvania was returned to Hungary, the other remained in Romania. By this 'Solomonic' judgement Germany gained Hungarian agreement to use Hungarian railway routes. Romania continued to supply Germany with oil and, not least of all, neither Hungarian nor Romanian grievances were satisfied, thus guaranteeing their continuing dependence on Germany.[44]

The period after the Second Vienna Award was a time of coming to terms with German dominance. Germany moved swiftly to extract from Hungary the price for assistance given during the conflict with Romania. Horthy was not entirely ungrateful, even if the pro-German groups within the army and government still failed to gain the upper hand. Within days of signing the Vienna Award the German minority in Hungary was granted extensive rights. Hungary committed herself to supplying Germany with industrial raw materials and agricultural produce. Legislation limiting the activities of the Arrow Cross was rescinded while its leaders were released from prison. In accordance with German wishes, and not entirely unwillingly, the Hungarian government put in place racist laws primarily aimed at the Jewish community. On 20 November Hungary joined the Tripartite Pact earlier signed by Germany, Italy and Japan. By this move the Hungarian government effectively rejected any further association with the Western powers and accepted German hegemony.[45]

To the rest of the world it looked as if Hungary had irrevocably committed herself to the German side. Horthy and his government chose to believe that this was not the case, that the option of neutrality was still there to be exercised. Within the government discussions were conducted on the desirability or otherwise of building bridges with other states. Inconclusive flirtations with Yugoslavia, with which a Pact of Frendship was signed on 12 December, and trade contact with the Soviet Union signalled a deep anxiety which inevitably overwhelmed the Hungarian politicians when considering the extent of their country's dependence on Germany. In reality these timorous moves could not disguise the fact that Hungary had no choice but to find the best possible position within the German bloc. It was not possible for her to exist outside it.

It has been suggested that in the spring of 1941 Prime Minister Pál Teleki considered the possibility of Germany losing the war. This therefore reinforced the idea of Hungary keeping her military resources for action in the final days of war.[46] Teleki's anxieties were shared by sections of the political elites and the intellectual circles. Professional groups which stood to benefit from Hungary's full commitment to Germany's war effort, namely the military leadership, university students and state employees, opposed the policy of 'wait and see'. Germany's military successes raised hopes of further territorial revision. In 1941 Germany's decision to attack the Soviet Union forced Hungary to make a commitment. Before the campaign was undertaken the Balkans had to be secured. Italian action in Greece drew Germany into that conflict and in March plans were made for the occupation of Yugoslavia. Hungarian participation in the occupation of Yugoslavia was purchased at the price of a promise that Hungarian territorial claims to the country would be recognised by Germany. Hungary's complicity in German aggression against Yugoslavia was two-fold.

In the first place German troops were allowed to cross Hungary, in the second, Hungarian troops entered Yugoslavia and occupied Baćska, the Baranya triangle and Muraköz. As a result of this last campaign Britain broke off relations with Hungary, making it clear that Hungary was viewed as an aggressor and Germany's ally. Teleki, sensing the collapse of his policy of avoiding direct association with Germany, committed suicide on the eve of German and Hungarian entry into Yugoslavia.

Hungary's final act of commitment to the German side came only days after the attack on the Soviet Union. While officially Horthy and the military leaders maintained that they did not wish to commit Hungarian troops to the conflict, they relented when they realised that participation in the conflict would entitle them to a share of the spoils. Apparently jealousy over Slovakia being rewarded with Ruthenia for her assistance in the campaign against the Soviet Union tipped the balance in favour of direct participation in the war. On 27 June the Hungarian Airforce and 40 000 troops were committed to the German war effort against the Soviet Union.

7 The Balkans: Yugoslavia, Albania, Bulgaria

At the turn of the century, the Balkan region was synonymous with instability. For some time it had been the focal point of intense international rivalries. These had been generated by the progressive weakening of the Ottoman Empire, which inevitably led to speculation and conflict as to which country would be able to grab its European territories. In 1878 the Treaty of Berlin, largely an attempt by the European Powers to regulate the Ottoman Empire's loss of control over its European possessions, established three independent states, Romania, Serbia and Montenegro. Nevertheless, the European Powers' consensus since the Crimean War that an Ottoman presence was necessary in South-Eastern Europe could only halt temporarily the disintegration of the Ottoman empire. The Balkans' strategic importance ensured that the region continued to arouse concern and rivalry among the European Powers. At the beginning of the twentieth century the growth of indigenous nationalism came to play an important role in the region. The newly independent states proved difficult to control. Their loyalty to their earlier patrons was fickle. Neither Russia, nor France and Britain, nor Germany and Austria–Hungary were able to control the Balkan countries' desire to challenge the Ottoman Empire. It was inevitable that the Balkan states would pose a threat to the precarious balance of power in the region, with incalculable implications for European relations.

For the West European Powers the region represented at worst, a tinder box, at best a region in a state of flux. In reality there was little concern for the demands and expectations of the people of the region. Though Austria–Hungary and Russia in principle welcomed any opportunity to consolidate their respective hold over the region, each was wary of undermining the balance of power by too blatantly supporting any particular group. When in 1912 the Balkan Wars virtually completed the removal of the Ottoman

4　The Balkan states after the First World War

Empire from European territories, they also signalled the limits of the Big Powers' control over the Balkan people.

Towards the end of the nineteenth century, nationalism, a dynamic expression of a desire to shake off foreign domination and tutelage, had manifested its strength in all European states, though nowhere was its potential for disruption bigger than in the Balkans. The new Balkan states claimed to represent not merely their own citizens but also their co-nationals in the whole region. The best example of national leaders both using and responding to calls for national unity was provided by the Serb Kingdom's aggressive policy of taking up the cause of all South Slavs in the Austro–Hungarian Empire. Unfortunately independence had its economic consequences. Lack of political experience and corruption meant that the new Balkan governments did not address rural and industrial backwardness. In addition the need to maintain standing armies placed a burden on government finances. The drive towards further wars was inevitable.

Thus the emerging Balkan states and the national groups still within the Ottoman and Habsburg Empires were an inevitable source of regional and European instability. They saw the state of affairs fixed at the Berlin Conference as merely the start of a process of emancipation. The Balkan states' attitude towards the balance of power in the region was based entirely on a narrow and short-sighted desire to capture land and to secure borders. They rightly perceived that the biggest threat to their borders and security came from neighbouring states rather than from the more distant West European powers. If an interest was shown in French, British or Italian policies towards the region and the East Mediterranean, this was only because the Balkan states wished to further their local interests, rather than any consistent policy on European alliances. This preoccupation with regional issues to the exclusion of wider European problems gave the Balkan states a reputation for being fickle and unprincipled.[1]

The first manifestation of the power of small Balkan states occurred in 1912.[2] By then a complex web of treaties bound Serbia, Bulgaria, Greece and Montenegro. The common bond was the desire to grab lands which the Ottoman Empire still held in Europe. On 8 October the Balkan states attacked the Ottoman Empire simultaneously. The European Powers hastened to intervene. They still felt apprehensive about the full implications of the

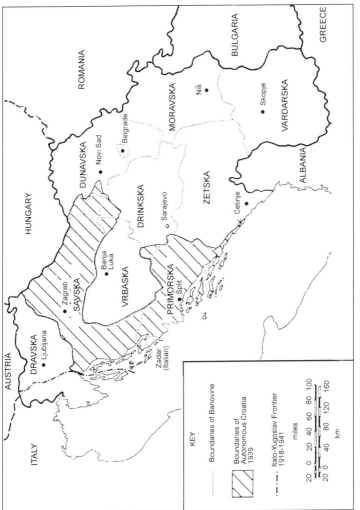

5   The administrative boundaries of the Kingdom of Yugoslavia, 1929–41

ITALY

AUSTRIA

HUNGARY

ROMANIA

BULGARIA

GREECE

ALBANIA

DRAVSKA
• Ljubljana

SAVSKA
• Zagreb

DUNAVSKA
• Novi Sad

Belgrade •

VRBASKA
Banja
Luka •

DRINKSKA
Sarajevo o

MORAVSKA
Niš •

PRIMORSKA
Split •

ZETSKA
Cetinje •

VARDARSKA
Skopje •

Zadar
(Italian)

KEY

.... Boundaries of Banovine

▨ Boundaries of
Autonomous Croatia
1939

–·–· Italo-Yugoslav Frontier
1918–1941

miles
20 0 20 40 60 80 100

km
20 0 40 80 120 160

dismantling of the Ottoman Empire. Attempts at mediation were too obviously aimed at dividing the Balkan states, and only temporarily halted the conflict. In June 1913 Bulgaria, fearing that she would be cut out of the division of spoils, attacked Greece and Serbia. The Balkan Wars led to the defeat of Bulgaria but also to the establishment of a new balance of power in the region. Serbia and Greece emerged enlarged and confident. Montenegro and Romania also gained territory. International interference in the region's conflict secured the emergence of Albania as an independent state, since neither Italy nor the Austro–Hungarian Empire wanted to allow the Serbs to gain control of the Adriatic coast. An independent Albania prevented the Serbs from realising that long-cherished dream.[3]

The political alignments which emerged in the Balkans during the First World War were firmly rooted in the parochial territorial conflicts of the region. War aims as defined by each of the Balkan states rarely related to the larger objectives of the war. Throughout the war the governing circles in each of the Balkan states conduced a fraught debate on whether to enter the war and, if so, which side would offer the highest reward. The military fate of Austria, Italy, Britain, France and Germany only mattered if promises made as an earlier inducement to enter the war could be improved upon. At the end of the war Serbia, Montenegro, Romania and Greece were on the winning side. Bulgaria first decided to join the Central Powers but towards the end of hostilities hoped to be released from responsibility for this by a quick change of government. The change was to no avail. Together with Hungary, Austria and the Ottoman Empire, Bulgaria was treated as a defeated country. Irrespective of the side on which it ended the war, each of the Balkan countries felt that it had either been treated with undue harshness, or that its enemies had been rewarded too lavishly. In any case, territorial adjustments were not the result of negotiated settlements but were imposed through the use of force and the establishment of local administrations. Decisions were sometimes made on the basis of war-time agreements, but some were then renegotiated. This was the case with commitments made to Serbia and Italy in respect of the Adriatic coast. Entirely new solutions were considered too, as was apparent when approval was given to Greece and Turkey ceding territories and exchanging populations. There were many occasions when the victorious powers had to recognise that they could not become involved in the myriad of small and large boundary changes which took place throughout the period 1918–21. Throughout the inter-war period the Balkans continued to be a volatile region, unconscious of its own vulnerability to internal instability and continuing exploitation by the larger states.

The foreign policies of the Balkan states were strongly affected by internal considerations in which the force of nationalism was probably the strongest single factor. Before and after the First World War, Balkan nationalism confused the issue of a given country's security needs with historic achievements and aspirations. This infused the foreign policies of the Balkan states with a rapacious desire to exploit any moment of weakness which a neighbour might experience, an unflinching determination to settle with maximum advantage new and old grievances, and a desire that the League of Nations act as guarantor of their security. Not surprisingly, while displaying a determination to benefit from aggression, each of the Balkan states faced the possibility of being attacked by a neighbouring state. This accounts for the total absence of any loyalty to any European power and a willingness to consider in turn Italy, France, Britain and Germany as an ally and supplier of military equipment.

During the economic depression of the early 1930s the Balkan states faced impoverishment and dependence on minimal foreign capital. Inevitably they looked to the wealthier West European states for investment and trade opportunities. Economic relations between Western Europe and the Balkans were always determined by strategic considerations. Italy provided Albania with financial assistance, thus consolidating her hold over a country which was considered an important sphere of influence. In the 1930s Germany came to appreciate the importance of subsidising trade with Eastern and South Eastern Europe. Political subordination went hand-in-hand with consistent economic support and that is what Germany wanted. France traditionally was very aware of the need to support Yugoslavia as a counterweight to Italy. Thus French investment in Yugoslavia was motivated in equal parts by economic and political considerations. Investments and subsidies for trade with the agricultural Balkan states tended to be short-term and inconsistent. When the Depression affected Europe in the early 1930s western subsidies dried up.

Purchases of low-quality agricultural goods, which together with tobacco were the main items exported to the West, were reduced. Western Europe in defending its agricultural prices refused, even for political reasons, to subsidise the backward economies of the Balkans. As a result, when anxiety about German aggression became a factor in European strategic considerations, Britain and France noted with regret that the ruling circles of those countries had little sympathy with their desire to limit German expansion. The Balkan states observed the escalation of the confrontation between Germany and the Western Democracies in a dispassionate way. Their own regional conflicts continued to determine their foreign policy.[4]

Yugoslavia

On the eve of the First World War Serbia was confident of its ability to assert control over the developments which dramatically unfolded following the assassination of Archduke Franz Ferdinand by a Serb terrorist. The two Balkan Wars had shown that it was possible to ignore the wishes of the Big European Powers. Serbia, with the recklessness of a small and nationally united state, did what none in Europe dared to, namely, challenge and ultimately defeat the Turkish Empire. During the First Balkan War in 1912 Montenegro, joined by Serbia, Bulgaria and Greece, attacked Turkey. British intervention led to the Treaty of London, which prevented the partition of the European parts of the defeated Ottoman Empire. Nevertheless in the course of the Second Balkan War in 1913, caused by rivalry between Serbia, Greece and Bulgaria, the Turks were confined to a small corner of Europe. Serbia's erstwhile ally, Bulgaria, was defeated, leaving Serbia as the most powerful state in the Balkans. As a result of the Treaty of Bucharest, signed in August 1913, Serbia and Greece divided Macedonia between them. The territory of the Serbian Kingdom was thus doubled. More importantly, Serbia's dominant position among the South Slavs was consolidated and her confidence increased sufficiently to make her government and King believe that the Austro–Hungarian Empire could be defeated next.

The assassination in Sarajevo on 28 June 1914 is generally seen as the starting point of the First World War. On 28 July Austria–Hungary declared war on Serbia. Germany declared war on Russia, Serbia's ally, who had mobilised in response to the crisis. As the complex web of treaties unravelled, Europe was overwhelmed by war. Neutrals and allies alike entered into the conflict with the same degree of grim determination. The Serbs were, rightly as it turned out, worried that the need to attract neutrals and to divide enemy ranks might lead Britain and France to make indiscriminate territorial promises. Militarily Serbia was of little significance and that increased her dependence on her allies. After initial victories Serb troops entered Hungarian territories but they were pushed back. By October 1915 Serbia was finished. The capital Belgrade was occupied by Austrian troops, and her troops defeated when Bulgaria joined the Central Powers and occupied most of Serbian territory. The Serb government and army fled through Albania and found temporary refuge in Corfu. For the duration of the war it could only wait for the liberation of its territories and in the meantime prepared plans for the end of hostilities.

Serbia shared with other Central European and Balkan states a desperate desire not to allow its fate to become a bargaining counter between larger powers. To avoid this, the Serbian government sought from the onset of the war to commit the Allied Powers to Serbia's war aims. In December 1914 the Serbian Prime Minister, Nikola Pašić, let it be known that the unification of Serbs, Croats and Slovenes was Serbia's key war aim. The defeat and break-up of the Austro–Hungarian Empire was clearly a precondition. Upon this demand all talks between the Serbs and their allies foundered. Tied up in their hostilities with Germany, neither Britain nor France wanted to commit itself to the destruction of the Habsburg Empire. As long as there was the slightest hope that Austria–Hungary could be induced to abandon Germany, its partition could not be put forward as a war aim.[5] The Serbs spent the war on diplomatic intrigues aimed at finding out what had been promised to potential and existing allies and on campaigns to maintain the Serb case in the forefront of all international discussions. Italy's entry into the war, while militarily desirable, was a diplomatic disaster for the Serbs, who sought access to the Adriatic coast. Even before the Bolsheviks had revealed the substance of

Allied promises, it was common knowledge that Italy's commitment to the Allied side had been purchased. It was assumed that
the Western Allies had promised Italy in the Treaty of London a
dominant position in the Aegean and Adriatic.[6]

In July 1917, by the Declaration of Corfu, the three main South
Slav communities, the Serbs, Croats and Slovenes, resolved the
internal differences which had been an obstacle to their unification. Earlier, in May 1915, a Yugoslav Committee had been established by refugees from the Austro–Hungarian Empire in Paris.
The committee was headed by a Croat, Ante Trumbić, and was
dominated by Croats. Their main aim was the creation of the
a South Slav state. In the first place they had tried to obtain
commitments from Paris and London where the refugees from
Austria–Hungary had congregated. A federal structure was seen
by the Yugoslav Committee as the best way of bringing the South
Slavs together into one state. The Corfu Declaration brought the
programmes of the Serb government and the Yugoslav Committee together. As a result of discussions between the Corfu government and the Yugoslav Committee the federal concept was
rejected. Thus the Corfu Declarations stated that the future kingdom of Serbs, Croats and Slovenes would be a parliamentary
monarchy, headed by the Karadjeordjevice dynasty.[7]

While the signatories of the Corfu Declaration concentrated on
obtaining the support of the Allied Powers, developments in the
Austro–Hungarian Empire took their own course. Most nationalities in the empire had come to expect that the war would lead to
their gaining self-rule. Italy encouraged *émigré* groups to mount
high-profile campaigns, hoping thus to hasten Austro–Hungary's
collapse. In April 1918 the Congress of Oppressed Nationalities
met in Rome. If the Italian leadership hoped that by fomenting
dissent among the national groups in the Empire they would militarily weaken it, they inadvertently also gave encouragement to
the South Slav leaders who henceforth assumed that Italy
accepted the creation of an independent Yugoslav state as a key
war aim.[8]

The common weakness of exile governments and authorities is
the loss of direct contact with developments back home. While the
Corfu government concentrated on persuading the Allies and the
US of the value of making a public commitment to the Yugoslav
case, developments in the Balkan regions took their own course.

In October 1918 a National Council was established in Zagreb. Its initial aim was to represent the joint interest of Serbs, Croats and Slovenes in the Austro–Hungarian Empire. By questioning the authority of those who had put their signatures to the Corfu Declaration, the National Council automatically also challenged the agreements made there. Its decision to assume the duties of a provisional government was confirmed when on 20 October 1918 Emperor Charles of Austria–Hungary, on signing the armistice terms, transferred to it state authority and control over the fleet in the Adriatic Sea.[9] Within days Bosnia–Hercegovina and Vojvodina were brought under the authority of the National Council. The haphazard process of bringing together disparate national groups was completed when Montenegro and Serbia proper agreed to join the Kingdom of Serbs, Croats and Slovenes headed by the National Council. The Corfu Government and the Yugoslav Committee hastened to join the National Council. The reason for this unexpected show of unity was fear of Italian aggression. The National Council had assumed responsibility for the Austrian fleet. The Serb government in Corfu commanded an army of approximately 100 000 men. Italy's obvious determination to grab lands in excess of those granted it by the London Agreement, which drew Italy to the Allied side, dictated haste and imposed unity on what was still a deeply divided population in the Balkans. On 1 December 1918 King Alexander of Serbia proclaimed the Kingdom of Serbs, Croats and Slovenes. In 1929, in line with common usage, it was officially renamed Yugoslavia.

The new state had yet to be united. The idea of South Slav solidarity was a myth. Only circumstances had dictated the need for co-operation. Throughout the inter-war years the forces which had brought the national groups together remained strong. At the same time unresolved issues relating to division of power within the state tended to work against that unity. At times it was impossible to overlook the fact that even Serb communities had little in common with each other: some had already experienced independence in the Serb Kingdom and others had lived in the Austro–Hungarian Empire. The new Yugoslav government faced the formidable task of welding into a state territories and peoples which had never been united before and had developed in different ways and at different paces.

The constitution adopted in September 1920 established a liberal parliamentary system in Yugoslavia. By 1929 the Western model of government broke down and was replaced by a royal dictatorship. Unresolved differences of opinion about the structure of the state bedevilled internal politics from the start. The Croats felt cheated by the creation of a centralised state. They would have preferred a federal structure. As a protest, and in spite of a good showing in the first elections, the Croatian Republican Peasant Party refused to take up its 50 seats in the Constituent Assembly, the Skupstina. The Skupstina was dominated by Serbs who also held most posts in the army. The perception that Yugoslavia was ruled by the Serbs took root swiftly, and the Serbs did little to dispel this perception. In the 1923 elections the Croat Radical Party secured 70 seats which it again refused to take up. The pattern was set, even though in 1925 the Croats were drawn into forming a government with the Serb Radical Party. The Croats were still not placated and held out variously either for a federal state structure or for an independent Croatia. Parliamentary consensus broke down and in 1928 King Alexander took over and henceforth ruled by decree.[10]

On 9 October 1934 Alexander was assassinated by Croat and Macedonian extremists during a visit to Marseilles. His ten-year-old son became heir, although Prince Paul, acting as Regent, continued Alexander's policies. Half-hearted attempts to break the *impasse* were generally unsuccessful. Only in August 1939, in the face of threatening international developments, the Serb Prime Minister Dragiša Cvetkovic reached an agreement with the Croat leader Vladko Maček. As a result a joint government was formed. Croat regions, including Bosnia–Hercegovina and Dalmatia, were granted a degree of self rule. Unfortunately this willingness to accommodate Croat aspirations, which was accompanied by a promise of similar concessions to Slovenes and Moslems came too late. The German invasion in 1941 drove a wedge between the communities, destroying the fragile compromise.

The emergence of the Kingdom of Serbs, Croats and Slovenes cut across a number of highly contentious First World War agreements. At an early stage of its establishment the young state faced a number of territorial disputes which were not of its making. During the peace negotiations the war-time allies disagreed about whether to honour the London Agreement. In any case even before the peace talks had started Italy had occupied Austro–Hungarian territories on the Adriatic coast. These included Istria, the town of Pula, strategic islands off the Croat coast and the Bay of Zara. The Serbs managed to stop them from reaching Ljubljana. The Italians also captured Rijeka (Fiume).

Britain, France and the US tried to hold the balance, only to incur Italian hostility. The US was first to break ranks and insist that the Treaty of London should be reviewed in the light of new developments. The Italian–Yugoslav conflict was discussed without resolution at the Paris Conference. Agreement was not reached either during the St. Germain Conference concerning Austria. While territorial issues relating to Austria had been resolved, the Adriatic coast remained a bone of contention.

Yugoslav distrust of French and British motives was confirmed when the flamboyant Italian poet D'Annunzio led a troop of volunteers to occupy the disputed town of Fiume. Even though the town had been declared a Free City under the protection of the League of Nations, nothing was done to remove him. The complicity of the Italian government in the escapade was widely suspected. The passivity of the League of Nations in the face of a blatant breach of international agreements made the Yugoslavs reluctant to vest any trust in the League. Two years after the end of the First World War, the Italian and Yugoslav governments finally arrived at a compromise. Italy retained the Zara district. Albania's independence was acknowledged by both states. In a further, uneasy compromise Fiume became an independent state.[11] But the rapprochement was only temporary. Relations with Italy never improved and anxiety about Italian policy in the Balkans continued. Italian interference in Albania and support for Hungary and Bulgaria all played on Yugoslav insecurity. In response King Alexander tried to build up regional security blocs with the explicit aim of limiting Italian influence.

In August 1920 Czechoslovakia and Yugoslavia concluded a treaty which, with Romania as an additional signatory, led to the creation of a regional security pact. Known as the Little Entente, this combination of agreements was aimed against the common enemy, Hungary. France also had an interest in supporting the Little Entente as a counterweight to German influence, though the government in Paris was anxious its support for Yugoslavia should not upset France's relations with Italy.

In 1934 another regional treaty reinforced Yugoslavia's security. The Balkan Entente signed by Yugoslavia, Greece, Romania and Turkey continued the previous anti-Italian policy.[12] France would have wanted to strengthen relations with Yugoslavia but the tensions in Yugoslav–Italian relations were a permanent obstacle. During the 1930s France was willing to sacrifice her Balkan options for the sake of securing Italian aid in preventing Germany from annexing Austria. Limiting her involvement in Yugoslav affairs was the price France paid for Italian support for the maintenance of Austrian independence. In 1934 the Italian government, itself anxious about German intentions, was willing to give France an assurance on the Austrian issue. When in 1934 France tried to put pressure on Belgrade to be more conciliatory towards Italy, distrust and anxiety pushed Yugoslavia towards Germany.[13] In 1935 Italian actions in Ethiopia led to League sanctions being invoked. While in principle the Yugoslavs were only too pleased to see Italy condemned, revelations about French and British attempts to reach an accommodation with Italy destroyed confidence in the League. The League's condemnation of Italy proved too weak to redeem the organisation's tarnished image in Yugoslav eyes.

A gradual rapprochement with Germany was facilitated by the Yugoslav Army's insecurity about its ability to defend the country. No trust could be placed in Britain and France. In the long term, Germany's influence was rising in the Balkans, resulting in increasing political dependence on Germany. In 1935 British enquiries and international tension caused by the Abyssinian crisis induced the Yugoslavs to take stock of their military and political situation. The General Staff warned that in the event of an Italian attack the army would not be able to defend the country. The military leadership cautioned against any agreements with Britain, since it was clear that Italy would be in a position to knock Yugoslavia out of the war before Britain could provide any assistance.[14]

Yugoslavia's economic situation made her particularly vulnerable to approaches from Germany. At the end of the First World War Yugoslavia's industrial capacity was negligible. In the absence of any industrial capital, state and private investment could not build up significant infrastructure. The limited industrial expansion that did take place was largely financed by foreign loans. Yugoslavia remained an agricultural country, with small and subsistence farming predominating. Her exports were

confined to agricultural goods and wood. The first was unprofita-
ble because of a glut of food on European markets, the second
made her dependent on Italy, the main purchaser of softwood.
The geography of the Balkans and common economic circumstances had largely determined trading patterns. Little trade
therefore took place between the poorly developed Little Entente
countries. Italy and increasingly Germany were Yugoslavia's
main trading partners. In 1935 Yugoslavia's vote in support of
sanctions against Italy caused a reduction in commercial links
with Italy. On the other hand trade with Germany steadily
increased. Since 1931 Germany had favoured bilateral trade with
the Balkan states. By using such blocked accounts Germany
increased each country's economic dependence. Trade agreements between them obliged the Balkan trading partners to
accept payment for their exports in credits accruing in Germany.
Such credits could only be used to buy German goods. When
Hitler came to power Yugoslavia's economic dependence was
increased, a process which was not viewed by the Yugoslavs as
undesirable. The Yugoslav economy clearly benefited from Germany's interest in the region.[15] In the second half of the 1930s, in
the wake of Germany's monopolisation of her economy, Yugoslavia tried to diversify her economic relations and to limit her political dependence on Germany. Unfortunately neither France nor
Britain were willing to provide equally advantageous trading
terms. By the end of 1938 Yugoslavia had no freedom to manoeuvre. The steady increase in trade with Germany now became
a stranglehold. In October 1939 Yugoslavia had to reduce con-
sumption of foodstuffs because of export commitments to Germany. Her economic dependence on Germany became absolute.[16]

   After 1936, however, the Italian Minister for Foreign Affairs,
Count Galeazzo Ciano, sought to counteract the growth of
German influence. German penetration into the Balkans, traditionally an Italian sphere of influence, had caused some disquiet
in Rome. An attempt was therefore made to resolve all outstanding issues with Yugoslavia. In March 1937 a treaty was signed by
both sides. Italy undertook to respect Yugoslav integrity and to
limit the activities of the Croat nationalist Ustaše in Italy. Italy
also agreed to extend her trade with Yugoslavia. On Albania
Italy refused to budge, restating that it was her sphere of influence.[17] The result of being courted both by Germany and Italy

was that Yugoslavia lost interest in the Austrian issue. When challenged to explain what would be the Yugoslav response in the event of Germany's Anschluss with Austria, the Yugoslav, Prime Minister, Milan Stojadinović, told the French, British and US Ambassadors that he would neither oppose nor condone it. Germany was only too willing to give an assurance that Yugoslav security would not be threatened which was all that Belgrade wanted to hear.[18]

Unlike the Austrian issue, Germany's aspirations towards Czechoslovakia did cause some concern, though only indirectly. Yugoslavia had always been anxious about Hungarian revisionism. Her commitment to the Little Entente and the Balkan Entente was a reflection of that concern. When analysing the implications of German aggression it was assumed that the break-up of Czechoslovakia would inevitably strengthen and encourage the Hungarians. Thus the Yugoslav response to the crisis did not hinge upon whether to defend the Czechoslovak state, but on what would be the effect of such a development on Hungary. Thus Stojadinović encouraged the Czechoslovak government to be conciliatory towards the Sudeten Germans but at the same time insisted that if Hungary was to benefit territorially from the break-up of Czechoslovakia this should only be done with Yugoslav and Romanian agreement.[19] Polish attempts to reconcile Hungary with Yugoslavia and weaken the Little Entente were only partially successful. On the eve of the Munich Conference, in return for parity in rearmament programmes, Hungary committed herself not to use force against any of the three Little Entente states.[20] The Munich Conference was accepted by the government in Belgrade as a constructive method of resolving a crisis, but its attention continued to be focused on Hungary. In the ensuing Vienna Award Hungary gained territories in Slovakia and Ruthenia, but the process remained strictly under German control. The Yugoslavs felt that this satisfied their minimum requirements. They accepted Hungary's limited territorial acquisitions and continued to keep a wary eye on any further developments.[21]

At the beginning of 1939 Stojadinović tried to avoid being drawn into the impending war. Sensing that Poland was most likely to be the next object of German aggression and that Germany was a threat to Yugoslavia, he tried to distance Yugoslavia from Germany and from Poland. Italy appeared to offer a counterweight to the now undesirable political dependence of Yugoslavia on Germany. Ciano encouraged Yugoslav dissociation from Germany. In his game of brinkmanship with Hitler, the Italian Minister for Foreign Affairs tried to improve and consolidate relations with the Balkan states. In return for closer economic and political ties with Italy Yugoslavia was expected to turn a blind eye to the Italian occupation of Albania.[22] Yugoslavia's search for security in the impending European conflict was accompanied by domestic intrigues. In February, after months of criticism, Stojadinović was removed. The accusations against him centred on his alleged willingness to accommodate Germany. Prince Paul, who was reputed to be anti-German, assumed closer controls over foreign policy making. Under his leadership talks with the Croats were resumed. Reconciliation with the Croats carried the further advantage of reducing Italian influence among the Croats. The British and French governments encouraged Yugoslavia in her policy of neutrality. Both countries felt that by consolidating relations with other Balkan states and by continuing to talk with the Hungarians, the Yugoslavs would be able to reduce German and Italian influence.

The Italian invasion of Albania on 7 April 1939 was an unpleasant shock to the Yugoslavs. In spite of a general improvement in relations between the two countries, Ciano had not kept Belgrade informed of his plans. He rightly suspected that, although Yugoslavia was willing to allow Albania to become an Italian sphere of influence, the Yugoslav government would not have agreed to the occupation of its southern neighbour. As a precaution, Italy had arranged for Hungary to station six divisions on the border with Yugoslavia. This proved unnecessary. In return for not raising objections to the Italian occupation of Albania, Yugoslavia was assured that Italy accepted that the Kosovo district, inhabited by an Albanian majority would remain in Yugoslavia. In talks with the government in Rome and Berlin, Yugoslav politicians gave assurances that their country would remain neutral. Under the current circumstances, that invariably was more beneficial to Italy and Germany than to the Western democracies seeking to contain Italian and German aggression. On the eve of the Second World War Yugoslavia politely declined an invitation to join the Anti-Comintern Pact.

In September 1939 Yugoslavia confirmed its commitment to neutrality. This decision was largely motivated by Italian neutrality. As long as Italy was unwilling to support Germany actively, Yugoslavia was able to keep out of the European conflict. This stance was not maintained easily. Italian plans for an attack on Greece involved pressure on the Yugoslavs to allow the passage of troops. The government in Belgrade refused to discuss these plans and held out against having Italian and German military missions in Yugoslavia. Nevertheless, anticipating the inevitable, Prince Paul encouraged the British and French to believe that were they to open the Salonica Front, he would assist them.[23] The fall of France in June 1940 appeared to destroy that hope. More than ever before, Yugoslavia was forced to rely entirely on its own resources. Unexpectedly, at this stage Yugoslavia played a card which had not been played throughout the whole of the inter-war period. Setting aside the anti-Soviet policies of that period, Yugoslavia appealed to the Russians for help. The Soviet Union agreed that it was not a good idea for Italy to have a free hand in the Balkans and moved swiftly to sign commercial agreements with Belgrade. The publicity given to the Soviet–Yugoslav rapprochement was meant to warn the Italians that the Soviet Union retained an interest in the region, and that excessive Italian involvement in the Balkans would be treated as encroachment on a Soviet sphere of influence. Only then did Yugoslavia belatedly grant the Soviet Union recognition.[24]

The Soviet move may have been why Hitler signalled to Mussolini that he was no longer prepared to tolerate Yugoslav independence. This enabled Italy to proceed with her plans, safe in the knowledge that Germany would not support the Yugoslavs. On 28 October 1940 Italy attacked Greece. Although the Greek port of Thessalonika was a major outlet to the sea for Yugoslavia, the government in Belgrade, fearful of a joint Italian and German attack, could do little. Initially Germany did little to assist Italy in Greece but the Italian failure to secure a victory drew Germany into the conflict. Yugoslavia, as a transit route to Greece, had to make a commitment. In the long term, Germany, in preparation for the ultimate destruction of the Soviet Union, needed to consolidate her hold of strategically important areas in the Balkans.[25] At the end of March 1941 Yugoslavia, after extensive bullying, committed herself to the Three Power Pact signed by Germany,

Italy and Japan on 27 September 1940. Unexpectedly, strong opposition to Yugoslavia abandoning its neutrality appeared in the ranks of the army. On 28 March 1941 a military coup was staged. It received popular support from various groups opposed to Yugoslavia's falling into the Axis camp. The young King Peter was willing to head it.

Hitler responded by attacking Yugoslavia on 6 April. Hungary and Bulgaria were drawn into the military plans, and assurances were given to both states that they would be allowed to take territories to which they had laid claim. After exceptionally savage bombing of Belgrade an armistice was signed on 17 April. Hungary was rewarded with territories between the Danube and Tisza rivers. Bulgaria grabbed Macedonia. In the final share-out Italy took Kosovo and Southern Slovenia. Northern Slovenia was attached to German Austria. Finally two nominally independent states were created, an Independent State of Croatia ruled by Ante Pavelić and Serbia, where Milan Nedić became the appointed Prime Minister. The young king left for London where he headed a government in exile.

Albania

At the end of the nineteenth century, the all-apparent and growing weakness of Ottoman rule in Europe raised the obvious question of what was to emerge in its place. Hence the Albanian region, which possesses little if any mineral and natural wealth, became the focus of international attention during the Balkan Wars. Serbia wanted free access to the Adriatic coast, something Austria–Hungary was determined to prevent at all costs. France and Britain also feared the extension of Serb influence, suspecting that this would increase the influence of Russia, Serbia's protector. In 1912, in the course of international mediation at the time of the First Balkan War, the establishment of an independent state of Albania was agreed upon as a means of blocking the expansion of Serbia towards the coast. This solution was acceptable to Italy.

Initially Albania was to remain under Ottoman suzerainty. The precise definition of the new state's border created a number of problems. The biggest threat to the state's existence was posed by the fact that while the European powers agreed among themselves on the desirability of establishing an independent Albania, the neighbouring states had no commitment to this decision. Montenegro and Serbia continued to scheme against Albania, while any likelihood of a change in the local balance of power automatically aroused Austro–Hungarian and Italian interests. On Albania's southern flank Greece warily kept an eye on developments, ready to step in and grab available territories.[26] The Second Balkan War confirmed the precarious nature of Albania's status, though it was once more shored up by the support of the European Powers. This time it was decided that Albania was to be an independent state.[27]

The origins of the modern state of Albania lay in the appointment of a minor German princeling to head an Albanian monarchy at the turn of the century. The independent-minded Albanian tribes had not been consulted. The patent nonsense of trying to establish a central authority in a country without proper transport and communications infrastructure and deeply divided by tribal and religious conflicts did not fully sink in until the First World War broke out and the Albanian government, with little support, collapsed. Albania's neutrality was not respected.[28] During the course of the war Albania became a battleground. Greece invaded Southern Albania. Italy and Serbia joined in occupying territories and attempted to establish permanent footholds. With Italian encouragement, and Serb connivance, an adventurer, Essad Pasha, raised mercenary forces and tried to capture the interior of Albania.[29] The government of France showed an unexpected interest in developments in Albania, primarily because of her concern for the Salonica Front. By 1917 France and Italy were trying to legitimise their intervention in Albania by encouraging indigenous administrations. Austria–Hungary followed suit by occupying Albanian territories. These ad-hoc attempts to control the Albanian region, and the devastating effects of fighting, took their toll. When the World War ended, French, Serb and Greek troops remained on Albanian territories, awaiting assurances of a favourable balance of power. There was no institution to express any Albanian view, even though the newly established Committee for the Defence of Kosovo tried to put forward the Albanian point of view. Likewise representations made to the Paris Conference went unheeded. Northern Albania was incorporated into Serbia

as compensation for the decision to grant Italy Istria, Fiume and Zadar. Greek claims to Southern Albanian territory were likewise recognised.[30]
Internally the rump Albania remained divided by traditional tribal conflicts. Not until 1920 was an attempt made to govern the country. In January that year a self-appointed group of influential men convened a meeting at Lushnja to overcome differences and to form a government. First elections took place in 1921. Although a semblance of democracy had been established, this is all that it was, for political power remained firmly entrenched in the hands of clan leaders. A period of instability followed during which clans and tribes continued to fight each other. Successive governments reflected not diversity of political ideas but the changing fortunes and altering alliances of the tribal system. Italy and Yugoslavia remained deeply involved in the conflicts, at various stages supporting one or other group, in the hope of maintaining their influence in the region. In December 1924 a leader of a minor tribe, Ahmed Zogu, supported by Yugoslav arms and troops, was more successful than his predecessors in capturing and holding the new Albanian capital, Tirana. By 1925 all opposition had been either eliminated or tied by means of patronage and tribal alliances to Zog who in 1928 was crowned King of Albania.[31]
In 1938 Zog married a Habsburg princess. Unlikely as it might appear, Zog did believe that he could secure for Albania an independent role in the Balkan region. His freedom of manoeuvre was severely limited, which did not prevent him from gaining maximum advantage by pitching Yugoslavia against Italy. Italy ultimately proved to be the stronger and more persuasive of partners. In 1926 Zog swapped Yugoslav support for Italian. Mussolini was willing to provide aid. But the path to dependence, once taken, was difficult to abandon.
At the Paris Peace Conference it was accepted that Italy had a special interest in Albania. During the 1920s and 1930s Mussolini made sure that Albania's dependence on Italy steadily increased. Albania's economic plight was desperate. Zog's internal policies consisted of buying the loyalty of those who could not be depended on to support him for other reasons. Over the years, the revenue raised by selling concessions to Italy was used to provide annual payments to loyal tribesmen and for bribes to those who might not be inclined to be loyal. In January 1925 Italy was granted a

total monopoly on shipping and trade concessions. The Society for the Economic Development of Albania was set up by Italy with the explicit aim of funnelling loans to Zog. The Italian government established the National Bank of Albania in which it retained a 51 per cent stake. The Bank had total control over Albania's finance. Quite unusually, Italy was also granted the right to settle colonists on Albanian territory. Italian largesse was conditional on other countries not gaining an economic foothold in Albania.[32] Zog obliged by making it impossible for other countries to obtain concessions in Albania. Though he did not feel entirely satisfied with the course of Italian–Albanian relations. In the 1930s he looked for alternative sources of patronage. One of his moves was to appeal to Britain, in the hope that London would form a counterweight to Italy. But Britain only warned Mussolini not to expand into the Western Mediterranean. Rome interpreted this message as indicating that Britain continued to view Albania as Italy's sphere of influence.[33] Badly thought out Yugoslav attempts to stir anti-Italian groups only increased Zog's insecurity and confirmed his subjugation to Italy. Albania's internal system was totally dependent on loyalty payments to wealthy landowners and townspeople. Any attempts to limit this expenditure would lead to Zog being overthrown. In 1935 Zog faced a major challenge to his position. He was able to put down a rebellion but his reliance on Italian funds increased. Extensive loans were made available and this completed Italy's stranglehold over Albania's economy and army.[34]

The Italian invasion of Albania on 6 April 1939, which was preceded by an ultimatum demanding total subjugation to Italy, caused some consternation. The question which needs to be asked is why Italy sought to occupy a country over which it had unchallenged control? At this late stage King Zog neither could nor sought any more to distance himself from Italy. Italy had known for some time that neither France nor Britain would challenge her domination of the Albanian region. Italian–Yugoslav negotiations had confirmed the latter's acceptance of Italian economic and political interest in Albania. One suggestion is that Italy was no longer satisfied with mere control over this strategic area. The Fascist regime needed a high-profile gesture, the significance of which had more to do with diplomacy than with the acquisition of territories. The Albanian–Italian confrontation coincided with growing German pressure on Romania and Hungary. The fear that Germany would consolidate her grip on Eastern Europe and the Balkans, which Italy saw as her sphere of influence, compelled the Italian Fascists to take action.

The conflict was initiated on 25 March by Italy presenting a new treaty proposal. In substance it merely confirmed and extended rights already enjoyed by Italy, and gave licence to the Italians to take action if Albanian territory was threatened. The extension of economic rights was also requested. The intention was that the Albanian King would reject the proposal, which he was supposed to see as an attempt to annex Albania. All Zog's attempts to use the Italian proposal as a basis for negotiations with other European powers failed. Neither the Western democracies nor the other Balkan states wanted to get involved in the rapidly evolving crisis. On the morning of 7 April Italian troops marched into Albania. King Zog and his family departed; he was reported as taking with him 'a bucket of rubies and emeralds as well as part of the gold reserve of the state bank, all of which was valued at about ten million dollars'.[35]

Bulgaria

The Treaty of San Stefano, signed by Russia and the Ottoman Empire in March 1878, provided for the creation of Bulgaria. The victorious Russians were able to insist that the frontiers of the new state should be generous and embrace territories south of the Danube up to the Aegean Sea, including Thrace and Macedonia. The Russian government's determination to weaken the Ottoman Empire further and to establish a firm foothold in the Balkan region was the only reason why a Bulgarian state was created at this stage. Unfortunately Russian policies caused a strong international reaction. Neither France nor Britain was happy to see Russia's position strengthened. The creation of a Bulgarian state also undermined a precarious balance of power which had only recently been established in the region. Neither Romania nor Greece was happy to see Macedonia thus disposed of.[36] As a result of international pressure Russia had to scale down its initial plans for Bulgaria. The Treaty of Berlin not only decreased Bulgaria's territory but also re-emphasised its continuing relationship

with the Ottoman Empire. The Bulgarian state was left with territories north of the Balkan Mountains. In an attempt to shore up
Ottoman power in Europe the Berlin Treaty stipulated that Bulgaria was to be autonomous but to acknowledge the suzerainty of
the Sultan. An assembly of nobles in due course elected a German
prince, Alexander Battenberg, as Bulgarian sovereign.

It was inevitable that attempts to maintain the already-weak
Ottoman rule in Europe would fail. Bulgaria's dependence on
Russia increased, facilitated by the growth of pro-Russian sentiments within the political leadership of the country.[37] Bulgarians
felt themselves cheated of territories which had been initially
assigned to their country at San Stefano. Big Power intervention
was blamed for this humiliation. This formative period influenced
future thinking, justifying distrust of the European states and pro-
pagating the myth that the country had been denied territories to
which it had a just claim. Internal conflicts, caused by Alexander's
dependence on the Russians, quarrels between Liberal and Conservative Parties and social unrest in urban and rural areas created
a volatile situation. In 1887 Ferdinand of Saxe-Coburg replaced
Alexander, who was forced to flee. In September 1908 Bulgaria
became fully independent and Ferdinand declared himself king.

In 1912 despite Russian and Austro–Hungarian discourage-
ment, the Balkan states allied with the aim of reducing the Ottoman presence in Europe by force of arms. But the Balkan Wars
defined the limits of co-operation between the allies. The Second
Balkan War was caused by a Bulgarian attack on Serbia and
Greece. Both had sought to reduce the growing influence of Bulgaria in the Aegean and Macedonia. Bulgaria was forced to give
up territories captured earlier. The Ottoman Empire, Greece,
Romania, Montenegro and Serbia all laid claim to Bulgarian territories. While the boundaries of the Balkan states were finally
consolidated, so were lines of hostility.[38] Bulgaria lacked a natural
ally in the Balkans. This would breed insecurity and with it would
come a potential for disruption.

The First World War gave Bulgaria an opportunity to reverse
the losses incurred during the Second Balkan War. The larger
European conflict was of no consequence to the Bulgarians. What
mattered was to be on the winning side at the end of the war and
extract the highest possible price from the side with which
Bulgaria had allied itself. Regional rather than European issues

determined participation in the war. When the Allied powers looked likely to win, the Bulgarian government held back from making commitments because they rightly surmised that commitments to Serbia would take precedence. The Allies were only willing to consider minor border adjustments in Macedonia, whereas Bulgaria sought major territorial changes. The Central Powers' determination to defeat Serbia opened up bigger possibilities both in Thrace and Macedonia. When in September 1915 Bulgaria threw in her lot with Germany and Austria–Hungary it seemed as if their victory was a foregone conclusion.[39] Unfortunately the Bulgarians ended up on the losing side. They were made to pay a price. The Treaty of Neuilly defined the country's territorial losses which were both humiliating and considerable. Greece took territories on the Aegean, while Romania gained Southern Dobrudja and the Macedonian regions. Bulgaria had to pay reparations of $450 million and accept restrictions on the size of her army, which was to be henceforth raised on a voluntary basis. The reparations payments were extracted annually until 1932 when they were finally cancelled. The keen sense of grievance was further accentuated by there being 16 per cent (approximately 1 million) of Bulgarian nationals who now found themselves under foreign rule.[40]

In the immediate aftermath of the First World War Bulgaria did not have to face minority problems or agrarian conflicts. Consolidation of territories, a major problem to the enlarged Eastern European and Balkan states, was not an issue either. The diminished territory of post-war Bulgaria was relatively free of national minorities, while there was no tradition of large landholding. The peasantry was stable, with few conflicts manifesting themselves within the villages.

The most important force in inter-war politics was the Agrarian Party. The first administration was formed by the Agrarian leader Alexandûr Stamboliiski. His objectives were by any standards progressive. Redistribution of land previously held by the state and churches, improvements in rural education, the imposition of a compulsory labour service, all formed part of a concerted attempt to address problems of rural backwardness. Unfortunately disaffection among the military and urban unrest fuelled by the post-war inflation led to strikes and disturbances. In his foreign policy Stamboliiski broke the mould by actively seeking to normalise relations with Bulgaria's main rival, the Kingdom of South Slavs. That initiative brought him into direct conflict with the all-powerful International Macedonian Revolutionary Organisation (IMRO) which had been until then financed and aided by the Bulgarian government. In June 1923 Stamboliiski faced an army and IMRO coup during which he was captured and died after being tortured.[41]

From 1922 until 1931 a coalition bloc calling itself the Democratic Concord dominated Bulgarian politics, though the IMRO continued its activities unchecked. The extremely popular Communist Party was a major contender in all internal conflicts even though it was officially banned in 1924. In due course the government's reputation was tarnished by the repressive measures taken against all who opposed it. The extreme right, the IMRO and the Communists continued attacking the government. It has been pointed out that despite being a society which contained relatively few natural demarcation lines and class conflicts, Bulgaria by the mid-1920s exhibited all the signs of a collapse of law and order.[42]

Order was restored when in May 1934 a group of conspirators led by military officers took power. During the following year democratic rights were further restricted and trade unions were abolished and replaced by corporatist workers' organisations. In 1935 King Boris took over by establishing a royal dictatorship.[43] While order prevailed and the IMRO's activities were finally curtailed, in reality Bulgarian society was riven with unresolved grievances and hatreds. Simmering discontent was merely held down by the use of force.

The Bulgarian government's sole foreign policy objective, to destroy the Neuilly Treaty, made that government vulnerable to exploitation by any European Power which would support that objective.[44] During the 1920s Italy appeared to be Bulgaria's obvious friend. Bulgarian–Yugoslav hostilities were just the sort of local difficulty which the Italian government wanted to encourage and then exploit. In the 1930s Bulgaria came to appreciate the importance of forging better relations with her neighbours.

The creation of the Balkan Entente in 1934 caused major anxiety in Sofia and confirmed the wisdom of mending fences with Yugoslavia. In January 1937 Bulgaria signed a Pact of Friendship with Yugoslavia. In 1938 and 1939, when German aggression caused the governments of Britain and France to reassess their previous policies of appeasement, attention was briefly focused on the Balkans. In an attempt to limit German access to the economic wealth of that region, the British government tried to encourage the Balkan states to forge regional security agreements. The earlier exclusion of Bulgaria from the Balkan Entente was viewed as potentially dangerous. As a result of the Salonika Agreement, signed on 31 July 1938, the countries of the Balkan Entente agreed to lift the restrictions which had been imposed on the Bulgarian army. In return Bulgaria conceded that Greece could remilitarize Thrace and the Bulgarians were assured that the other Balkan states would not use force against them.[45]

In Bulgaria, the subject of its place in the European balance of power was closely linked to domestic issues. The nature of internal conflicts, and the bewildering realisation that Bulgaria had no negotiating position and was merely a pawn, inevitably led to a critical consideration of options. Russia, notwithstanding the Bolshevik Revolution and its exclusion from European politics, still appeared to some to be a credible partner. Bulgaria's very existence had been closely associated with Russia's Black Sea and Balkan policy. Germany also commanded loyalty which went beyond the immediate period of the First World War. All discussion of the Neuilly Treaty restrictions invariably linked Bulgaria's situation with that of Germany, which shared the same fate. Germany's determination to challenge the Versailles Treaty impressed the Bulgarian Army. Bulgaria had strong economic and cultural links with Germany. In 1939 sales to Germany made up 70 per cent of Bulgarian exports.[46] In the final analysis these considerations only played a limited role in determining Bulgaria's place in the European balance of power, for the brutal truth was that Bulgaria was not sufficiently important to merit major investment, either in diplomatic, military or economic terms.

When Germany attacked Poland, Bulgaria could not remain unaffected by the crisis even though the King and his political advisers tried to keep out of the conflict. Initially Britain and France preferred the Balkan states to remain neutral and to co-operate in denying economic resources to Germany. In the long run both sides tried to ensure that neutrality was applied in such a way as not to injure their interests. Whereas initially the British government wanted to make sure that Germany did not gain total control of Romanian oil and sought to preemptively purchase all production, later plans for a second front in the Balkans increased pressure on Bulgaria not to commit herself to Germany. Unfortunately, the French government was not convinced that Bulgaria was worth courting, while the British government realised that its inactivity in the face of German aggression destroyed Britain's standing in the Balkans. Although residual pro-British feelings remained in Bulgaria, the benefits to be derived from closer contacts with Germany ultimately prevailed. On 16 September 1939 the Bulgarian government declared neutrality. This in effect reduced the likelihood that it would throw in its lot with the British.[47]

During the next two years that neutrality was whittled down to nothing. Germany's victories offered Bulgaria opportunities to regain territories lost during the Second Balkan War and at the end of the First World War. Inevitably with each territorial gain Bulgaria's dependence on Germany increased. Somewhat improbably King Boris believed he had a choice of patrons in his desire for territorial revision. The signing of the Soviet–German Pact of Non-Aggression brought together two countries for which there was a sentimental regard in Bulgaria. Russophiles, mindful of Russian support before the First World War, looked to benefit from any Soviet actions against the common enemy. It was calculated that, were the Soviet Union to lay claim to the Romanian territories of Bessarabia and Bukovina, this would allow the Bulgarians to demand the return of Southern Dobrudja, with its majority Bulgarian population. The Soviet Union repeatedly informed the Bulgarians that they would support such claims.[48]

The decision to tie Bulgaria's fate to that of Germany came with the shift in the internal balance of power in favour of the pro-German faction in the government, and with Boris's approval. In February 1940 a new government was formed with Professor Bogdan Filov, a renowned anti-Semite and admirer of all things German. This government was willing to consider German offers of support with more sympathy than those from the Soviet Union. Molotov had put it to Filov that Bulgaria and the Soviet Union should sign a Pact of Mutual Assistance. The Bulgarian government nevertheless held out for German support and let it be known that it would seek territorial gains in Romania but wanted Germany to give prior approval for its action. The balance in favour of Germany was tipped with the fall of France. In August

THE BALKANS: YUGOSLAVIA, ALBANIA, BULGARIA   213

1940, following Soviet entry into Bessarabia, Bulgaria, jointly with Hungary, laid formal claim to Romanian territories. Although this action merely confirmed what had been suspected earlier, namely that Germany had agreed to the Balkans being a Soviet sphere of influence, Bulgarians celebrated the return of Southern Dobrudja as a sign of German goodwill. Soviet attempts to tie Bulgaria to the Soviet bloc were rejected when King Boris and Filov preferred to travel to Berlin. Unfortunately for them, the German government was preoccupied with two issues. Preparations for action against the Soviet Union and the need to relieve Italian troops in Greece took priority over Bulgarian territorial claims. In November 1940 pressure was put on Bulgaria to join the Three Power Pact and to allow her territory to be used as a base for action against Greece. The first was uneasily rejected, the second unofficially conceded.[49]

On 1 March 1941 Bulgaria joined the Three Power Pact. When Germany attacked Greece and Yugoslavia, it was claimed that Bulgarian troops were involved in action, though officially neutrality continued to be maintained. But German victories Bulgaria received Macedonia. All of Bulgaria's territorial claims had thus been satisfied. But Germany was not willing to put up with the Bulgarian government's claim to maintaining neutrality. Bulgaria was firmly in the German camp and she had benefited from German aggression. When the German armed forces attacked the Soviet Union, the Bulgarian government did not send troops to fight with German units. Instead, symbolically, a medical field station was offered for the Eastern Front. Interestingly, diplomatic relations between the Soviet Union and Bulgaria were not broken off throughout the Second World War.

The final act of commitment to the German war effort came with the German and Italian declaration of war on the United States after Pearl Harbor. In spite of earlier American attempts to keep Bulgaria out of the conflict, on 13 December 1941 Bulgaria declared war against the US and Britain.

8 The Baltic States: Lithuania, Latvia, Estonia

The phrase 'The Baltic States' used here refers jointly to the small states of Lithuania, Latvia and Estonia on the southern coast of the Baltic Sea. While this may suggest a collective identity, they did not identify with each other. The region, in addition to having a history of conquest by different states, at various times came under the political influence of different powers. The three states contain populations of diverse ethnic origins and cultures. Nevertheless in the twentieth century historic developments have affected the three states in a similar way, thus justifying their grouping under one heading.

Developments in the region were determined by the course of relations between the major north European states. Germany and Russia always had a direct interest in the Baltic coast and any rivalry between the two had a bearing on developments in the Baltic region. That in turn affected the degree of freedom enjoyed by the Baltic people. Of the three states only Lithuania had existed as an independent state before the end of the First World War. In the fourteenth century the Polish and Lithuanian Kingdoms formed a union which dominated the region. Lithuania's fate continued to be closely tied to that of Poland. In 1795, when Austria, Prussia and Russia completed the destruction of the Polish Kingdom, Lithuania became part of the Russian Empire. For historic reasons, Lithuanians were predominantly Catholic. Its nobility had assimilated Polish traditions and political ideas, in the process losing its own identity. The separation of the nobility from its compatriots was further encouraged by the Russian administration. Within the Russian Empire, Lithuania, in common with the other two Baltic States, was allowed a degree of autonomy. The assembly of nobles was given extensive powers and rights of decision-making. This changed after the 1863 Polish rebellion, with which the Lithuanian nobility strongly associated. The Russian response to the failed uprising was to undermine the influence of the national elite and the organisations from which

6   The Baltic states. From Georg von Rauch, *The Baltic States: The Years of Independence*. Copyright © 1974 by C. Hurst & Co. Used by permisssion of the University of California Press.

the Lithuanian population derived its sense of national identity. Lithuania was thus the first to experience the brutal russification policies which aimed at destroying the power of the local nobility and the eradication of all vestiges of national solidarity. The Emancipation Act of 1861 which abolished serfdom in the Russian Empire, was particularly favourable to the Lithuanian peasants. One of its aims was to undermine the economic influence of the local nobility. The result was that a wealthy and stable peasant stratum emerged in the Baltic regions, while the rest of European Russia continued to be characterised by poverty and agricultural backwardness.

Though geographically close, the other countries developed as a result of different pressures. In the twelfth century the areas which subsequently came to be known as Latvia and Estonia had been conquered by the German Crusading Order of the Brothers of the Sword and the Teutonic Order. German political power was thus established firmly in the region, with German landowners ruling over the local peasantry, while merchants of the Hanseatic League dominated the coast.

Conflicts between the north European states affected the Baltic directly. Whereas in the sixteenth century Sweden was the main protagonist in the region, by 1721, as a result of reversals in her military fortunes, Sweden was forced to hand over Latvia and Estonia to the Russian Empire. The Tsarist regime had no wish to enter into direct conflict with the economically more-developed German nobility and the well-organised towns of the newly acquired Baltic region. The German landowners continued to enjoy all their previous privileges, including the right to an assembly. Religious observance in the German-dominated area followed developments in Germany. Thus in due course Protestantism became the main religion of the region. Only in 1881 did Tsar Alexander II authorise a policy of 'russification'. The Orthodox Russian Church, with a degree of success, sought to entice peasants away from the Lutheran Church. German culture nevertheless continued to have a very strong influence on the intellectual development of the region. Higher levels of education ensured contacts with cultural developments in Western Europe.

By the beginning of the twentieth century the educated elites in all Baltic regions were affected by the growth of nationalism.

There was no perception of a common identity among the people of the three Baltic States; nevertheless Russian policies towards national groups in the Empire had the result of accentuating similarities. Thus intellectual debates and cultural developments increasingly focused on the fact that, the national aspirations of the Baltic people were one. The First World War inevitably accelerated this trend by highlighting shared hardships. The growing perception that the Baltic people shared a common fate led to a search for solutions which were essentially similar. The desire to express a common Baltic identity and solidarity thus transcended their different historic traditions.[1]

In 1914, when the First World War broke out, the nationalist aspirations of the Baltic peoples were initially confined to hoping that the autonomy conceded after the 1905 revolutions, would be extended. The military defeat of the Russian Empire and the February Revolution which followed in 1917 created unexpected opportunities for the emergence of independent Baltic States.

At the beginning of the war, the Baltic people, with a limited understanding of the magnitude of the European conflict, generally supported the Russian war effort. German victories by September 1915 had extended its army's control over Lithuania and the province of Courland. The German High Command was given absolute administrative control over the occupied territories and developed long-term plans for the Baltic provinces. The Baltic provinces, the so-called *Land Oberost*, occupied a very important place in German plans for a post-war settlement. Their economic potential and strategic importance was such that it was decided to annex the region to Germany.[2] To justify their policies, the High Command put forward their plans as no more than encouraging the local people to claim the right to self-determination. This in turn opened up further the debate which had been taking place among the politically active population of the occupied regions. When, by February 1918, the German Armies established control over the remainder of the Baltic region, the debate on the subject of self-determination was extended to Estonia and Latvia. German plans for the *Land Oberost* never were genuinely meant to allow the Baltic people independence. German colonisation had been started in 1916 and proceeded throughout this period. Nevertheless, by raising the issue of the region's future after the collapse of the Russian Army and administration, the German High Command unwittingly facilitated the growth of national expectations among the people of the Baltic provinces.

The Lithuanians in particular expected genuine, not merely nominal, independence within the German Empire.[3] They were the first to recognise the opportunities offered by Germany's public support for their rights of self-determination. In September 1917 a Lithuanian Provincial Council (Taryba) was convened. The Taryba concentrated on obtaining from Germany genuine recognition of Lithuanian rights to independence. Only after a promise was given that the new state would remain within the German sphere of influence did Kaiser Wilhelm II authorise the establishment of an independent state of Lithuania. This followed German pressure on the Soviet representatives at the armistice talks at Brest-Litovsk to accept Lithuanian independence. At the same time the Bolsheviks were forced to agree that the territories of future Estonia and Latvia would remain under temporary German occupation.

The steps towards the emergence of Estonian and Latvian states were made at the time when Russian administration appeared to disintegrate after February 1917. In April 1917 the Provisional Government in Petrograd had decided to divide the remaining nominally Russian-controlled Baltic territories into Estonia and Latvia. Estonia was allowed to establish an elected provincial assembly. No such concession was made to the Latvian population. In November 1917 the Latvians were able to proclaim a National Council which in due course issued a declaration stating that an independent Latvian republic had been established. Clearly such proclamations had only a transitory importance. Taking advantage of the impasse in the German–Russian military confrontation the Estonians followed suit with their own proclamation of independence. But the Committees in the two countries were still a long way from being able actually to exercise independence and form stable and independent administrations. In the first half of 1918 the fate of the Baltic peoples continued to depend on the outcome of the war.

These first, uncertain steps towards the creation of independent Baltic States were checked by the events which followed the signing of the German armistice with the Allied Powers on 9 November 1918. Far from clarifying the situation, the armistice between Germany and the Allied Powers introduced new complexities. The most important of them arose out of the fact that the conditions of the armistice left unresolved Germany's role in territories which she had hitherto occupied. While the armistice clearly specified conditions for the German withdrawal from occupied territories in the west, Article 12 stated that, in the east, German troops would have to pull back to German territories 'as soon as the Allies shall consider this desirable'. This clause was introduced into the armistice conditions because of a general anxiety about developments in the east where the collapse of the Russian Empire and the military defeat of Germany and Austria led to local administrations emerging in a haphazard way. The continuing presence of the German Army in the east appeared to offer some assurance of short-term stability. The implications of the Bolshevik take-over in Russia were still being digested. A blind eye was therefore turned to the continuing German presence in Eastern Europe in order to forestall the spread of Bolshevik control. In the following year the reluctance of sections of the German High Command to relinquish the *Land Oberost* was encouraged by the Western preference for Germany to form a barrier against the Red Army. The newly emerging administrations in the Baltic States had little power to influence the course of deliberations taking place in Berlin and Paris.[4]

During the closing months of 1918 and in 1919, the Baltic coast became the battleground on which Soviet troops were confronted to prevent their entry into Poland and Germany. The picture continued to be profoundly complex. The emerging Baltic States' governments recognised that they did not have the military power with which to oppose the Red Army. They therefore welcomed the assistance of the German troops on their soil. White Russian forces too were willing to aid the Baltic States, but their commitment to Baltic independence was less clear because of their desire to restore the Russian Empire. Britain supported the Baltic States' governments and the White Russians. In the midst of these conflicts the region was succumbing to fratricidal struggles, as the entry of Soviet troops into the Baltic States was accompanied by the setting up of local Soviet governments, which drew on support from local revolutionary workers.[5] Finland and Poland took a direct interest in these conflicts. They too were trying to define their respective borders and spheres of interest.

Thus when, in November 1918, Soviet troops entered Estonia and established an Estland Workers' Commune, British naval units aided by Finnish troops assisted the Estonian government in defeating the Red Army. In December, Soviet entry on to Latvian territory was followed by the establishment of a Soviet government. In this case German volunteer units, from troops who had not been pulled out of the region, were helped by the British Navy to defeat the Red Army. In January 1919 the Lithuanian government was overthrown by a local Soviet aided by the Russians. The entry of Polish troops led to the defeat of the Red Army and toppled the revolutionary government. By the autumn of 1919 the Russian Soviet government was forced to accept military defeat in the Baltic region. In February 1920 it recognised Estonia. By the summer of 1920 Latvia and Lithuania were also granted recognition.

The new Baltic States learned a painful lesson from these events, namely that none of the bigger neighbours would respect their integrity. Military assistance, when given, had been motivated by self-interest. The sovereignty of the Baltic States was only tolerated because the Big Powers who had an interest in the region jointly agreed that it was in their mutual interest to allow the small states sufficient control over their affairs to keep out rival powers. Any increase in the influence of one power in the Baltic States was viewed by the other powers as provocative and justifying intervention. The Baltic people were forcefully reminded that their sovereignty depended not on their armed forces but on the balance of power in the region.

In each of the cases where foreign intervention assisted the Baltic governments to defeat an invader, a price was paid. Thus in January 1919 when Soviet troops entered Latvian territory they were pushed back by German units raised from the Baltic German population and the local Latvian population. The defeat of the Soviet troops was followed by the German troops imposing their will upon those they had earlier assisted. Swelled by volunteers from the Reich, German units in Lithuania overthrew the Lithuanian government and replaced it with a puppet administration. Frustrated and angry at their humiliation by the Versailles Treaty, the German High Command approved action to retain a foothold in the east. Combined Latvian and Lithuanian forces were finally able to defeat the Germans in June, when the Allies put pressure on Gustav Noske, the German Minister of the Interior, to order the withdrawal of Germans from the Baltic area. By 13 December 1919 the German adventurers, for that was all they had become, had returned to Germany.[6]

Similarly Polish support for Lithuania was not disinterested. The Poles laid claim to the city of Vilnius and its surrounding areas. In April 1919 Poland's assistance was welcomed by the Lithuanian government which had been overthrown by the Red Army. The Poles and Lithuanians jointly toppled the Lithuanian Soviet government which had been installed in Vilnius. But then the Poles refused to return the city to Lithuania. They were forced to relinquish it when, in the wake of a military impasse with the Soviet Union, international mediation was sought. One of the conditions imposed by the Big Power mediators was that Vilnius should return to Lithuania. This the Poles did, but in October 1919, by a rather obvious ruse, the Poles reclaimed the disputed town. Officially it was stated that a Polish General, Lucjan Żeligowski exceeded instructions with his troops and captured Vilnius. But when he offered the town to the Polish state, which then accepted the gift, no one was fooled by this unsophisticated incident. The Vilnius incident left a lasting dislike of Poles in Lithuania.

After the initial period of instability, the setting up of administrative structures proceeded with relative ease. The proximity of the Soviet state and memories of the Red Army's attempts to create puppet Soviets in the Baltic areas discredited the revolutionary model. Liberal and constitutional ideas which the Baltic intellectuals had advocated during the Tsarist period guided the new governments. The constitutions of the newly created Baltic States 'read as if they had been lifted from a textbook on egalitarian-participatory democratic theory.'[7] In addition to a bill of rights which mirrored the most progressive examples in Western Europe, constitutions introduced in the new states provided for assemblies which had powers well in excess of the executive. Thus successive governments were heavily dependent on the elected assemblies, with Prime Ministers and the executive function subordinate to the legislature. At the time this was seen as a guarantee of democratic stability. Later it proved to be a source of weakness as there were few incentives for political parties to compromise in order to form or support a government. Instead most political and administrative decisions were made in the parliaments, a cumbersome and unwieldy process that hindered effective government.

In view of the rural character of all three states, Agrarian Parties were the strongest ones, closely followed by the Socialist Party. The dominance of the Catholic faith in Lithuania, ensured that the Christian Democratic bloc of parties held sway in that country. National minorities were also well represented. The German population, even though it supported a number of parties, cooperated closely. The Poles formed a sizeable minority with considerable electoral strength in Lithuania. Jewish parties also participated in the political life of the Baltic States. From such comprehensive democracy all three Baltic States ultimately succumbed to dictatorship.

In December 1926 two officers, Augustinas Voldemaras and Anatanas Smetona staged a military coup in Lithuania. In addition to support from the Nationalist Parties, they were assured of the tacit backing of the Christian Democratic Party. Economic discontent was a key factor in support given to Voldemaras and Smetona. In 1929 Smetona removed Voldemaras and established a dictatorship. The political system which developed under his leadership is difficult to define in simple terms. It certainly was nationalist, authoritarian and anti-democratic. Though some elements of a strictly Fascist regime were introduced, there appears not to have been a conscious intention to model the Lithuanian dictatorship on any other example.[8]

In Estonia, authoritarianism emerged from the economic Depression of the 1930s and the apparent impotence of the assembly to deal with its consequences. After 1929 criticism of the parliamentary system was widespread. Attempts to strengthen the executive so that it could be more decisive in dealing with the economic problems failed. The Veterans Association put forward a proposal calling for a directly elected government. The leader of the Agrarian Party, Konstantin Pats, supported this. When the proposal was endorsed by a referendum, the legal framework of a dictatorship was established. In March 1934 Pats became acting President. Pats dissolved first the Veterans Association and then the elected assembly, and postponed general elections indefinitely. Under his dictatorship, political opponents were routinely imprisoned and killed.[9]

In Latvia the establishment of a dictatorship occurred in circumstances similar to those in Estonia. Economic problems which Latvia experienced in the wake of the Depression created the preconditions for political instability. Political polarisation and conflict between the Communists and Socialists on the one extreme, and the right-wing Thunder Cross organisation on the other, paralysed all debates. In March 1934 Karlis Ulmanis, leader of the Farmers Union, supported by the nationalist movements and paramilitary organisations precipitated the fall of the government. Ulmanis then formed a new government and took action against the Left and Right. Henceforth he ruled by decree, although his actions had been supported by the Right and Centre parties on the grounds that he had defended democracy.[10]

Economic problems were the main source of discontent during the inter-war period. Governments of all three Baltic States concentrated on internal stability and reforms. These, rather than foreign relations and disputes concerning security, determined the course of political change. At the outset the single most important issue in the Baltic States was that of land ownership. In Latvia and Estonia most major landowners were German. In Lithuania, Polish and Russian landowners controlled the large estates. In all, proposals for the redistribution of land had two aims. One was to create a politically stable peasantry. The other was to reduce the economic power of foreigners, in particular the German minority. Both aims were to be achieved by the state taking over large estates and breaking them up into smaller units. Generally speaking land redistribution was successfully implemented. In due course the Baltic States managed to establish a reputation for good-quality agricultural produce which was exported to other European states, rivalling the already well-established Danish producers. The encouragement of agricultural co-operatives increased rural stability and guaranteed economic progress.[11]

Whereas the establishment of independent states gave an impetus towards land redistribution and the modernisation of agricultural production, in industry the reverse was the case. Before the First World War, the Baltic provinces had benefited from being part of the vast protected Russian market. In addition, the Baltic ports had acted as outlets for goods coming from and into Russia. The First World War devastated the area, not merely because of military activities, but also because the Russian authorities dismantled and removed industrial plants from the war zones into the interior. Workers and their families were usually expected to accompany factories thus being removed. Loss of skilled labour and industrial dislocation made post-war recovery very difficult.[12]

After the war the Baltic coast continued to be a strategic transit route for trade between Russia and the rest of the world. The German government in particular continued to take an interest in retaining a foothold in that region This was motivated by economic and military considerations.[13] The British government too, hopeful that pre-war trading patterns would be rebuilt, kept an eye on the Baltic States.[14] But the Estonian and Latvian economies never recovered from the loss of the Russian markets; in the 1930s their main export continued to be agricultural produce and timber. Their markets unfortunately were heavily affected by the world Depression, which in turn undermined confidence in post-war recovery. The political consequence of economic instability was the growth of nationalism.

In the case of Lithuania the loss of Vilnius and surrounding areas meant that the country was cut off from the Soviet Union by a strip of land controlled by Poland. As a result Lithuania was not able to benefit from the trade which subsequently developed between the Soviet Union and Europe. In comparison with Estonia and Latvia, Lithuania had very little industrial capacity and attempts to built it up during the inter-war period had only limited success.

At first glance it would seem only natural that the three Baltic States would stick together, clearly realising that their size, recent emergence as independent states, and most obviously their strategic position would be permanent sources of weakness. All three in varying degrees had reason to be apprehensive of the Soviet Union and of Germany. Latvia and Estonia, which had been drawn into the Russian Civil War and on whose territories the Soviet Union had encouraged the creation of Soviet governments, feared the Soviet Union's political interference more than that of Germany. Lithuania's territory had been part of the *Land Oberost* during the war. That period and the activities of the German freebooters immediately after the war had fanned strong anti-German sentiments in Lithuania. Unfortunately Polish occupation of the

ancient capital of Vilnius and continuing Polish–Lithuanian hostilities meant that Lithuania was more insecure than the two other
Baltic States. The aim of her foreign policy was to obtain guarantees by means of international pacts.

Thus while each of the Baltic States continued to feel unsure of
its future, there was no common agreement on how security could
be obtained, least of all because there was no shared perception as
to which of the European Powers was the real enemy and which
could be counted upon to be an ally. These basic considerations
stood in the way of the Baltic States coming together into a viable
regional security pact. While each recognised the need for such a
pact, they differed in their fear of the three powers which dominated the Baltic coast.

French and British support for the newly emerged states in Eastern Europe could never be taken for granted. In the case of the
Baltic States, the primary preoccupation was with the Soviet
Union. That determined British and French policy towards the
Baltic States. During the Russian Civil War British and French
governments had hoped that the Baltic region would act as a barrier against the spread of the Communist regime. By 1921, realising that the Soviet Union was not going to collapse, the focus
shifted away from that region. It was recognised that the Baltic
States were there to stay, though little attention was paid to their
needs. The involvement of the Royal Navy units in defending
Latvia and Estonia during the Russian Civil War encouraged a
pro-British orientation in those countries, but little was made of
this sentiment since the British government had limited use for
the region, beyond seeking to maintain trading routes to the
Soviet Union. This meant that no security assurances were given
by the government in London to the Baltic States during the inter-
war period. The Scandinavian states likewise distanced themselves from that part of the Baltic coast. With the exception of
Finland, which for historic reasons showed a passing interest in
Estonia and Latvia, Scandinavia remained aloof. Neutrality, a
formula which had been so advantageous to Sweden and Norway
during the First World War, came to be seen as the best foreign
policy option for the future.[15]

Politicians in the Baltic States were only too well aware that
they had to take the initiative in nurturing the interest of the
Great Powers in their independence. At the same time they did

investigate the possibility of regional arrangements. An important initiative towards consolidating the Baltic States was made by Zigrids Meierovics, the Latvian Minister for Foreign Affairs in the early 1920s. By all accounts Meierovics stood head and shoulders above the average East European politician. Realism seems to have been the hallmark of his policies. His aim was to stabilise the region, which meant persuading the Soviet Union that it faced no threat from the Baltic States. The representatives of five governments in the region were persuaded to attend the founding meeting of the Baltic League in August 1920. In addition to delegates from the three Baltic States there were representatives of Poland and Finland. Although he wanted Poland to be a member of the emerging Baltic League Meiereovics realised that it was important not to become involved in Polish–Soviet conflicts. On the other hand, if Lithuanian commitment to the proposal was to be secured, the Polish–Lithuanian conflict needed to be scaled down.

In March 1922, after a number of conferences, a joint accord was signed in Warsaw. The Lithuanian government was not included among the signatories and the Finnish Parliament refused to ratify the agreement. In essence the accord provided for consultations in the event of an unprovoked attack on any of the signatories. Limited though it was, the Warsaw Accord marks the high point of Baltic co-operation. It is debatable whether it was aimed at actually guaranteeing the security of any of the signatories, although it was an important factor in the signatories' negotiations with other regional powers, most notably the Soviet Union.[16]

A number of developments prevented this general agreement being translated into a fully fledged security pact with the potential to draw into its fold other states. In April 1922 Germany and the Soviet Union signed the Rapallo Treaty. While the Baltic States were alarmed at the prospect of co-operation between the two powers which dominated the region, the Western Powers reaction was to seek some form of reconciliation with Germany and the Soviet Union. In 1924 Britain and France recognised the Soviet government. This, as far as the Baltic States were concerned, signalled British and French acceptance of the Soviet Union's role in the Baltic region.

Baltic security debates naturally hinged upon the understanding of Soviet and German objectives. In addition, any debate on the subject of Baltic security had to take into account the Polish government's aspirations. The government in Warsaw had its own plans for a Baltic League but one which would have given it a dominant role in the area between Germany and the Soviet Union. Polish plans, while in principle complementary to the Meierovics plans, in reality aimed to make the Polish government the arbiter of issues relating to the Baltic States. Thus there were always potential conflicts between Poland's interests in Baltic unity. Soviet hostility towards any regional bloc in an area considered to be its sphere of influence and a vital security zone, warned Latvia against becoming too closely associated with the Meierovics initiative. The Baltic States could not ignore these hints and the prospects for the negotiation of a Baltic League were destroyed.[17] Lack of unity meant that the Soviet Union was able to manipulate each of the Baltic States in turn. The Lithuanian government was the first to sign a Non-Aggression Pact with the Soviet Union on 28 September 1926. In March 1927 a Latvian–Soviet Pact was signed. The government of Estonia refused to sign any treaty with the Soviet Union. As a result Latvian–Estonian relations, the bedrock upon which plans for regional co-operation had been briefly built, loosened and the region became more volatile and susceptible to outside pressure.

The first major change in the European balance of power came in January 1934 with the signing of the German–Polish Non-Aggression Pact. In the months preceding its signing the Poles had been approached by the Soviet Union. Moscow had been looking for ways of reducing Polish–German co-operation. Baltic politicians observed this initiative with deep distrust. They believed that the carrot which the Soviet Union was holding out to the Poles was a free hand in the Baltic region. But Josef Beck, the Polish Minister for Foreign Affairs, was not interested in negotiations with the Soviet Union. To him co-operation with Germany offered bigger opportunities. As a result of the failure to woo the Poles away from Germany the Soviet Union undertook a conciliatory approach in relation to the Baltic States. It was generally suspected that this was the outcome of a major review of foreign policy which the Kremlin had undertaken after the collapse of the Rapallo Agreement with Germany. It was noted by German diplomats that growing disenchantment with Germany had caused the Soviet Union to focus its attention on the risks posed by the Baltic States' hostility. The result was that in February 1934 the Soviet Union signalled that it no longer opposed any security agreements which the governments of the Baltic States might choose to sign among themselves. Furthermore it was indicated to the Baltic statesmen that were they to choose to proceed with regional security pacts, these would receive full Soviet approval.[18]

Having received such obvious encouragement the governments of Latvia and Estonia signed a Treaty for the Organisation of an Alliance on 17 February 1934. The door was left open for Lithuania to join. The next move was made by the Lithuanian government, which had also been affected by the changing political situation in Europe. Closer German–Polish co-operation gave rise to anxiety that Polish hostility towards Lithuania would increase. The Lithuanians believed that the Poles had been held in check hitherto by an anxiety that any action against Lithuania would be viewed by Berlin as an attempt to reduce German influence in the Baltic States. Thus in April 1934 the Lithuanian government called for the signing of a regional pact. On 3 November the three countries finally signed the Baltic Entente.

Historians are divided on the importance of this treaty. In the past it has been suggested that it was of no relevance, failing to add anything new to the earlier Baltic League concept.[19] Recently historians have been less harsh, seeing the Baltic Entente as a genuine attempt to resist the conflicting pressures which buffeted the three small states.[20] But any foreign policy decisions made by the governments of the Baltic States could not influence the course of relations between the major states dominating the region. The reality is that in 1934 the Baltic States were faced with an increasingly complex and shifting pattern of international relations. Their governments were all, in varying degrees, placed in the invidious position of being offered a choice of associating with one of the two regional powers. Whatever choice they made, it was inevitable that the other side was going to view their choice as a hostile act. Adherence to one side offered some prospect of security, but would automatically incur the hostility of the other one. At the same time it was realised that staying neutral and refusing to choose gave no guarantee of security.

Between 1934 and 1940 the Foreign Ministers of the Baltic States met 11 times. On the background of the growth of German and Italian belligerence they tried to maintain and increase co-operation. Although most politicians of the Baltic States fully realised that the League's role in upholding international agreements was slight, they subscribed to its principles, hoping thus to demonstrate their commitment to collective security. In 1936 the Spanish Civil War formed the main topic of international discussions. The Baltic politicians had to face a different problem. A disturbingly aggressive speech made by Andrey Zhdanov, the powerful Secretary of the Leningrad Communist Party, once more raised doubts about Soviet aims. Irrespective of where the Ministers for Foreign Affairs looked they saw little to comfort them. The meetings continued even when the major dilemmas facing the Baltic States proved intractable. While the meetings served no clear purpose they were nevertheless an enduring symbol of unity in a rapidly changing international situation.

The Entente was of a purely defensive character. There had been no tradition of military cooperation between the armies of the Baltic States. No attempts had been made to standardise weapons and munitions production. In fact each of the states obtained supplies from different sources. The Latvians made purchases in Britain, the Estonians in Germany and Russia, while Lithuania used German and French equipment and ammunition.[21] While the Baltic States could be counted upon to field 500 000 soldiers, the quality of manpower was considered to be low and that of the officer corps insignificant. Lack of joint military planning does not fully account for the apparent failure to underpin the political significance of the Baltic Entente with a military convention. The Estonians were anxious not to become embroiled in the Lithuanian conflict with Poland. The Vilnius and Memel issues, the latter a bone of contention with Germany, were explicitly excluded from the scope of the Entente. Thus the Entente's strength lay in providing a forum for political discussions.

In March 1938, in the wake of the German Anschluss, Poland took steps against Lithuania. The resolution of the existing political impasse with Lithuania was something the Poles had tried to deal with during the early 1930s. The establishment of diplomatic relations with Lithuania was of considerable importance to the Polish government, which aspired to regional leadership. In spite of the general satisfaction with Poland's relations with Germany,

Beck had hoped to strengthen Poland's position by building a Central European bloc. This was to form a counter to the growth of German and Soviet influence in that region. Naturally, the Poles assumed that they would play a dominant role in the scheme which came to be known as the 'Third Europe' plan. Beck's vision included the Scandinavian states, the Baltic countries, Hungary, Romania, Yugoslavia and possibly also Italy. While the Scandinavian countries showed scant interest in the plan, Lithuania's hostility towards Poland made it difficult to bring the Baltic States into the Polish sphere of influence. Beck had decided that no concessions should be made to the Lithuanians. The Polish Ministry for Foreign Affairs knew that the new Lithuanian Minister for Foreign Affairs, Stasys Lozoraitis, was in favour of opening talks with the Poles. This convinced Beck that his determination not to make concessions was correct. He maintained that the Lithuanians wanted to negotiate but needed to be pushed into this politically difficult decision.[22] The result of this reasoning was that on 11 March 1938, under the pretext of seeking an explanation for a border incident in which a Polish frontier guard had been killed, a 48-hour ultimatum was issued to the Lithuanian government demanding the resumption of diplomatic relations.

When the Lithuanian Cabinet discussed the matter, the otherwise unpalatable decision to bow to Polish pressure was made easier by an announcement from the head of the Lithuanian armed forces, General Rastikis, that the army was not capable of facing any military confrontation with the Poles. The ultimatum was accepted and in due course talks were opened.

In the autumn of 1938 the deterioration in Lithuania's relations with Germany gave added impetus to the resumption of relations with Poland. The Lithuanian government realised that without Polish support it would not be able to withstand German pressure for the return of its only sea port of Memel (Kłajpeda). The Poles were given an informal Lithuanian assurance that, were they to back her in dealings with Germany, Lithuania and the other two Baltic States would be willing to enter into political and military alliances with Poland. Unfortunately, at the end of 1938 and the beginning of 1939 the Polish Minister for Foreign Affairs was not receptive to such messages. Although Beck started having doubts about Hitler's commitment to the Polish–German Declaration of Non-Aggression, he was

confident of his ability to resolve all problems through direct negotiations with Germany.[23]

The Czechoslovak crisis and the ensuing Munich Conference
had no direct bearing on the Baltic States, but served as a warning
to them. Unity appeared to offer little benefit, in particular when
faced with a real threat. Neither the Latvian nor the Estonian governments were willing to aid Lithuania in her dispute with Poland.
Pro-Polish sentiments prevailed over any loyalty towards the
potential victim. After the Munich Conference all three Baltic
States accepted that Germany and the Soviet Union, either jointly
or individually, would determine the future course of events in the
region. It was obvious that whatever was going to be Germany's
next move, the independence of the Baltic States was bound to be
affected. After the Munich crisis the general assumption was that
Germany would next force the resolution of either the Danzig or
the Memel issues.[24]

In 1938 the activities of the German minority in the Lithuanian
city of Memel increasingly suggested that Berlin was involved in
coordinating, if not in outright directing, an anti-Lithuanian campaign. In September 1937 the Lithuanian government had expro-
priated land around Memel. Most of it had been owned by the
German community. While this appeared to have been the main
reason for conflict between Germans in Memel and the government, at the time of the Czechoslovak crisis the activities of the
Nazi party became noticeably more aggressive.[25] The situation
came to a head when the district legislature was dissolved and
new elections were called for the 11 December 1938. Ernst Neu-
mann, the Memel Gauleiter, conducted the German minority's
campaign on the assumption that the city would be incorporated
in the Reich. Nevertheless, at that stage Berlin was not willing to
sanction action which could have been viewed by the Poles as provocative. The Poles and Lithuanians were seen drawing together,
both clearly disturbed by the growth of German belligerence. Germany did not wish to accelerate this process by unnecessarily
alarming the Lithuanians. Even after the Memel Germans won
an outright majority in the elections to the district assembly,
demands for an Anschluss with Germany were played down on
instructions from Berlin.[26]

The first move towards defusing the state of tension was made
by the Lithuanian government at the end of 1938. A general

willingness to negotiate over outstanding issues was communicated to Berlin. Britain and France also tried to stabilise the situation by requesting Berlin to make a commitment to respect the status of the city port of Memel. Berlin was not willing to make any such commitment. The governments of Latvia and Estonia viewed the Memel issue with deep disquiet. They had both tried to maintain good relations with Berlin and now wished to emphasise that they would not be drawn into the conflict. Britain encouraged this attitude, hoping that the Memel issue could be treated as a minor local difficulty. In that way it was less likely to escalate into an incident which would precipitate the outbreak of a European war.

In March 1939 Hitler's troops invaded Prague. In European capitals the state of tension and foreboding was already high. It was generally known that at the same time Germany had made economic demands to Romania and that some talks had been taking place between Poland and Germany concerning Danzig. On 20 March Ribbentrop unexpectedly demanded that Lithuania cede the port of Memel and the surrounding area to Germany. By 22 March the Lithuanian government, having failed to obtain any support from neighbouring states, bowed to German pressure.[27] Germany's victory was sealed with Hitler's visit to Memel on 22 March.

Not surprisingly the Soviet Union was deeply alarmed by these developments. The spread of German control around the Baltic coast brought them closer to the militarily sensitive region of Leningrad. Even if the Polish government still appeared determined to retain its foothold in Danzig, the Soviet Union distrusted the Poles, suspecting the military regime of a willingness to support any anti-Soviet adventure on which the Nazis might embark. At this stage it appeared that the Soviet leadership still sought to consolidate its political influence over the Baltic. In the coming months the Soviet negotiators made it clear to the French and British that if the Soviet Union considered its security was threatened, it would invade the Baltic States. On 28 March all three Baltic States received assurances from Litvinov that the Soviet Union was committed to the maintenance of their independence. German actions and the Soviet reaction strained the Baltic Entente's unity to its limits. Under pressure, each state looked for powerful allies, hoping thus to deflect the aggressive intentions of what each considered to be their main adversary. Lithuania henceforth would accept German dominance; Estonia anxious about the Soviet Union sought German guarantees, while Latvia, fearful of Germany, solicited assurance from Berlin that it would respect Latvian neutrality.[28] In June 1939 German–Estonian and German–Latvian Pacts of Non-Aggression were signed. This freed the Nazi government to concentrate on its main objective. Hitler was clearly demonstrating that while it was important to secure the Baltic coast, the resolution of the Polish issue was the priority. German economic penetration of the Baltic States established a stranglehold over the region.

After the German occupation of Prague, Britain embarked on an unexpected, poorly thought-out and inconsistent policy of encouraging Eastern European states to oppose German aggression. In this plan first Poland and then the Soviet Union were seen as vital elements. Eastern European countries were to receive British moral support, though neither finance nor war materials were provided to underpin any military opposition to Germany.[29] The role of the Baltic States in this opposition only arose in the context of the Franco-British talks with the Soviet Union, which were reluctantly initiated by the British Prime Minister in May 1939. Until then the Foreign Office had, not always successfully, pressed for the government to retain trading links with the Baltic States, with a view to limiting the spread of German economic and, inevitably, also political influence. The truth was that the Foreign Office had not managed to persuade the government of the potential the Baltic States had in Britain's anti-German schemes. During the Polish–Lithuanian war of notes in 1938 and at the time of the Memel crisis in March 1939, when approached by the Lithuanians, the British government refused to get involved.

After March 1939 the Chamberlain Cabinet took the view that, although direct aid could not be offered to Eastern European states, it was desirable that they should not be drawn into the German sphere of influence and, furthermore, that they should combine together to resist German demands. The contradictions in this were painfully exposed when the Soviet Union demanded that Britain and France accept that the Soviet Union had a right to enter the territory of a neutral state to oppose German aggression against a state with which the Soviet Union had borders. What Molotov had in mind was the possibility of German penetration of the Baltic States, which he believed would only be done in preparation for an attack on the Soviet Union. The British recoiled from accepting a formula which suggested lack of respect for the sovereignty of neutral states. Chamberlain had in mind a general Anglo–Soviet agreement to oppose German aggression, not one whose precise and effective commitments might lead the German government to believe that Britain was leading in a policy of encirclement. In any case, British politicians feared that were it to be known that the British government was willing to conduct negotiations on the basis that the sovereign rights of independent states could be overlooked, the goodwill of neutral states would be lost. In the circumstances the Foreign Office warned that in addition to the Baltic States, the Balkans, Scandinavia, Belgium and Switzerland would all lose confidence in Britain. The Soviet leaders refused to see the issue of Baltic independence in separation from the threat German aggression would pose to their security. They were only prepared to continue the talks if precise circumstances were discussed and prior agreements made for action in the event of direct or indirect German aggression taking place.

At the root of British and Soviet inability to agree on the issue of Baltic independence lay a much more obvious fundamental obstacle. Franco–British political and military talks with the Soviet Union were hampered by the lack of political will to agree on joint action with the Soviet Union. Furthermore the Baltic States had repeatedly requested that Britain should not negotiate with the Soviet Union. By July the British government refused to accept the Soviet point of view. However, when faced with the prospect of a breakdown of talks, a Franco–British Military Mission was sent to Moscow to complete the military talks. The matter remained unresolved and Britain and France never agreed with the Soviet interpretation of indirect aggression. Nevertheless the real reason why the matter was not pushed to its conclusion was because, in the meantime, the Soviet Union and Germany concluded negotiations for the signing of the Non-Aggression Pact.[30]

Nazi Germany and the Soviet Union had initiated diplomatic talks after a speech made by Stalin on 10 March 1939. In it the Soviet leader made an unusual departure from previous pronouncements on the need to oppose Nazi Germany, and instead signalled the Soviet Union's willingness to negotiate with states seeking to maintain peaceful relations. Initial tentative soundings led to trade talks. On 23 August Ribbentrop arrived in Moscow to conclude negotiations for a pact. Naturally the Baltic States featured prominently in exchanges between the two sides. In conclusion Germany accepted that Finland, Estonia and Latvia were Soviet spheres of influence. The Soviet government conceded Lithuania to Germany. Following the defeat of Poland another agreement was signed by the two on 28 September. In return for a Soviet renuciation of claims to Polish territories west of the Curzon Line, Germany accepted that Lithuania would be in the Soviet sphere of influence. The Baltic people, in spite of the secrecy surrounding the treaties, rightly guessed that their fate had been agreed by Nazi Germany and the Soviet Union. But the full meaning and the implications of the pacts were far from clear.[31]

One of the consequences of Soviet–German co-operation during this period was the evacuation of ethnic Germans from Estonia and Latvia to the German-occupied territories of Poland. Already in September 1939 Hitler authorised Himmler's plans for removing Germans from the Baltic States on grounds that there they were exposed to the threat of the Soviet Union taking over the region.[32] Calculations made at the end of the war estimated that 130 000 Baltic Germans were moved into German-occupied territories. The Nazi state assumed the mantle of protector of all German communities outside the Reich. Even though the Baltic Germans had not wanted to leave areas which their ancestors had inhabited for hundreds of years, they were made to do so. To Himmler the prime concern was not their protection but the need to settle newly occupied territories.[33]

It is possible to speculate that Soviet plans for the Baltic States were not clearly formulated in September 1939. Soviet policy makers repeatedly showed that they had little respect for the concept of the territorial integrity of an independent state. Nevertheless at some point a decision was made to go beyond controlling that vital region, to incorporating the Baltic States in the Soviet Union.[34] Continuing anxiety about Germany's long-term objectives must have played a key role. In the days following the defeat of Poland, the Soviet Commissar for Foreign Affairs, Molotov, proceeded piecemeal. At the end of September and during the first week of October the Baltic leaders were invited to Moscow for discussions. All were forced to accept the Soviet Union's right to station troops and establish military bases on their territories. Anxiety about Germany was cited as the main reason for such preparations. The Estonian Minister for Foreign Affairs, Selter, arrived in Moscow on 23 September. The result was the signing of a Soviet–Estonian Pact on 28 September. On 2 October the Latvian Minister, Munters, arrived in Moscow, where he signed the Soviet–Latvian Alliance. Lithuania signed a Military Pact with the Soviet Union on 10 October.[35]

Baltic politicians made discreet attempts to sound out Germany, with a view to either halting or moderating Soviet demands. The fact that Ribbentrop refused to be drawn into the issue of Soviet relations with the Baltic States confirms that Nazi Germany and the Soviet Union were acting in accordance with prior agreements.[36] None of the Baltic States considered taking military action. That would have meant certain destruction. The recent fate of Poland acted as a warning to all European states. The lesson drawn was that negotiations with the aggressor would at worst lead to subjugation, whereas resistance meant total annihilation. The neutral states of Eastern Europe lived in hope that the worst fate which would befall them would be similar to that which befell Czechoslovakia. Nazi policies in the Czech and Slovak territories appeared to be mild whereas Poland from the outset was subject to harsh treatment.

On 30 November 1939 the Soviet Union attacked Finland. During the Soviet–Finnish War the Baltic States decided to adhere to strict neutrality. When the case of the Soviet attack was surprisingly referred to the League of Nations, the Baltic delegates jointly abstained from the vote to expel the Soviet Union. One could argue that these were insignificant gestures. They were nevertheless an attempt to maintain a precarious independence.

Military setbacks faced by the Red Army during the war with Finland, combined with the German successes in France in May 1940, had a bearing on the Soviet decision to complete the process of establishing control over the Baltic States. Soviet pronouncements had been a confusing mixture of ideological threats and demands for military facilities. In mid-June 1940 Soviet policy makers decided to clear up the Baltic issue. Lithuania was first accused of being anti-Soviet and of having conspired with Estonia and Latvia to transform the Baltic Entente into an anti-Soviet treaty. On 14 June Molotov instructed the Lithuanian government to dismiss those who were responsible for the anti-Soviet policy and to allow the Red Army free access to Lithuanian territory. After discussing the issue and aware of the fact that the army did not wish to oppose the Soviet demands, the Lithuanian government accepted the Soviet conditions.[37]

Although the Latvian government was repeatedly reassured that the Soviet Union's disagreements with its Lithuanian counterpart would have no bearing on relations with Latvia, on 16 June similar accusations were levelled against the Ulmanis Government. The Latvian government accepted the demand to form a new government and to allow the Red Army right of entry on to its territory.[38] The Estonian government received an ultimatum which was in all respects similar to the ones which had been issued to the governments in Lithuania and Latvia. This was reluctantly accepted.[39]

At the same time the Soviet authorities went to great lengths to give their actions the appearance of a popular expression of support for the Soviet Union. Communists organised demonstrations and stage-managed rallies took place. General elections were called and duly took place on 14–15 July. The presence of the Soviet secret service and the Red Army ensured that the newly elected governments did as they were instructed. They all duly requested incorporation into the Soviet Union. There is no doubt that all the events of the summer of 1940 were organised in Moscow by Andrey Zhdanov.[40] The Red Army, which had already been allowed to occupy strategic points after September 1939, assumed total control of the Baltic States by 1 August. Germany occupied the Baltic States as a result of military victories in June 1941. The three states became German Protectorates.

Although the British and American governments did not accept the legality of the process, the issue was not one which they could fruitfully discuss with the Soviet government. After the German attack on the Soviet Union in June 1941, the question of the restoration of the Baltic States became an issue in British–US relations with the Soviet Union. Nevertheless in the context of war-time co-operation, in particular because the Soviet Union carried the brunt of fighting against Nazi Germany in Europe, it was inevitable that the Soviet refusal to make commitments to the restoration of the Baltic States could not be allowed to cloud relations between the war-time allies. It was accepted that the post-war fate of the Baltic States would be determined by the Soviet Union.

Notes and References

1. FRIENDS? FRANCE AND BRITAIN

1. W. Sukiennicki, *East Central Europe during World War I: From Foreign Domination to National Independence*, Vol. II, East European Monographs, Boulder, 1984, pp. 911–13.
2. P. S. Wandycz, *France and Her Eastern Allies, 1919–1925: French–Czechoslovak–Polish Relations from the Paris Peace Conference to Locarno*, University of Minnesota Press, Minneapolis, 1962, pp. 11–16.
3. Ibid., pp. 46–8.
4. Ibid., pp. 193–4.
5. Ibid., pp. 216–18.
6. M. Alexander, *The Republic in Danger. General Maurice Gamelin and the Politics of French Defence, 1933–1940*, Cambridge University Press, Cambridge, 1992, pp. 306–9.
7. P. S. Wandycz, *The Twilight of French Eastern Alliances, 1926–1936: French–Czechoslovak–Polish Relations from Locarno to the Remilitarization of the Rhineland*, Princeton University Press, Princeton, 1988, pp. 397–400.
8. R. J. Young, *In Command of France. French Foreign Policy and Military Planning, 1933–1940*, Harvard University Press, Cambridge, Massachusetts, 1978, pp. 92–6.
9. Ibid., pp. 96–8.
10. P. S. Wandycz, *The Twilight of French Eastern Alliances, 1926–1936*, pp. 422–31.
11. Ibid., p. 446.
12. R. J. Young, *France and the Origins of the Second World War*, Macmillan, Basingstoke, 1996, pp. 14–17.
13. J. Nere, *The Foreign Policy of France from 1914 to 1945*, Routledge & Kegan Paul, London, 1974, pp. 71–6.
14. P. S. Wandycz, *France and Her Eastern Allies, 1919–1925*, pp. 366–7.
15. N. Jordan, *The Popular Front and Central Europe: The Dilemmas of French Impotence, 1918–1940*, Cambridge University Press, Cambridge, 1992, pp. 68–9.
16. R. J. Young, *In Command of France*, pp. 122–9.
17. N. Jordan, *The Popular Front and Central Europe*, pp. 98–107.
18. Ibid., pp. 183–4.
19. M. S. Alexander, *The Republic in Danger*, pp. 306–11.

20. Ibid., 303–4.
21. R. J. Young, *In Command of France*, pp. 195–8.
22. N. Jordan *The Popular Front and Central Europe*, pp. 274–9.
23. Ibid., pp. 207–13.
24. A. Adamthwaite, *France and the Coming of the Second World War 1936–1939*, Frank Cass, London, 1977, pp. 227–9.
25. Ibid., pp. 227–9.
26. Ibid., p. 228.
27. M. S. Alexander *The Republic in Danger*, p. 11.
28. R. J. Young, *France and the Origins of the Second World War*, pp. 130–1.
29. M. S. Alexander, *The Republic in Danger*, pp. 351–6.
30. W. Sukiennicki, *East Central Europe During World War I: From Foreign Domination to National Independence*, Vol. I, East European Monographs, Boulder, New York, 1984, pp. 163–72.
31. B. Bond, *British Military Policy between the Two World Wars*, Clarendon Press, Oxford, 1980, pp. 24–32.
32. Ibid., pp. 75–8.
33. M. Howard, *The Continental Commitment: The Dilemma of British Defence Policy in the Era of Two World Wars*, Pelican, London, 1974, pp. 114–19.
34. B. Bond, *British Military Policy between the Two World Wars*, pp. 248–52.
35. B. Bond, *British Military Policy between the Two World Wars*, pp. 225–9.
36. I. Colvin, *The Chamberlain Cabinet*, Victor Gollancz Ltd, London, 1971, pp. 102–15.
37. Ibid., pp. 135–45.
38. D. C. Watt, *How War Came: The Immediate Origins of the Second World War, 1938–1939*, Heinemann, London, 1989, pp. 148–52.
39. Bernd-Jurgen Wendt, ' "Economic Appeasement" – a Crisis Strategy', in W. J. Mommsen and L. Kettenacker (eds), *The Fascist Challenge and the Policy of Appeasement*, George Allen & Unwin, London, 1983, pp. 157–72.
40. D. E. Kaiser, *Economic Diplomacy and the Origins of the Second World War*, Princeton University Press, Princeton, New Jersey, 1980, pp. 11–12.
41. Ibid., pp. 80–99.
42. Ibid, pp. 170–5.
43. Ibid., 175–96.
44. G. C. Pender, *British Rearmament and the Treasury, 1932–1939*, Scottish Academic Press, Edinburgh, 1979, pp. 100–5.
45. Ibid., 303–9.
46. Ibid., pp. 303–4.
47. Bernd-Jurgen Wendt ' "Economic Appeasement" – A Crisis Strategy', p. 169.
48. M. Howard, *The Continental Commitment*, pp. 74–8.
49. Ibid., pp. 284–5.

50. Ibid, pp. 300–4.
51. Ibid., pp. 328–30.
52. A. J. Prażmowska, *Britain, Poland and the Eastern Front, 1939*, Cambridge University Press, Cambridge, 1987, pp. 80–8.
53. Ibid., p. 81.
54. Ibid., p. 82.
55. Ibid., pp. 80–100.
56. R. Douglas, *The Advent of War, 1939–40*, Macmillan Press, London, 1978, pp. 23–8.
57. A. J. Prażmowska, *Britain, Poland and the Eastern Front, 1939*, pp. 142–50.
58. Ibid., pp. 33–41.
59. D. C. Watt, *How War Came: The Immediate Origins of the Second World War, 1938–1939*, pp. 454–60.
60. A. J. Prażmowska, *Britain, Poland and the Eastern Front,1939*, pp. 179–81.
61. A. J. Prażmowska, *Britain and Poland 1939–1943: The Betrayed Ally*, Cambridge University Press, Cambridge 1995, pp. 49–53.

2. THE SOVIET UNION: THE IDEOLOGICAL ENEMY?

1. T. J. Uldricks, *Diplomacy and Ideology: The Origins of Soviet Foreign Relations, 1917–1930*, Sage, London, 1979, pp. 27–8.
2. M. Light, *The Soviet Theory of International Relations*, Wheatsheaf, Guildford, 1988, pp. 27–31.
3. Ibid., pp. 31–43.
4. E. H. Carr, *The Bolshevik Revolution, 1917–1923*, Vol. 3, Pelican Books, London, 1988, pp. 21–8.
5. R. K. Debo, *Survival and Consolidation: The Foreign Policy of Soviet Russia, 1918–1921*, McGill-Queen's University Press, Montreal & Kingston, 1992, pp. 106–10.
6. E. H. Carr, *The Bolshevik Revolution, 1917–1923*, Vol. 3, p. 53.
7. Ibid., pp. 128–40.
8. Ibid., p. 403.
9. E. H. Carr, in *The Bolshevik Revolution, 1917–1923*, Vol. 3, p. 220, suggests that the Polish–Soviet war and the failure of the Polish offensive in August 1920 marked the end of the naive conviction that the Red Army could sweep forward into Western Europe and by its presence unleash revolutionary forces. I. Deutscher, in *Stalin: A Political Biography*, Oxford University Press, Oxford, 1961, agrees with this view. R. K. Debo, *Survival and Consolidation*, pp. 153–5, suggests that the Soviet leaders had made the decision to enter into direct talks with the Western Powers at the beginning of 1920. During trade talks with Britain the Soviet Union indicated its wish to normalise relations.

10. R. K. Debo, *Survival and Consolidation*, pp. 192–3.
11. E. H. Carr, *The Bolshevik Revolution*, Vol. 3, pp. 214–17.
12. Ibid., pp. 218–20.
13. Ibid., pp. 132–4.
14. K. McDermott and J. Agnew, *The Comintern: A History of International Communism from Lenin to Stalin*, Macmillan, Basingstoke, 1996, p. 23.
15. Ibid., pp. 45–9.
16. T. J. Uldricks, *Diplomacy and Ideology*, pp. 157–60.
17. I. Deutscher, *Stalin*, p. 391.
18. Ibid., pp. 404–6.
19. R. K. Debo, *Revolution and Survival: The Foreign Policy of Soviet Russia, 1917–18*, Liverpool University Press, Liverpool, 1979, pp. 211–29.
20. G. F. Kennan, *Soviet Foreign Policy, 1917–1941*, D. van Nostrand, Princeton, 1960, pp. 39–41.
21. J. Haslam, *Soviet Foreign Policy, 1930–1933*, Macmillan, Basingstoke, 1983, pp. 67–70.
22. Ibid., pp. 97–106.
23. T. J. Uldricks, 'Soviet Security Policy in the 1930s', in G. Gorodetsky (ed.), *Soviet Foreign Policy, 1917–1991: A Retrospective*, Frank Cass, London, 1994, pp. 65–74.
24. J. Haslam, *The Soviet Union and the Struggle for Collective Security in Europe, 1933–1939*, Macmillan, Basingstoke, 1984, pp. 36–7.
25. Ibid., pp. 48–51.
26. H. Bulhak, 'Polska a Rumunia 1918–1939' in H. Bulhak, T. Cieślak et al. (eds), *Przyjaźnie i antagonizmy. Stosunki Polski z państwami sąsiednimi w latach 1918–1939*, Zakład Narodowy Imienia Ossolińskich, PAN, Wrocław, 1977, pp. 333–7.
27. D. Lungu, *Romania and the Great Powers, 1933–1940*, Duke University Press, Durham, 1989, pp. 99–103.
28. K. McDermot and J. Agnew, *The Comintern*, pp. 134–8.
29. I. Deutscher, *Stalin*, pp. 422–5.
30. Ibid., pp. 423–4.
31. J. Haslam, *The Soviet Union and the Struggle for Collective Security*, pp. 110–14.
32. Ibid., pp. 120–4.
33. I. Deutscher, *Stalin*, pp. 378–80.
34. J. Erickson, *The Soviet High Command: A Military–Political History, 1918–1941*, Westview, Boulder, p. 465.
35. J. Haslam, *The Soviet Union and the Struggle for Collective Security*, pp. 158–60.
36. Ibid., p. 162.
37. Ibid., pp. 164–5.
38. Ibid., pp. 215–16.

39. A. J. Prażmowska, *Britain, Poland and the Eastern Front, 1939*, pp. 137–40.
40. J. Haslam, *The Soviet Union and the Struggle for Collective Security*, pp. 225–9.
41. G. Roberts, *The Soviet Union and the Origins of the Second World War: Russo–German Relations and the Road to War, 1933–1941*, St Martin's Press, New York, 1995, pp. 72–81.
42. A. Read and D. Fisher, *The Deadly Embrace: Hitler, Stalin and the Nazi–Soviet Pact, 1939–1941*, W.W. Norton, New York, 1988, pp. 250–6.
43. P. Salmon, 'Great Britain, the Soviet Union and Finland at the beginning of the Second World War', in J. Hiden and Th. Lane (eds), *The Baltic and the Outbreak of the Second World War*, Cambridge University Press, Cambridge, 1992, pp. 96–101.
44. J. Erickson, *The Soviet High Command*, pp. 542–52.
45. Ibid., pp. 552–5.
46. G. Roberts, *The Soviet Union and the Origins of the Second World War: Russo–German Relations and the Road to War, 1933–1941*, pp. 106–11.
47. D. Lungu, *Romania and the Great Powers, 1933–1940*, p. 231.
48. J. Erickson, *The Soviet High Command*, pp. 578–9.

3. CZECHOSLOVAKIA

1. V. S. Mamatey, 'The Establishment of the Republic', in V. S. Mamatey and R. Luza (eds), *A History of the Czechoslovak Republic, 1918–1948*, Princeton University Press, Princeton, New Jersey, 1973, pp. 5–10.
2. Ibid., pp. 3–5.
3. A. Komjathy and R. Stockwell, *German Minorities and the Third Reich*, Holmes & Meier, New York, 1980, pp. 17–18.
4. V. S. Mamatey, 'The Establishment of the Republic', pp. 10–12.
5. V. Olivova, *The Doomed Democracy: Czechoslovakia in a Disrupted Europe, 1914–38*, Sidgwick & Jackson, London, 1972, pp. 29–34.
6. Ibid., pp. 38–40.
7. V. S. Mamatey, 'The Establishment of the Republic", pp. 22–7.
8. V. S. Mamatey, 'The Establishment of the Republic", pp. 27–30; J.W. Bruegel, *Czechoslovakia before Munich: The German Minority Problem and British Appeasement Policy*, Cambridge University Press, Cambridge, 1973, pp. 22–37.
9. J.W. Bruegel, *Czechoslovakia before Munich*, pp. 38–47.
10. V. Olivova, *The Doomed Democracy*, pp. 107–17.
11. V.S. Mamatey, 'The Development of Czechoslovak Democracy 1920–1938', in V. S. Mamatey and R. Luza, *A History of the Czechoslovak Republic*, pp. 108–9.
12. Ibid., pp. 156–60.

13. A. Teichova and P. L. Cottrell, 'Industrial Structures in West and East Central Europe during the Inter-war Period', in A. Teichova and P. L. Cottrell (eds), *International Business and Central Europe, 1918–1939*, Leicester University Press, St. Martin's Press, New York, 1983, pp. 40–1.

14. D. H. El Mallakh, *The Slovak Autonomy Movement, 1935–1939: A Study in Unrelenting Nationalism*, East European Quarterly, Boulder, 1979, pp. 45–9.

15. Ibid., p. 54–7.

16. V. S. Mamatey, 'The Development of Czechoslovak Democracy, 1920–1938', pp. 156–7.

17. D. H. El Mallakh, *The Slovak Autonomy Movement, 1935–1939*, pp. 113–28.

18. Ibid., pp. 129–35.

19. Ibid., p. 217.

20. J. W. Bruegel, *Czechoslovakia before Munich*, pp. 65–73.

21. R. Luza, *The Transfer of the Sudeten Germans: A Study of Czech–German Relations, 1933–1936*, Routledge & Kegan Paul, London, 1964, p. 40.

22. A. Komjathy and R. Stockwell, *German Minorities and the Third Reich*, pp. 20–1.

23. Ibid., pp. 20–1.

24. Ibid., pp. 21–3.

25. J. W. Bruegel, *Czechoslovakia before Munich*, pp. 144–50.

26. A. Komjathy and R. Stockwell, *German Minorities and the Third Reich*, pp. 33–6.

27. P. S. Wandycz, 'Foreign Policy of Edvard Beneš, 1918–1938', in V. S. Mamatey and R. Luza (eds), *A History of the Czechoslovak Republic, 1918–1948*, pp. 216–20.

28. J. Kozeński, *Czechosłowacja w Polskiej Polityce Zagranicznej w latach 1932–1938*, Instytut Zachodni, Poznań, 1964, pp. 33–4.

29. Z. Zeman with A. Klimek, *The Life of Edvard Beneš, 1884–1948*, Clarendon Press, Oxford, 1997, pp. 88–91.

30. J. Kozeński, *Czechosłowacja w Polskiej Polityce Zagranicznej w latach 1932–1938*, pp. 35–9.

31. P. S. Wandycz, 'Foreign Policy of Edvard Beneš, 1918–1938', p. 226.

32. J. Kozeński, *Czechosłowacja w Polskiej Polityce*, pp. 32–3.

33. Ibid., pp. 56–61.

34. J. W. Brugel, *Czechoslovakia before Munich*, p. 175–83.

35. Ibid., pp. 184–6.

36. A. Komjathy and R. Stockwell, *German Minorities and the Third Reich*, pp. 30–2.

37. Ibid., pp. 33–6.

38. N. Henderson, *Failure of a Mission: Berlin 1937–1939*, London, 1940, pp. 130–3.

39. Z. Zeman with A. Klimek, *The Life of Edvard Beneš, 1884–1948*, pp. 122–3.

40. J. Kozeński, *Czechosłowacja w polskiej polityce zagranicznej w latach 1932–1938*, pp. 127–8.
41. Ibid., pp. 254–5.
42. Ibid., pp. 267–70.
43. R. Luza, *The Transfer of the Sudeten Germans: A Study of Czech–German Relations, 1933–1962*, pp. 145–50.
44. A. J. Prażmowska, 'Poland's Foreign Policy: September 1938–1939', *Historical Journal*, Vol. 29, No. 4 (1986), pp. 856–7.
45. Th. Prochazka, 'The Second Republic, 1938–1939', in V. S. Mamatey and R. Luza, *A History of Czechoslovak Republic, 1918–1948*, pp. 257–9.

4. ROMANIA

1. S. Fischer-Galati, *20th Century Rumania*, 2nd ed., Columbia University Press, New York, 1991, pp. 218–25.
2. K. Hitchins, *Rumania, 1866–1947*, Clarendon Press, Oxford, 1994, pp. 142–8.
3. Ibid., pp. 150–4.
4. E. Boia, *Romania's Diplomatic Relations with Yugoslavia in the Interwar Period, 1919–1941*, East European Monographs, Boulder, 1993, p. 25.
5. Ibid., p. 25.
6. Ibid., pp. 63–4.
7. H. Roberts, *Rumania: Political Problems of an Agrarian State*, Oxford University Press, Oxford, 1951, pp. 50–5.
8. Ibid., pp. 69–70.
9. M. Pearton, *Oil and the Romanian State*, Clarendon Press, Oxford, 1971, pp. 96–8.
10. H. L. Roberts, *Rumania: Political Problems of an Agrarian State*, pp. 97–100.
11. S. Fisher-Galati, 'Fascism in Romania', in P. F. Sugar (ed.), *Native Fascism in the Successor States, 1918–1945*, ABS-CLIO, Santa Barbara, 1971, pp. 112–17.
12. D. E. Kaiser, *Economic Diplomacy and the Origins of the Second World War: Germany, Britain, France, and Eastern Europe, 1930–1939*, Princeton University Press, Princeton, 1980, pp. 73–80.
13. Ibid., pp. 130–8.
14. Ibid., pp. 158–9.
15. Ibid., pp. 264–5.
16. M. Pearton, *Oil and the Romanian State*, pp. 189–97.
17. D. Kaiser, *Economic Diplomacy and the Origins of the Second World War*, pp. 264–73.
18. Ibid., pp. 266–70.

19. K. Hitchins, *Rumania, 1866–1946*, pp. 434–7.
20. E. Boia, *Romania's Diplomatic Relations with Yugoslavia in the Interwar Period, 1919–1941*, pp. 76–7.
21. Ibid., pp. 126–7.
22. D. B. Lungu, *Romania and the Great Powers, 1933–1940*, Duke University Press, Durham, 1989, pp. 52–6.
23. Ibid., pp. 55–6.
24. Ibid., pp. 103–7.
25. H. L. Roberts, *Rumania: Political Problems of an Agrarian State*, pp. 214–16.
26. D. B. Lungu, *Romania and the Great Powers, 1933–1940*, p. 151.
27. Ibid., pp. 120–4.
28. S. Fisher-Galati, 'Fascism in Romania', p. 118.
29. A. Komjathy and R. Stockwell, *German Minorities and the Third Reich: Ethnic Germans and East Central Europe between the Wars*, Holmes & Meier, New York, 1980, pp. 115–20.
30. K. Hitchins, *Rumania, 1866–1947*, pp. 437–9.
31. H. Bulhak, 'Polska a Rumunia 1918–1939', in H. Bulhak, T. Cieślak et.al. (eds), *Przyjaźnie i Antagonizmy. Stosunki Polski z państwami sąsiednimi w latach 1918–1939*, Narodowy Zakład Imienia Ossolińskich, Wrocław, 1977, pp. 336–9.
32. Ibid., pp. 338–40.
33. D. B. Lungu, *Romania and the Great Powers*, pp. 124–5.
34. Ibid., pp. 151–8.
35. H. L. Roberts, *Rumania: Political Problems of an Agrarian State*, p. 215.
36. D. B. Lungu, *Romania and the Great Powers, 1933–1940*, pp. 170–3.
37. D. C. Watt, *How War Came: The Immediate Origins of the Second World War, 1938–1939*, Heinemann, London, 1989, pp. 271–88.
38. Ibid., pp. 174–91.
39. Valeriu Florin Dobrinescu, *The Diplomatic Struggle over Bessarabia*, The Center for Romanian Studies, The Romanian Cultural Foundation, Iaéi, 1996, pp. 67–71.
40. Ibid., pp. 74–6.
41. Ibid., p. 155.
42. K. Hitchins, *Rumania, 1866–1947*, p. 444.
43. Ibid., pp. 204–6.
44. Valeriu Florin Dobrinescu, *The Diplomatic Struggle over Bessarabia*, pp. 155–7.
45. Ibid., pp. 163–5.
46. Ibid., pp. 447–50.
47. M. Pearton, *Oil and the Romanian State*, pp. 223–6.
48. E. Boia, *Romania's Diplomatic Relations with Yugoslavia*, pp. 294–8.
49. S. Fischer-Galati, *20th Century Rumania*, pp. 64–9.

5. POLAND

1. R. Leslie (ed.) *The History of Poland since 1863*, Cambridge University Press, Cambridge, 1980, pp. 110–17.
2. Ibid., pp. 125–9.
3. A. Garlicki, *Józef Piłsudski, 1867–1935*, Scolar Press, Aldershot, 1995, pp. 89–105.
4. K. Lundgreen-Nielsen, *The Polish Problem at the Paris Peace Conference: A Study of the Policies of the Great Powers and the Poles, 1918–1919*, Odense University Press, Odense, 1979, pp. 233–45; P. Wandycz, 'Dmowski's Policy at the Paris Peace Conference: Success or Failure?', in P. Latawski (ed.), *The Reconstruction of Poland, 1914–1923*, Macmillan, Basingstoke, 1992, pp. 117–29.
5. A. M. Cienciała and Titus Komarnicki, *From Versailles to Locarno: Keys to Polish Foreign Policy, 1919–1925*, University Press of Kansas, Lawrence, Kansas, 1984, pp. 59–90.
6. Z. Landau, 'The Economic Integration of Poland, 1918–1923', in P. Latawski (ed.), *The Reconstruction of Poland, 1914–1923*, pp. 133–44.
7. Z. Landau and J. Tomaszewski, *Trudna niepodległość. Rozważania o gospodarce Polski 1918–1939*, Książka i Wiedza, Warsaw, 1978, pp. 63–71.
8. A. Polonsky, *Politics in Independent Poland 1921–1939*, Clarendon Press, Oxford, 1972, pp. 455–9.
9. A. Garlicki, *Józef Piłsudski, 1867–1935*, pp. 145–59.
10. A. Polonsky, *Politics in Independent Poland*, pp. 483–93.
11. A. Cineciała, *From Versailles to Locarno*, pp. 19–40.
12. A. Cienciała, *From Versailles to Locarno*, pp. 255–75.
13. A. J. Prażmowska, 'The Role of Danzig in Polish–German Relations on the Eve of the Second World War', in J. Hiden and T. Lane (eds), *The Baltic and the Outbreak of the Second World War*, Cambridge University Press, Cambridge, 1992, pp. 74–86.
14. A. J. Prażmowska, 'Poland's Foreign Policy: September 1938–September 1939', *The Historical Journal*, Vol.29, No. 4. (1986), pp. 853–73.
15. Paweł Starzeński, *Trzy lata z Beckiem*, Polska Fundacja Kulturalna, London, 1972, pp. 160–6.
16. M. Jedrzejewicz (ed.), *Diplomat in Berlin, 1933–1938: Papers and Memoirs of Josef Lipski, Ambassador of Poland*, New York, Columbia University Press, 1969, pp. 453–4.
17. *Official Documents Concerning Polish–German and Polish–Soviet Relations, 1933–1939*, Ministry for Foreign Affairs, the Polish Government, London, 1940, Doc. 34, pp. 41–2; Doc. 36, pp. 43–4.
18. O. Terlecki, *Pulkownik Beck*, Krajowa Agencja Wydawnicza, Kraków, 1985, pp. 233–8.

19. A. J. Prażmowska, *Britain, Poland and the Eastern Front, 1939*, Cambridge University Press, Cambridge, 1987, pp. 38–56.
20. Ibid., pp. 861–73.
21. A. Ciechała, *Poland and the Western Powers, 1938–1939: A Study in the Interdependence of Waster and Western Europe*, Routledge and Kegan Paul, London, 1968; pp. 26–8; P. S. Wandycz, *The Twilight of French Eastern Alliances, 1926–1936*, pp. 438–45.
22. D. E. Kaiser, *Economic Diplomacy and the Origins of the Second World War*, Princeton University Press, Princeton, 1980, pp. 208–12.
23. Ibid., pp. 210–12.
24. A. J. Prażmowska, 'Poland's Foreign Policy', pp. 862–5.
25. A. J. Prażmowska, *Britain, Poland and the Eastern Front, 1939*, pp. 47–56.
26. Ibid., pp. 865–72.
27. Ibid., pp. 80–105.
28. Marek Tarczyński (ed.), *Wacław Stachiewicz. Wierności dochować żołnierskiej*, Oficyna Wydawnicza 'Rytm', Warszawa, 1998, pp. 115–20.
29. Ibid., 102–5.
30. Ibid., 107–34.
31. A. J. Prażmowska, 'Poland's Foreign Policy: September 1938–September 1939', pp. 870 1.
32. J. Haslam, *The Soviet Union and the Struggle for Collective Security in Europe, 1933–1939*, Macmillan, London, 1984.
33. A. J. Prażmowska, *Britain, Poland and the Eastern Front*, pp. 147–50.
34. Marek Tarczyński (ed.), *Wacław Stachiewicz*, pp. 127–31.
35. A. J. Prażmowska *Britain and Poland, 1939–1943: The Betrayed Ally*, Cambridge University Press, Cambridge 1995, pp. 1–8.

6. HUNGARY

1. C. M. Macartney, *October Fifteenth: A History of Modern Hungary, 1929–1945*, Edinburgh University Press, Edinburgh, 1956, pp. 8–10.
2. Ibid., pp. 12–15.
3. M. Ormos, *From Padua to the Trianon, 1918–1920*, Social Science Monographs, Boulder, Colorado, 1990, p. 22.
4. Ibid., pp. 28–31.
5. P. Pastor, *Hungary between Wilson and Lenin: The Hungarian Revolution of 1918–1919 and the Big Three*, East European Quarterly, Boulder, 1976, pp. 25–8.
6. Ibid., pp. 38–42.
7. M. Ormos, *From Padua to the Trianon, 1918–1920*, pp. 53–62.
8. G. Juhasz, *Hungary's Foreign Policy, 1919–1945*, Akademia Kiado, Budapest, 1979, p. 20.

9. Ibid., pp. 22–3.
10. M. Ormos, *From Padua to the Trianon, 1918–1920*, pp. 240–1.
11. G. Juhasz, *Hungarian Foreign Policy, 1919–1945*, pp. 22–3.
12. C. A. Macartney, *October Fifteenth: A History of Modern Hungary, 1929–1945*, p. 4.
13. G. Juhasz, *Hungarian Foreign Policy, 1919–1945*, pp. 49–50.
14. L. Dombrady 'Trianon and Hungarian National Defense', in B. K. Kiraly and L. Veszpremy (eds), *Trianon and East Central Europe. Antecedents and Repercussions: War and Society in East Central Europe*, Vol. XXXII, Social Science Monographs, Boulder, 1995, pp. 261–2.
15. Ibid., pp. 264–6.
16. M. Molnar, *From Bela Kun to Janos Kadar: Seventy Years of Hungarian Communism*, Berg, Oxford, 1990, pp. 14–29.
17. C.A. Macartney, *October Fifteenth: A History of Modern Hungary, 1929–1945*, pp. 26–9.
18. M. Molnar, *From Bela Kun to Janos Kadar*, pp. 56–7.
19. M.C. Macartney, *October Fifteenth: A History of Modern Hungary, 1929–1945*, pp. 36–45.
20. Ibid., pp. 46–60.
21. F.L. Carsten, *The Rise of Fascism*, Methuen, London, 1970, pp. 173–81.
22. G. Juhasz, *Hungarian Foreign Policy, 1919–1945*, pp. 55–7.
23. Ibid., pp. 59–65.
24. C.A. Macartney, *October Fifteenth: A History of Modern Hungary, 1929–1945*, pp. 85–8.
25. Ibid., pp. 137–40.
26. G. Juhasz, *Hungarian Foreign Policy, 1919–1945*, pp. 114–15.
27. Ibid., pp. 137–9.
28. M. Koźminski, *Polska i Węgry przed drugą wojna Światową (Październik 1938 – Wrzesień 1939). Z dziejów dyplomacji i irredenty*, Zakład Narodowy Imienia Ossolińskich, Wydawnictwo Polskiej Akademii Nauk, Wrocław, 1970, pp. 48–52.
29. D. E. Kaiser, *Economic Diplomacy and the Origins of the Second World War: Germany, Britain, France, and Eastern Europe, 1930–1939*, Princeton University Press, Princeton, 1980, pp. 155–7.
30. Ibid., pp. 176–177.
31. G. Juhasz, *Hungarian Foreign Policy, 1919–1945*, pp. 131–3.
32. Ibid., pp. 54–7.
33. Ibid., p. 58.
34. Ibid., pp. 141–3.
35. Ibid., pp. 143–4.
36. M. Koźminski, *Polska i Węgry przed drugą wojna światową*, pp. 166–71.
37. Ibid., p. 227.
38. G. Juhasz, *Hungarian Foreign Policy, 1919–1945*, pp. 158–9.

39. Ibid., p. 159.
40. M. Koźminski, *Polska i Węgry przed drugą wojną światową*, pp. 319–20.
41. G. Juhasz, *Hungarian Foreign Policy, 1919–1945*, pp. 163–5.
42. N. A. F. Dreiszinger, *Hungary's Way to World War II*, Hungarian Herlicon Society, Toronto, 1968, pp. 118–19.
43. Ibid., pp. 121–3.
44. G. Juhasz, *Hungarian Foreign Policy, 1919–1945*, pp. 172–5.
45. N.A.F. Dreisziger, *Hungary's Way to World War II*, pp. 138–45.
46. G. Juhasz, *Hungarian Foreign Policy, 1919–1945*, p. 182.

7. THE BALKANS: YUGOSLAVIA, ALBANIA, BULGARIA

1. H. L. Roberts, 'Politics in a Small State: The Balkan Example', in C. and B. Jelavich (eds), *The Balkans in Transition: Essays on the Development of Balkan Life and Politics since the Eighteenth Century*, Archon Books, Hampden, Connecticut, 1974, pp. 384–9.
2. B. Jelavich, *History of the Balkans: Twentieth Century*, Vol. 2, Cambridge University Press, Cambridge, 1983, pp. 95–7.
3. Ibid, pp. 96–100.
4. H. L. Roberts, 'Politics in a Small State: The Balkan Example', pp. 390–3.
5. A. N. Dragnich, *The First Yugoslavia: Search for a Viable Political System*, Hoover Institution Press, Stanford University, Stanford, 1983, pp. 6–7.
6. I. J. Lederer, *Yugoslavia at the Paris Peace Conference: A Study in Frontiermaking*, Yale University Press, New Haven, 1963, pp. 5–14.
7. Ibid., pp. 6–9.
8. Ibid., pp. 29–35.
9. Ibid., pp. 41–5.
10. A. N. Dragnich, *The First Yugoslavia*, pp. 57–73.
11. I. J. Lederer, *Yugoslavia at the Paris Peace Conference*, pp. 306–8.
12. F. Singleton, *Twentieth-Century Yugoslavia*, Macmillan, London, 1976, pp. 80–1.
13. J. B. Hoptner, *Yugoslavia in Crisis, 1934–1941*, Columbia University Press, New York, 1963, pp. 22–4.
14. Ibid., pp. 41–3.
15. F. C. Littlefield, *Germany and Yugoslavia, 1933–1941*, East European Monographs, Columbia University Press, New York, 1988, pp. 25–30.
16. Ibid., pp. 34–5.
17. Ibid., pp. 52–5.

18. J. B. Hoptner, *Yugoslavia in Crisis, 1934–1941*, pp. 109–13.
19. A. Garlicka, *Polska–Jugoslavia 1934–1939. Z Dziejów Stosunków politycznych*, Zakład Narodowy Im. Ossolińskich, Wrocław, 1977, pp. 156–7.
20. Ibid., p. 160.
21. Ibid., 117–19.
22. Ibid., pp. 178–9.
23. J. B. Hoptner, *Yugoslavia in Crisis, 1934–1941*, pp. 170–2.
24. F. C. Littlefield, *Germany and Yugoslavia, 1933–1941*, pp. 77–8.
25. Ibid., pp. 89–90.
26. M. Vickers, *The Albanians: A Modern History*, I.B. Tauris, London, 1995, pp. 65–71.
27. Ibid., pp. 79–81.
28. Ibid., pp. 85–7.
29. S. Paollo and A. Puto, *The History of Albania from its Origins to the Present Day*, Routledge and Kegan Paul, London, 1981, pp. 164–6.
30. M. Vickers, *The Albanians: A Modern History*, p. 96.
31. B. Jurgen Fischer, *King Zog and the Struggle for Stability in Albania*, East European Monographs, Boulder, 1984, pp. 127–38.
32. M. Vickers, *The Albanians: A Modern History*, pp. 118–19.
33. S. Pollo and A. Puto, *The History of Albania*, pp. 200–3.
34. Ibid., pp. 208–11.
35. B. Jurgen Fischer, *King Zog and the Struggle for Stability in Albania*, p. 293.
36. C. and B. Jelavic, *The Establishment of the Balkan National States, 1804–1920*, University of Washington Press, Seattle, 1977, pp. 153–7.
37. R. J. Crampton, *A Short History of Modern Bulgaria*, Cambridge University Press, Cambridge, 1987, pp. 21–6.
38. C. and B. Jelavich, *The Establishment of the Balkan National States, 1804–1920*, pp. 219–21.
39. R. J. Crampton, *A Short History of Modern Bulgaria*, pp. 65–9.
40. Ibid., pp. 83–4.
41. Ibid., pp. 93–9.
42. B. Jelavich, *History of the Balkans: Twentieth Century*, Vol. 2, pp. 170–1.
43. R. Lee Wolf, *The Balkans in Our Time*, Harvard University Press, Cambridge, Massachusetts, 1956, pp. 133–6.
44. R. J. Crampton, *A Short History of Modern Bulgaria*, p. 119.
45. Ibid., pp. 120–1.
46. M. Lee Miller, *Bulgaria During the Second World War*, Stanford University Press, Stanford, 1975, pp. 6–7.
47. Ibid., pp. 13–14.
48. Ibid., pp. 15–16.
49. Ibid., pp. 33–9.

8. THE BALTIC STATES: LITHUANIA, LATVIA, ESTONIA

1. J. D. White, 'Nationalism and Socialism in Historical Perspective', in G. Smith (ed.), *The Baltic States: The National Self-Determination of Estonia, Latvia and Lithuania*, Macmillan, Basingstoke, 1994, pp. 13–19.
2. A. Strazhas, 'The *Land Oberost* and Its Place in Germany's *Ostpolitik*, 1915–1918', in V. S. Vardys and R. J. Misiunas (eds), *The Baltic States in Peace and War, 1917–1945*, Pennsylvania State University Press, University Park and London, 1978, pp. 42–7.
3. J. Hiden and P. Salmon, *The Baltic Nations and Europe: Estonia, Latvia and Lithuania in the Twentieth Century*, Longman, London, 1994, pp. 26–9.
4. Ibid., pp. 32–8.
5. J. D. White, 'Nationalism and Socialism in Historical Perspective', pp. 33–5.
6. C. L. Sullivan, 'The German Campaign in the Baltic: The Final Phase', in V. S. Vardys and R. J. Misiunas (eds), *The Baltic States in Peace and War, 1917–1945*, pp. 30–41.
7. V. Stanley Vardys, 'The Rise of Authoritarian Rule in the Baltic States' in V. Stanley Vardys and Romuald J. Misiunas (eds), *The Baltic States in Peace and War, 1917–1945*, p. 66.
8. J. Hiden and P. Salmon, *The Baltic Nations and Europe*, pp. 52–8.
9. Ibid., pp. 50–3.
10. V. Stanley Vardys, 'The Rise of Authoritarian Rule in the Baltic States', pp. 74–6.
11. G. von Rauch, *The Baltic States: The Years of Independence. Estonia, Latvia, Lithuania, 1917–1940*, Hurst, London, 1970, pp. 87–91.
12. J. Hiden and P. Salmon, *The Baltic Nations and Europe*, pp. 76–8.
13. J. Hiden, *The Baltic States and Weimar Ostpolitik*, Cambridge University Press, Cambridge, 1987, pp. 93–6.
14. Ibid., pp. 97–8.
15. J. Hiden and P. Salmon, *The Baltic Nations and Europe*, pp. 62–6.
16. H. I. Rodgers *Search for Security. A Study in Baltic Diplomacy, 1920–1934*, Archon, Hamden, Connecticut, 1975, pp. 22–9.
17. Ibid., pp. 33–8.
18. Ibid., pp. 88–95.
19. Ibid., pp. 106–7.
20. J. Hiden and P. Salmon, *The Baltic Nations and Europe*, pp. 96–7; D. M. Crowe, *The Baltic States and the Great Powers: Foreign Relations, 1938–1940*, Westview Press, Boulder, 1993, pp. 23–8.
21. E. Anderson, 'The Baltic Entente: Phantom or Reality?', in V. S. Vardys and R. J. Misiunas (eds), *The Baltic States in Peace and War, 1917–1945*, pp. 129–31.

22. P. Łossowski, 'Stosunki polsko-litewskie 1918–1939', in H. Bulhak, T. Cieślak et al. (eds), *Przyjaźnie i Antagonizmy. Stosunki Polski z państwami sąsiednimi w latach 1918–1939*, Zakład Narodowy im. Ossolińskich, Wrocław, 1977, pp. 168–70.
23. Ibid., pp. 171–4.
24. J. Hiden and P. Salmon, *The Baltic Nations and Europe*, p. 97.
25. D. M. Crowe, *The Baltic States and the Great Powers*, pp. 31–3.
26. Ibid., pp. 39–44.
27. G. von Rauch, *The Baltic States: The Years of Independence*, pp. 197–199.
28. Ibid., pp. 200–3.
29. A. J. Prażmowska, *Britain, Poland and the Eastern Front, 1939*, pp. 116–20.
30. D. Kirby 'Incorporation: The Molotov–Ribbentrop Pact' in G. Smith (ed.), *The Baltic States: The National Self-Determination of Estonia, Latvia and Lithuania*, pp. 70–2.
31. G. von Rauch, *The Baltic States*, pp. 208–12.
32. D. M. Crowe, *The Baltic States and the Great Powers*, pp. 118–20.
33. A. C. Bramwell, 'The Re-settlement of Ethnic Germans, 1939–1941', in A. C. Bramwell (ed.), *Refugees in the Age of Total War*, Unwin Hyman, London, 1988, pp. 121–3.
34. J. Hiden and P. Salmon, *The Baltic Nations and Europe*, pp. 111–14.
35. G. von Rauch, *The Baltic States*, pp. 212–13.
36. D. Kirby, 'Incorporation: The Molotov–Ribbentrop Pact' in G. Smith, (ed.) *The Baltic States*, pp. 72–4.
37. D. M. Crowe, *The Baltic States and the Great Powers*, pp. 155–8.
38. Ibid., pp. 158–61.
39. Ibid., pp. 161–2.
40. G. von Rauch, *The Baltic States*, pp. 217–27.

Timeline

1918

March 3	Brest–Litovsk Peace Treaty signed between Germany and Russia
May	Romania signs the Treaty of Bucharest with the Central Powers
June	France recognises the Czechoslovak National Council as the official representative of that country
October 27	Austria–Hungary signs armistice
November	Józef Piłsudski-led government emerges in Poland
November 3	Austria–Hungary signs armistice in Padua
November 11	Germany signs armistice at Campiègne
December 1	King Alexander proclaims the emergence of the Kingdom of Serbs, Croats and Slovenes (in 1929 renamed Yugoslavia)

1919

March	Founding Congress of the Third International (Comintern)
March 21	Béla Kun Soviet Republic established in Hungary
June 28	Versailles Treaty signed with Germany
August 1	Fall of the Hungarian Soviet Republic
September 10	St Germain Treaty signed with Austria
November 27	Neuilly-sur-Seine Treaty signed with Bulgaria

1920

February	Soviet Union and Estonia sign Treaty of Peace at Dorpat
March	Hungarian Soviet Republic proclaimed in Budapest
April 25	Poland commences campaign against the Red Army
June 4	Trianon Treaty signed by Hungary
August	Founding of the Baltic League
August 10	Sèvres Treaty signed with Turkey
August 14	Alliance signed between Czechoslovakia and the Kingdom of Serbs, Croats and Slovenes (Yugoslavia) initiating the Little Entente

1921

February 19	Franco–Polish Political Agreement and Military Convention signed
March 3	Polish Romanian Alliance signed
March 18	Poland and Soviet Union sign Treaty of Peace at Riga
April 23	Romanian–Czechoslovak Alliance signed
June 7	Yugoslav–Romanian Alliance signed

1922

April 16	Rappalo Treaty signed

1923

January 11	Franco–Belgian occupation of the Ruhr

1924

January 21	Lenin dies
January 24	Franco–Czechoslovak Treaty of Alliance signed

1925

October	Locarno Treaty signed
October 16	Treaty of Mutual Guarantee between France and Poland and between France and Czechoslovakia

1926

May	*Coup d'état* staged by Józef Piłsudski in Warsaw
June	Franco–Romanian Treaty of Friendship signed
September 28	Soviet–Latvian Non-Aggression Pact signed

1927

March	Latvian–Soviet Pact signed
April	Treaty of Friendship and Co-operation signed between Italy and Hungary

1928

| December | Stalin initiates policy of 'Socialism in One Country' |

1933

| December 20 | Soviet Politbureau approves policy of 'Collective Security' |
| October | Germany leaves the League of Nations |

1934

January	German–Polish Declaration of Non-Aggression signed
February 9	Signing of the Balkan Entente by Turkey, Greece, Romania and Yugoslavia
March 17	Rome Protocol signed by Hungary and Italy
October 1	King Alexander of Yugoslavia assassinated in Marseilles
November 3	Baltic Entente signed by Latvia, Estonia and Lithuania

1935

May 2	Franco–Soviet Pact of Mutual Assistance signed
May 16	Czechoslovak–Soviet Treaty of Mutual Assistance signed
October	Italy invades Abyssinia

1936

March 7	Germany remilitarises the Rhinland
October	Protocol of Co-operation signed by Italy and Germany
November 26	Anti-Comintern Pact signed by Japan and Germany

1938

March 11/12	German occupation of Austria *Anschluss*
September 15	Chamberlain visits Hitler in Berchtesgaden
September 30	Munich Agreement signed by Germany, Italy, France and Britain
November 1	First Vienna Award

1939

March 10	Stalin's speech to the 18th Party Congress
March 15	Germany occupies Prague
	Hungary occupies sub-Carpathian–Ruthenia
March 16	Slovakia becomes a German Protectorate
March 22	Germany occupies the Lithuanian port of Memel
March 31	British guarantee to Poland
April 7	Italian invasion of Albania
April 13	British guarantee to Romania and Greece
August 23	Ribbentop and Molotov sign Non-Aggression Pact
August 25	Agreement of Mutual Assistance signed by Britain and Poland
September 1	German attack on Poland
September 3	Britain and France declare war on Germany
September 16	Bulgaria declares neutrality
September 28	Soviet–Estonian Pact signed
October 2	Soviet–Latvian Alliance signed
October 10	Soviet–Lithuanian Military Alliance signed
November 30	Soviet Union attacks Finland
December 12	Hungarian–Yugoslav Pact of Friendship signed

1940

May 10	Germany invades Holland
June 22	Armistice signed between France and Germany
August 29	Second Vienna Award
September 27	Three Power Pact signed by Germany, Italy and Japan

1941

March 1	Yugoslavia joins the Three Power Pact
March 28	Military coup in Yugoslavia
April 6	German attack on Yugoslavia
June 22	Germany invades the Soviet Union
December 13	Bulgaria declares war against the US and Britain

Bibliography

The Balkans

Crampton, R. J., *A Short History of Modern Bulgaria*, Cambridge University Press, Cambridge, 1987.

Dragnich, Alex N., *The First Yugoslavia. Search for a Viable Political System*, Hoover Institution Press, Stanford University, Stanford, 1983.

Fischer, Bernd Jurgen, *King Zog and the Struggle for Stability in Albania*, East European Monographs, Boulder, 1984.

Garlicka, Anna, *Polska–Jugostavia 1934–1939. Z Dziejów Stosunków politycznych*, Zakład Narodowy Im. Ossolińskich, Wrocław, 1977.

Hoptner, J. B., *Yugoslavia in Crisis, 1934–1941*, Columbia University Press, New York, 1963.

Jelavich, Barbara, *History of the Balkans: Twentieth Century*, Vol. 2, Cambridge University Press, Cambridge, 1983.

Jelavic, Charles and Barbara, *The Establishment of the Balkan National States, 1804–1920*, University of Washington Press, Seattle, 1977.

Lederer, Ivo J., *Yugoslavia at the Paris Peace Conference: A Study in Frontiermaking*, Yale University Press, New Haven, 1963.

Littlefield, Frank C., *Germany and Yugoslavia, 1933–1941*, East European Monographs, Columbia University Press, New York, 1988.

Miller, Marshall Lee, *Bulgaria During the Second World War*, Stanford University Press, Stanford, 1975.

Paollo, Stefan and Arben Puto, *The History of Albania from its Origins to the Present Day*, Routledge and Kegan Paul, London, 1981.

Roberts, Henry L., 'Politics in a Small State: The Balkan Example', in Charles and Barbara Jelavich (eds), *The Balkans in Transition: Essays on the Development of Balkan Life and Politics since the Eighteenth Century*, Archon Books, Hampden, Connecticut, 1974.

Singleton, Fred, *Twentieth-Century Yugoslavia*, Macmillan, London 1976.

Vickers, Miranda, *The Albanians: A Modern History*, I. B. Tauris, London, 1995.

Wolf, Robert Lee, *The Balkans in Our Time*, Harvard University Press, Cambridge, Massachusetts, 1956.

The Baltic States

Anderson, Edgar, 'The Baltic Entente: Phantom or Reality?', in V. Stanley Vardys and Romuald J. Misiunas (eds), *The Baltic States in Peace and War, 1917–1945*, Pennsylvania State University Press, London, 1978.

Bramwell, Anna C., 'The Re-settlement of Ethnic Germans, 1939–1941', in Anna C. Bramwell (ed.), *Refugees in the Age of Total War*, Unwin Hyman, London, 1988.

Crowe, David M., *The Baltic States and the Great Powers: Foreign Relations, 1938–1940*, Westview Press, Boulder, 1993.

Hiden, John, *The Baltic States and Weimar Ostpolitik*, Cambridge University Press, Cambridge, 1987.

Hiden, John and Patrick Salmon, *The Baltic Nations and Europe: Estonia, Latvia and Lithuania in the Twentieth Century*, Longman, London, 1994.

Łossowski, Piotr, 'Stosunki polsko-litewskie 1918–1839', in Henryk Bulhak, Tadeusz Cieślak et al. (eds), *Przyjaźnie i Antagonizmy. Stosunki Polski z państwami sąiednimi w latach 1918–1939*, Zakład Narodowy im. Ossolińskich, Wrocław, 1977.

Kirby, David, 'Incorporation: The Molotov–Ribbentrop Pact', in Graham Smith (ed.), *The Baltic States: The National Self-Determination of Estonia, Latvia and Lithuania*, Macmillan, Basingstoke. 1994.

Prażmowska, Anita J., *Britain, Poland and the Eastern Front, 1939*, Cambridge University Press, Cambridge, 1987.

Rauch, Georg von, *The Baltic States: The Years of Independence. Estonia, Latvia, Lithuania, 1917–1940*, Hurst, London, 1970.

Rodgers, Hugh I., *Search for Security: A Study in Baltic Diplomacy, 1920–1934*, Archon Books, Hamden, Connecticut, 1975.

Strazhas, Aba, 'The *Land Oberost* and Its Place in Germany's *Ostpolitik*, 1915–1918', in V. Stanley Vardys and Romuald J. Misiunas (eds), *The Baltic States in Peace and War, 1917–1945*, Pennsylvania State University Press, University Park and London, 1978.

Sullivan, Charles L., 'The German Campaign in the Baltic: The Final Phase', in V. Stanley Vardys and Romuald J. Misiunas (eds), *The Baltic States in Peace and War, 1917–1945*, Pennsylvania State University Press, University Park and London, 1978.

Vardys, V. Stanley, 'The Rise of Authoritarian Rule in the Baltic States', in V. Stanley Vardys and Romuald J. Misiunas (eds), *The Baltic States in Peace and War, 1917–1945*, Pennsylvania State University Press, London, 1978.

White, James D., 'Nationalism and Socialism in Historical Perspective', in Graham Smith (ed.), *The Baltic States: The National Self-Determination of Estonia, Latvia and Lithuania*, Macmillan, Basingstoke, 1994.

France

Adamthwaite, Anthony, *France and the Coming of the Second World War, 1936–1939*, Frank Cass, London, 1977.

Alexander, Martin, *The Republic in Danger: General Maurice Gamelin and the Politics of French Defence, 1933–1940*, Cambridge University Press, Cambridge, 1992.

Jordan, Nicole, *The Popular Front and Central Europe: The Dilemmas of French Impotence, 1918–1940*, Cambridge University Press, Cambridge, 1992.

Nere, J., *The Foreign Policy of France from 1914 to 1945*, Routledge & Kegan Paul, London, 1974.

Sukiennicki, Wiktor, *East Central Europe during World War I: From Foreign Domination to National Independence*, Vol. II, East European Monographs, Boulder, 1984.

Wandycz, Piotr S., *The Twilight of French Eastern Alliances, 1926–1936: French–Czechoslovak–Polish Relations from Locarno to the Remilitarization of the Rhineland*, Princeton University Press, Princeton, 1988.

Wandycz, Piotr S., *France and Her Eastern Allies, 1919–1925:. French–Czechoslovak–Polish Relations from the Paris Peace Conference to Locarno*, University of Minnesota Press, Minneapolis, 1962.

Wandycz, Piotr S., *The Twilight of French Eastern Alliances, 1926–1936: French–Czechoslovak–Polish Relations from Locarno to the Remilitarization of the Rhineland*, Princeton University Press, Princeton, 1988.

Young, Robert J., *In Command of France: French Foreign Policy and Military Planning, 1933–1940*, Harvard University Press, Cambridge, Massachusetts, 1978.

Young, Robert J., *France and the Origins of the Second World War*, Macmillan, Basingstoke, 1996.

Great Britain

Bond, Brian, *British Military Policy between the Two World Wars*, Clarendon Press, Oxford, 1980.

Colvin, Ian, *The Chamberlain Cabinet*, Victor Gollancz, London, 1971.

Douglas, Roy, *The Advent of War. 1939–40*, Macmillan, London, 1978.

Howard, Michael, *The Continental Commitment: The Dilemma of British Defence Policy in the Era of Two World Wars*, Pelican, London, 1974.

Kaiser, David E., *Economic Diplomacy and the Origins of the Second World War*, Princeton University Press, Princeton, New Jersey, 1980.

Pender, G. C., *British Rearmament and the Treasury, 1932–1939*, Scottish Academic Press, Edinburgh, 1979.

Prażmowska, Anita J., *Britain, Poland and the Eastern Front, 1939*, Cambridge University Press, Cambridge, 1987.

Prażmowska, Anita J., *Britain and Poland, 1939–1943: The Betrayed Ally*, Cambridge University Press, Cambridge 1995.

Sukiennicki, Wiktor, *East Central Europe During World War I: From Foreign Domination to National Independence*, Vol. I, East European Monographs, Boulder, New York, 1984.

Watt, Donald Cameron, *How War Came: The Immediate Origins of the Second World War, 1938–1939*, Heinemann, London, 1989.

Wendt, Bernd-Jurgen, ' "Economic Appeasement" – a Crisis Strategy', in Wolfgang J. Mommsen and Lothar Kettenacker (eds), *The Fascist Challenge and the Policy of Appeasement*, George Allen & Unwin, London , 1983.

Soviet Union

Bulhak, Henryk, 'Polska a Rumunia 1918–1939', in Henryk Bulhak, Tadeusz Cieclak et al. (eds), *Przyjaznie i antagonizmy. Stosunki Polski z panstwami sasiednimi w latach 1918–1939*, Zaklad Narodowy Imienia Ossolińskich, PAN, Wrocław, 1977.

Carr, E. H., *The Bolshevik Revolution, 1917–1923*, Vol. 3, Pelican, London, 1988.

Debo, Richard K., *Revolution and Survival: The Foreign Policy of Soviet Russia, 1917–18*, Liverpool University Press, Liverpool, 1979.

Debo, Richard K., *Survival and Consolidation: The Foreign Policy of Soviet Russia, 1918–1921*, McGill-Queen's University Press, Montreal & Kingston, 1992.

Deutscher, Isaac, *Stalin: A Political Biography*, Oxford University Press, Oxford, 1961.

Erickson, John, *The Soviet High Command: A Military–Political History, 1918–1941*, Westview Press, Boulder.

Haslam, Jonathan, *Soviet Foreign Policy, 1930–1933*, Macmillan, Basingstoke, 1983.

Haslam, Jonathan, *The Soviet Union and the Struggle for Collective Security in Europe, 1933–1939*, Macmillan, Basingstoke, 1984.

Kennan, George F., *Soviet Foreign Policy, 1917–1941*, D. van Nostrand, Princeton, 1960.

Light, Margot, *The Soviet Theory of International Relations*, Wheatsheaf, Guildford, 1988.

Lungu, Dov, *Romania and the Great Powers, 1933–1940*, Duke University Press, Durham, 1989.

McDermott, Kevin and Jeremy Agnew, *The Comintern: A History of International Communism from Lenin to Stalin*, Macmillan, Basingstoke, 1996.

Prażmowska, Anita J., *Britain, Poland and the Eastern Front, 1939*, Cambridge University Press, Cambridge 1986.

Read, Anthony and David Fisher, *The Deadly Embrace: Hitler, Stalin and the Nazi–Soviet Pact 1939–1941*, W. W. Norton, New York, 1988.

Geoffrey Roberts, *The Soviet Union and the Origins of the Second World War: Russo–German Relations and the Road to War, 1933–1941*, St Martin's Press, New York, 1995.

Salmon, Patrick, 'Great Britain, the Soviet Union and Finland at the beginning of the Second World War', in John Hiden and Thomas Lane (eds), *The Baltic and the Outbreak of the Second World War*, Cambridge University Press, Cambridge, 1992.

Uldricks, Teddy J., *Diplomacy and Ideology: The Origins of Soviet Foreign Relations, 1917–1930*, Sage, London, 1979.

Uldricks, Teddy J., 'Soviet Security Policy in the 1930s', in Gabriel Gorodetsky (ed.), *Soviet Foreign Policy, 1917–1991: A Retrospective*, Frank Cass, London, 1994.

Czechoslovakia

Bruegel, J.W., *Czechoslovakia before Munich: The German Minority Problem and British Appeasement Policy*, Cambridge University Press, Cambridge , 1973.

Henderson, Nevile, *Failure of a Mission: Berlin, 1937–1939*, London, 1940.

Komjathy, Anthony and Rebecca Stockwell, *German Minorities and the Third Reich*, Holmes & Meier, New York, 1980.

Kozeński, J., *Czechosłowacja w Polskiej Polityce Zagranicznej w latach 1932–1938*, Instytut Zachodni, Poznań, 1964.

Luza, Radomir, *The Transfer of the Sudeten Germans: A Study of Czech–German Relations, 1933–1936*, Routledge & Kegan Paul, London, 1964.

Mallakh, Dorothea H. El, *The Slovak Autonomy Movement, 1935–1939: A Study in Unrelenting Nationalism*, East European Quarterly, Boulder, 1979.

Mamatey, Victor S., 'The Establishment of the Republic', in Victor S. Mamatey and Radomir Luza (eds), *A History of the Czechoslovak Republic, 1918–1948*, Princeton University Press, Princeton, New Jersey, 1973.

Olivova, Vera, *The Doomed Democracy. Czechoslovakia in a Disrupted Europe, 1914–38*, Sidgwick & Jackson, London, 1972.

Prażmowska, Anita J., 'Poland's Foreign Policy: September 1938–1939', *Historical Journal*, Vol. 29, No. 4, 1986.

Prochazka, Theodor, 'The Second Republic, 1938–1939', in Victor S. Mamatey and Radomir Luza (eds), *A History of the Czechoslovak Republic, 1818–1948*, Princeton University Press, Princeton, New Jersey, 1973.

Teichova, Alice and P. L. Cottrell, 'Industrial Structures in West and East Central Europe during the Inter-war Period', in Alice Teichova and P. L. Cottrell (eds), *International Business and Central Europe, 1918–1939*, Leicester University Press, St Martin's Press, New York, 1983.

Wandycz, Piotr S., 'Foreign Policy of Edvard Beneš, 1918–1938' in Victor S. Mamatey and Radomir Luza (eds), *A History of the Czechoslovak Republic 1918–1948*, Princeton University Press, Princeton, New Jersey, 1973.

Zeman, Zbynek with Antonin Klimek, *The Life of Edvard Beneš 1884–1948*, Clarendon Press, Oxford, 1997.

Rumania

Boia, Eugene, *Romania's Diplomatic Relations with Yugoslavia in the Interwar Period, 1919–1941*, East European Monographs, Boulder, 1993.

Bulhak, Henryk, 'Polska a Rumunia, 1918–1939', in Henryk Bulhak, Tadeusz Cieślak et al. (eds), *Przyjaźnie i Antagonizmy. Stosunki Polski z państwami sąsiednimi w latach 1918–1939*, Narodowy Zakład Imienia Ossolińskich, Wrocław, 1977.

Fisher-Galati, Stephen, 'Fascism in Romania', in Peter F. Sugar (ed.), *Native Fascism in the Successor States, 1918–1945*, ABS–CLIO, Santa Barbara, 1971.

Fisher-Galati, Stephen, *Twentieth Century Rumania*, 2nd edn, Columbia University Press, New York, 1991.

Hitchins, Keith, *Rumania, 1866–1947*, Clarendon Press, Oxford, 1994.

Kaiser, David E., *Economic Diplomacy, 1930–1939 and the Origins of the Second World War: Germany, Britain, France, and Eastern Europe 1930–1939*, Princeton University Press, Princeton, 1980, pp. 73–80.

Komjathy, Anthony and Rebecca Stockwell, *German Minorities and the Third Reich: Ethnic Germans and East Central Europe between the Wars*, Holmes and Meier, New York, 1980.

Lungu, Dov B., *Romania and the Great Powers, 1933–1940*, Duke University Press, Durham, 1989.

Maurice Pearton, *Oil and the Romanian State*, Clarendon, Oxford, 1971.

Roberts, Henry L., *Rumania: Political Problems of an Agrarian State*, Oxford University Press, Oxford, 1951.

Watt, Donald Cameron, *How War Came: The Immediate Origins of the Second World War, 1938–1939*, Heinemann, London, 1989.

Poland

Cienciała, Anna M. and Titus Komarnicki, *From Versailles to Locarno: Keys to Polish Foreign Policy, 1919–1925*, University Press of Kansas, Lawrence, Kansas, 1984.

Garlicki, Andrzej, *Józef Piłsudski, 1867–1935*, Scolar Press, Aldershot, 1995.

Haslam, J., *The Soviet Union and the Struggle for Collective Security in Europe, 1933–1939*, Macmillan, London, 1984.

Jedrzejewicz, M. (ed.), *Diplomat in Berlin, 1933–1938: Papers and Memoirs of Josef Lipski, Ambassador of Poland*, New York, Columbia University Press, 1969.

Kaiser, David E., *Economic Diplomacy and the Origins of the Second World War*, Princeton University Press, Princeton, 1980.

Landau, Zbigniew, 'The Economic Integration of Poland, 1918–1923', in Paul Latawski (ed.), *The Reconstruction of Poland, 1914–1923*, Macmillan, Basingstoke, 1992.

Landau, Zbigniew, and Jerzy Tomaszewski, *Trudna niepodległość. Rozważania o gospodarce Polski 1918–1939*, Książka i Wiedza, Warsaw, 1978.

Leslie, Robert, (ed.), *The History of Poland since 1863*, Cambridge University Press, Cambridge, 1980.

Lundgreen-Nielsen, Kay, *The Polish Problem at the Paris Peace Conference: A Study of the Policies of the Great Powers and the Poles, 1918–1919*, Odense University Press, Odense, 1979.

Polonsky, Anthony, *Politics in Independent Poland, 1921–1939*, Clarendon Press, Oxford, 1972.

Prażmowska, A. J., 'Poland's Foreign Policy: September 1938–September 1939', *The Historical Journal*, Vol. 29, No. 4, 1986.

Prażmowska, A. J., *Britain, Poland and the Eastern Front, 1939*, Cambridge University Press, Cambridge, 1987.

Prażmowska, A. J., 'The Role of Danzig in Polish–German Relations on the Eve of the Second World War', in J. Hiden and T. Lane (eds), *The Baltic and the Outbreak of the Second World War*, Cambridge University Press, Cambridge, 1992.

Prażmowska, A. J., *Britain and Poland 1939–1943: The Betrayed Ally*, Cambridge University Press, Cambridge, 1995.

Terlecki, Olgierd, *Pułkownik Beck*. Krajowa Agencja Wydawnicza, Kraków, 1985.

Wandycz, Piotr, 'Dmowski's Policy at the Paris Peace Conference: Success or Failure?' in Paul Latawski (ed.), *The Reconstruction of Poland, 1914–1923*, Macmillan, Basingstoke, 1992.

Official documents concerning Polish–German and Polish–Soviet relations 1933–1939, Ministry for Foreign Affairs, the Polish Government, London, 1940.

Hungary

Carsten, F. L., *The Rise of Fascism*, Methuen, London, 1970.

Dombrady, Lorand, 'Trianon and Hungarian National Defense', in Bela K. Kiraly and Laszlo Veszpremy (eds), *Trianon and East Central Europe: Antecedents and Repercussions. War and Society in East Central Europe*, Vol. XXXII, Social Science Monographs, Boulder, 1995.

Dreiszinger, Nandor A.F., *Hungary's Way to World War II*, Hungarian Herlicon Society, Toronto, 1968.

Juhasz, Gyula, *Hungary's Foreign Policy, 1919–1945*, Akademia Kiado, Budapest, 1979.

Kaiser, David E., *Economic Diplomacy and the Origins of the Second World War: Germany, Britain, France, and Eastern Europe, 1930–1939*, Princeton University Press, Princeton, 1980.

Koźmiński, Maciej, *Polska i Węgry przed drugą wojną Światową (Październik 1938 – Wrzesień 1939). Z dziejów dyplomacji i irredenty*, Zakład Narodowy Imienia Ossolińskich. Wydawnictwo Polskiej Akademii Nauk, Wrocław, 1970.

Macartney, C. M., *October Fifteenth: A History of Modern Hungary, 1929–1945*, Edinburgh University Press, Edinburgh, 1956.

Molnar, Miklos, *From Bela Kun to Janos Kadar. Seventy Years of Hungarian Communism*, Berg, Oxford, 1990.

Ormos, Maria, *From Padua to the Trianon, 1918–1920*, Social Science Monographs, Boulder, Colorado, 1990.

Pastor, Peter, *Hungary between Wilson and Lenin: The Hungarian Revolution of 1918–1919 and the Big Three*, East European Quarterly, Boulder, 1976.

Index